Romance and Readership
in Twentieth-Century France

OXFORD STUDIES IN MODERN EUROPEAN CULTURE

GENERAL EDITORS

Elizabeth Fallaize, Robin Fiddian, and Katrin Kohl

The Oxford Studies in Modern European Culture series is conceived as a response to the changing modes of study of European literature and culture in many universities. Designed to combine focus with breadth, each title in the series presents a range of texts or films in dialogue with their historical and cultural contexts—not simply as a reflection of history but engaged in a mediation with history, conceived in broad terms as cultural, social, and political history. Flexible, interdisciplinary approaches are encouraged together with the use of texts outside the traditional canon alongside more familiar works. In order to make the volumes accessible not only to students of modern languages but also to those studying the history or politics of modern Europe, all quotations are offered both in the original language and in English.

ROMANCE AND READERSHIP IN TWENTIETH-CENTURY FRANCE

Love Stories

Diana Holmes

OXFORD
UNIVERSITY PRESS

OXFORD

UNIVERSITY PRESS

Great Clarendon Street, Oxford OX2 6DP

Oxford University Press is a department of the University of Oxford.
It furthers the University's objective of excellence in research, scholarship,
and education by publishing worldwide in

Oxford New York

Auckland Cape Town Dar es Salaam Hong Kong Karachi
Kuala Lumpur Madrid Melbourne Mexico City Nairobi
New Delhi Shanghai Taipei Toronto

With offices in

Argentina Austria Brazil Chile Czech Republic France Greece
Guatemala Hungary Italy Japan Poland Portugal Singapore
South Korea Switzerland Thailand Turkey Ukraine Vietnam

Oxford is a registered trademark of Oxford University Press
in the UK and in certain other countries

Published in the United States
by Oxford University Press Inc., New York

© Diana Holmes 2006

British Library Cataloguing in Publication Data
Data available

Library of Congress Cataloging in Publication Data
Data available

Typeset by Laserwords Private Limited, Chennai, India
Printed in Great Britain
on acid-free paper by
Biddles Ltd., King's Lynn, Norfolk

ISBN 0-19-924984-9 978-0-19-924984-8

10 9 8 7 6 5 4 3 2 1

Acknowledgements

Warm thanks to Penny Welch and Elizabeth Fallaize for their astute and helpful readings of work in progress, and for their encouragement.

And thanks to the many colleagues, friends, and family members who have encountered parts of this work in the form of conference papers, or just in conversation, and responded with questions, comments, or suggestions.

Finally, thanks to the students who have followed my courses on women's writing and cinema while I have been writing this book, and contributed their interest, enthusiasm, and critical insights.

Contents

Introduction

Writing and reading romances is generally thought of as something that women do. The association of women with romance has often been used to confirm gender stereotypes: women are the sentimental sex, by nature more interested in private, emotional matters than in political or philosophical concerns, narcissistically inclined to consume stories that reproduce and embellish their own personal dramas. I have a vivid memory of wanting to distance myself from this demeaning construction of who I was: mid-teens, newly but firmly self-identified as a serious reader unlimited by mere gender, I was asked by my grandma to change her books while I was at the library. This meant approaching the Romance section, being seen to select amongst the thin pink and blue volumes of the Mills and Boon series. I grabbed a couple, concealed them and headed straight for the serious end of the library where I felt I belonged, to choose—what? Certainly a wide range of books, from Dickens to Camus via Agatha Christie and Edgar Wallace (crime, somehow, was adult and respectable in a way that romance just wasn't), but always including a Brontë or an Austen or a Georgette Heyer, or an early Margaret Drabble, or a translated *Angélique* (spicy, but with the touch of seriousness conferred by being originally in French)—in other words, stories of love. If I review my current reading practices, the books I read in bed at night or on holiday, for pleasure, I find the same pattern: the majority are by women writers, and most of them are, usually amongst other things, love stories. I don't think that I am unusual in this.

As a feminist, one's first reaction to the generally derogatory suggestion that women just write and read about love is to prove the contrary, and this can certainly be done. Women novelists have of course ranged across genres, from the philosophical and political novel (in France, most famously, Sand, Beauvoir) to the formally experimental (Duras, Sarraute), the sociological (Ernaux), the *roman policier* (Fred Vargas), and so on. But once this case has been made, the fact still remains that the mass-market romance, with its almost exclusively female authorship and readership, has been the most consistently popular (even if also the most critically despised) genre of the last hundred years. Moreover, throughout the same period, there has been an important layer of very widely read 'middlebrow' women's writing centred on the love story, in France as in the UK and the USA, and a significant proportion of 'literary' fiction written by women (and mainly read by women?) has also continued to make love central, in terms of both narrative and themes. It is not, of course, that men don't write or read about love—but the identification of romance predominantly with women has a solid basis in fact. Rather than refuse the evidence, we may ask—and this book does ask—why, exactly, is romance a genre favoured by women writers, and what pleasures does it provide that explain its persistent popularity with readers? In France, even more than in other western cultures, formulaic, easy-to-read popular fiction is seen as the negative shadow against which authentic literature defines itself, and to be generically associated with the *roman à l'eau de rose* (popular romance) is to run the risk of critical scorn. Yet even at the beginning of the twenty-first century, romance remains a much-used genre for 'serious' women writers. Why?

A number of illuminating studies of the popular romance have been published over the last twenty years, and this book draws on their research and their insights. But, on the whole, popular romantic fiction has been studied in isolation from other forms of women's writing, as if there could be no real common ground between the personal vision and linguistic creativity of the 'literary' text, and the formula-driven transparency of the novel written for a mass-market collection. The gulf between them is, indeed, wide, but it is bridged in part by what is best described as middlebrow fiction—easy to read, providing the pleasure of immersion in an imaginary world, but also questioning, exploring, demanding a degree of cerebral engagement. The popular and the 'highbrow'—my awkward use of quotation marks signals the difficulty of denoting the different types of literature without implying pejorative judgements of either—are also best seen in relationship for another reason. The popular romance, with its familiar fairytale structure, contributes to a cultural construction of love that is woven into the collective imagination, including that of 'literary' writers, and we shall see that its structures and themes are strongly present, albeit in more self-aware and complex forms, in the work of authors—and particularly women authors—who belong in the category of serious literature. The genre of romance spans the hierarchy of fiction, from the mass-produced, disposable sort, to novels that achieve, in Bourdieu's formulation, 'cultural legitimacy', or in other words are consecrated not by the market alone, but by an elite audience of peer competitors and representatives of the dominant class. Crossing and connecting these levels, romance represents a mainly female domain, and can be seen as a space in which women elaborate a mythology that—like all mythologies—makes sense of their experience by recasting it as story, expressing and shaping a widely shared sense of reality.

It was around the end of the nineteenth century that a vast popular market for literary fiction opened up in France, and that the *roman d'amour* became a clearly identified genre for purposes of marketing, and one that was firmly associated with a female readership—though as Chapter 1 shows, the romance can trace its roots all the way back through the history of storytelling. My study therefore begins at the French 'Belle Époque', or close to the turn from nineteenth to twentieth centuries. It was clearly impossible, in a book of some 60,000 words, to make a comprehensive study of the romances written and read in France over more than a century, so the organization of chapters, and the selection of particular periods and texts, demand some explanation. The history of the popular romance in France, in some ways unique and in others typical of western Europe, is traced from chapter to chapter, with particular emphasis on key periods of its development. Otherwise, each chapter focuses on two or three 'literary' romance texts, selected because they were recognized as important either by critical consensus, or by massive sales, or in many cases by both, and selected too because they are sufficiently available—including, in most cases, in translation—for many readers to be familiar with them. Certain texts that were equally good examples of the genre were excluded because they have already been the subject of extensive recent analysis, in my work and/or in that of others (for example Marguerite Duras's *L'Amant*, Annie Ernaux's *Passion simple*).

Chapter 1 attempts a brief history and a theory of romance. The remaining chapters focus on periods at which the romance played a particularly interesting role in the cultural history of women in France. Chapter 2 examines the development of popular fiction at the Belle Époque, and the divergence of the *roman d'amour* into, on the one hand, the strait-laced, Catholic-influenced 'moral romance' and, on the other, the contestatory 'feminist romance'. Colette's romance diptych *La Vagabonde* and its rather less studied sequel *L'Entrave*, are read as exceptional examples of a genre practised by many of her female contemporaries. Chapter 3 moves beyond the First World War to the 1930s, and on into the Occupation. Romance is seen in its most politically reactionary form in the work of Delly, and in its capacity to espouse, equally, a progressive politics, particularly in the work of Resistance writers Elsa Triolet and Édith Thomas. In Chapter 4, Simone de Beauvoir's feminist analysis of romantic love is set against the passionate love story that forms a major strand of her novel *Les Mandarins*, and both Beauvoir's texts and the early novels of Françoise Sagan are seen within the contradictory gender ideology of the 1950s, when the push towards female emancipation was countered by a strong imperative towards marriage and the couple—a life defined, in other words, by the romance narrative. The rejection of romance by the post-1968 feminist movement is examined in Chapter 5, and the return of the genre in the 1980s is explored through the study of Marie Cardinal's novel of mature romance *Une vie pour deux*, Régine Deforges's blockbuster *La Bicyclette bleue*, and Mireille Best's lesbian love story *Camille en octobre*. Chapter 6 brings the story up to the present with an analysis of the contemporary Harlequin romance in France, a brief study of a lesbian version of the Harlequin formula, and an exploration of the 'postmodern' romances of Emmanuèle Bernheim (*Vendredi soir*) and Camille Laurens (*L'Amour, roman*). The film version of the Bernheim text allows me a brief foray into the question of romance in cinema.

In *Beyond Feminist Aesthetics: Feminist Literature and Social Change* (1989), Rita Felski argues that literature is not (contrary to some contemporary theory) merely a self-referential system, but is rather

> a medium which can profoundly influence individual and cultural self-understanding in the sphere of everyday life, charting the changing preoccupations of social groups through symbolic fictions by means of which they make sense of experience. (7)

Felski's formulation captures the way in which I want to envisage romance in this book, as a genre that is not merely a source of transient pleasure—though it is certainly that—but also a place in which women writers and their readers find a recognizable shape for their desires, apprehensions, fantasies, and often conflicted senses of identity and thus (at best) make better sense of them, personally, politically, and ethically. Felski's definition of the task of the feminist critic is equally useful: 'to situat(e) historically specific analysis of particular communicative practices in relation to changing constellations of power and the range of options available to women' (65). This study of romance aims to explore the major feminine genre of the past (almost) century and a half in relation to those changing 'constellations of power' that have shaped women's lives and cultural practices, across the boundaries of class and across the hierarchy of aesthetic forms.

1 A Feminine Genre: Romance and Women

Defining the genre

> La femme de lettres aime et chante presque exclusivement l'amour,
> voilà le fait . . . C'est la grande question, l'éternelle question pour les
> femmes et les romans de femme. L'amour, l'amour, l'amour![1]
>
> (Bertaut 1909: 231)

> Qu'elle était judicieuse, la remontrance d'un de mes maris: 'Mais tu ne
> peux donc pas écrire un livre qui ne soit d'amour . . . Est-ce qu'il n'y a
> pas autre chose dans la vie?' Si le temps ne l'eût pressé de courir—car
> il était beau et charmant—vers des rendez-vous amoureux, il m'aurait
> peut-être enseigné ce qui a licence de tenir, dans un roman et hors du
> roman, la place de l'amour . . .'[2]
>
> (Colette 1991a: 285–6)

Although, as Colette ironically observes, romantic love is one of life's
most compelling experiences for both sexes, writing and reading about
love are strongly associated, at least in contemporary western cultures,
with women. It has not always been so, for the love story is an archetypal
narrative of western literature, the majority of which has been authored
by men, and romance pervades oral and written story-telling as far back
as can be traced. Fairy tales, their origins lost in time, mutate as they
travel through centuries and shifting cultures, but continue to make
the discovery of mutual, passionate love the condition of living happily
ever after. When, in twelfth-century France, literature first began to be
written in the vernacular or 'romanz' language rather than in Latin, the
narrative of love and courtship soon became the dominant literary mode,
so that the word 'romance' took on the meaning it has retained to this
day. Old legends from the oral tradition were taken up and reworked

---

[1] 'The woman of letters cares for and sings of nothing but love, that is a fact . . . Love is the one
great, eternal question for women and for women's novels. Love, love, love!'

[2] 'How wise one of my husbands was when he remonstrated: "But is it impossible for you to write
a book that isn't about love . . .? Aren't there other things in life?" If he had not been in such a hurry
to get to his amorous rendezvous—for he was handsome and charming—he might perhaps have
taught me what can take the place of love, in a novel or out of it' (Colette 1979: 18–19).

to fit different cultures and different historical moments, so that the same story was told in numerous versions. Perhaps the most powerful of these was *Tristan et Iseult*, the tale of two passionate young lovers forced apart by the inexorable demands of family and social duty. Their story echoed through the courtly romances of medieval Europe, gathering the potency of a founding romantic myth whose legacy can be traced through centuries of love stories.[3]

It is the very pervasiveness of love as theme and narrative component that makes a closer definition of romance essential, for the majority of literature touches in some way on erotic and emotional relationships, but not every story containing love is best thought of as romance. The concept of genre is useful here, not in the sense of a fixed, ahistorical form, but in the sense of a consensual literary structure that provides an *horizon d'attente* (horizon of expectation) for readers and a *modèle d'écriture* (model of writing) for authors,[4] and that within these broad patterns of consistency can shift, adapt, and respond to a changing context. Romance, as I will argue, takes on a recognizable set of formal and thematic parameters, and acquires a particular and lasting social importance, towards the end of the nineteenth century, but the modern genre has deep taproots that lead all the way back through literary history to medieval romances, and to a pre-literary oral culture. What defines the romance, from *Tristan et Iseult* to the Harlequin series, is first the centrality of the love plot: what drives the plot, what motivates the turning of the pages, is the question of whether and how the two primary characters will achieve, or fail to achieve, a lasting union with each other. Other characters may populate the story, but they are secondary: they may merely function as what one analyst of the popular modern romance calls 'utilités' ('utilities', Constans 1999: 20) and another 'fricatives' (Paizis 1998: 75), or they may introduce important external dimensions to the drama of the relationship, but they are rarely centre stage. The basic narrative structure of romance—on which innumerable variations have been played—is that of meeting, negotiation of a series of obstacles both internal (psychological and emotional) and external (social and material), leading to a dénouement that may be happy (the couple united) or unhappy (separation and loss).

---

[3] In *L'Amour et l'Occident* (first published 1939) Denis de Rougemont asserts but deplores the lasting legacy of the Tristan myth, which he defines as a primitively irrational belief in the irresistible and anti-social power of love. The continuing potency of the myth, he argues, 'se trahit dans la plupart de nos romans et de nos films, dans leur succès auprès des masses' ('can be seen in most of our contemporary novels and films, and in their popular success', de Rougemont 1972: 17).

[4] These concepts are used in most modern genre theory; see, e.g., Todorov 1970: ch. 1, 'Les Genres littéraires'; Schaeffer 1989; Combe 1992.

Whatever the ending, love is a transcendent value in romance. It is a uniquely powerful emotion, as *Tristan et Iseult* establishes through the narrative device of a love-potion, which both lovers drink, inadvertently, while in each other's presence, with the result that 'Love, waylayer of all hearts, ... planted her victorious standard in their two hearts and bowed them beneath her yoke' (von Strassburg 1960: 195). More contemporary romances dispense with the material catalyst of the love-potion, but depict love as equally inexorable. But it is the difficulty of realizing desire that forms the stuff of the narrative. The romance deals with the conflict between a personal will to absolute fulfilment, and the intractability of the real, which most often takes the form of social imperatives that frustrate the desire to be with the loved one. Tristan and Iseult know briefly the supreme happiness of a consummated love, during their shared exile in a magical forest that has overtones of the Garden of Eden. Here, as one version has it, they live in perfect harmony, each providing all that the other needs: 'They made an even number: there was simply one and one' (von Strassburg 1960: 263). Marital, dynastic, and chivalric duties will put an end to their idyll, and the story ends with their separation and death. Tristan and Iseult experience, and then lose, perfect happiness in each other. Whether happy or sad in its dénouement, the romance is always structured as a quest for union with the beloved, and its narrative material is provided by the hurdles that lie in the path of that imagined perfection.

The feminization of romance

The constant elements of the romance genre then are the narrative centrality of a single love relationship, the narrative structure of a quest for love's fulfilment through conflict with a series of obstacles, and the representation of love as a powerful, indeed a transcendent force. Romance for writers of both sexes—and the majority of published writers have always been male, in France as elsewhere—has been a means of imagining the ideal relationship with the Other, and of exploring or rehearsing the conflicts between individual desire and all that contains and limits that desire, in particular the demands of society. Within these broad parameters, the genre (like all genres) has evolved and changed, both in response to external social forces, and internally, in reaction to or imitation of other literary works. But from the medieval period on, as French literature developed, diverged into the genres of theatre, poetry, and prose fiction and into numerous sub-genres, it returned (as did all European literatures) again and again to the romance plot. This was particularly the case with the novel, the French word for which, 'roman', retains the connection with medieval courtly romance, and implies a semantic link with romance in the sense of 'stories of love'. Some of the most celebrated early examples of the novel form, for example Honoré d'Urfé's seventeenth-century bestseller *L'Astrée* (1607–27) and (in a much more austere mode) Madame de Lafayette's *La Princesse de Clèves* (1678), are centrally concerned with the desire for and the possible consummation of love. In the eighteenth century, 'the love-interest was … central to most novels' (Hall 2000: 111) and the 'roman sentimental' dominated a growing market in which women authors such as Marie-Jeanne Riccobini and Isabelle de Charrières published alongside the better-known names of Antoine-François Prévost and Denis Diderot. Love, courtship, the possibility of reconciling the satisfaction of personal desire with social duty, these were staple ingredients of the novel form from the outset.

But from the latter part of the eighteenth century, and increasingly in the nineteenth, the romance started to be identified as a feminine mode of writing and reading. First, the Napoleonic era ushered in a more radical separation between male and female spheres, as women, under the succession of new regimes, were legally, economically, and politically excluded from the public domain and from the exercise of power or authority. At an ideological level, this meant the attribution to men of all those virtues that the post-Enlightenment century valued, whether these were the bourgeois virtues of rationality, pragmatism, and restraint, or, in the milieu of the artistic avant-garde, the qualities of creativity, intellectual daring, and political engagement. In these terms, it is clear that romance, with the importance it accords to marital and domestic arrangements, its emphasis on the quality of personal and emotional experience, its deployment of a narrative formula with its roots in myth and fairy tale, belonged firmly on the feminine—hence the inferior—side of the binary line. Moreover, the enormous popularity of the novel made it ripe for revalorization from a somewhat despised new arrival on the literary scene, to a serious literary form: the novel needed the credentials of virility, and this entailed the deprecation of women novelists. During this phase of the novel's rise to success, women's contribution to the genre was deemed to be 'limited by their intellectual and biological inferiority: they [were] granted the "feminine" virtues, finesse, sensitivity, spontaneity, but "male" virtues, strength, imagination, creative capacity, [were] deemed necessary to create truly "great" novels' (Hall 2000: 103).

The novel that consecrates the divide between the intellectually and aesthetically serious novel, and the foolishly feminine romance, is Flaubert's *Madame Bovary* (1857). Itself a formal *tour de force* as well as a deeply persuasive expression of moral disillusionment, *Madame Bovary* condemns the discourse of romance as both tawdry and pernicious. Fed on a diet of *romans d'amour*, Emma misinterprets the world around her, imagining searing passion where there is only sexual appetite and self-interest, failing to recognize the fatal incongruence between her dreams and reality.

> L'amour, croyait-elle, devait arriver tout à coup, avec de grands éclats et des fulgurations—ouragan des cieux qui tombe sur la vie, la bouleverse, arrache les volontés comme des feuilles et emporte à l'abîme le cœur entier.[5] (Flaubert 1983: 124)

If the romantic young student Léon shares Emma's escapist fantasies for a while, his masculine pragmatism soon asserts itself: what for Emma is a matter of life or death is for him a youthful interlude, to be left behind in his pursuit of a career and wealth. For Emma's second lover, Rodolphe, romance is merely a cynical strategy of seduction. Though Flaubert famously empathized with his heroine ('Madame Bovary, c'est moi'), and with her bitter dissatisfaction with a narrow destiny, his perspective on her is also detached and critical, and makes of her not the exceptional individual she longs to be, but rather a *petite bourgeoise* typical of her sex and class. Though Emma's dreams invite more readerly sympathy than the prosaic materialism that surrounds her, the form they take is treated caustically. Emma's imagination fails to rise above the clichés provided by the mass-produced fiction of the day, thus her dreams never attain the dignity of uniqueness, but are shared with her fellow consumers, who—it is clear—are mainly women.

In its acute observation of the ordinary, its refusal of idealism, and its depiction of the social texture of its time, *Madame Bovary* is one of the great realist novels. Realism, and its offspring naturalism, dominated French narrative fiction in the second half of the nineteenth century, and both defined themselves as the very antithesis of the emotion-centred, idealizing mode of romance. The realist project was mimetic and, in their depiction of reality, realists and naturalists accorded aesthetic priority to the concealed, darker face of the contemporary world, or to what Naomi Schor summarizes as the 'unsightly' (Schor 1988: 63). The Goncourt brothers produced, and extolled the virtues of, a literature that would face the harsh reality of modern urban living, defining realism's aims

---

[5] 'Love, she believed, had to come suddenly, with a great clap of thunder and a lightning flash, a tempest from heaven that falls upon your life, like a devastation, scatters your ideals like leaves and hurls your very soul into the abyss' (Flaubert 1992: 80).

as 'des études sur le vrai, sur le vif, sur le saignant' ('studies of what is true, live, and bloody', Gengembre 1997: 47). Love is certainly not absent from the great realist texts: Zola, theorist and most famous practitioner of naturalism, but also a great and a popular storyteller, incorporates romance plots into the complex tapestries of his novels. *Germinal* is a novel about politics, power, and the mining industry, but it is enriched by the narrative strand of the love story between Étienne and Catherine, and its final, sad consummation; *Au Bonheur des Dames* dramatizes the rise of consumer capitalism under the Second Empire, but its epic social history is underpinned by a love story between a retail magnate and a shop girl. However, naturalism, like realism, remained firmly on the virile side of the gender divide: rational and scientific in its aims (Zola famously compared his work to that of a surgeon dissecting a dead body), unflinching before the harsh realities from which the gentler sex had to be shielded, situated squarely in the public, social domain. If the most successful woman novelist of the nineteenth century, George Sand, was never quite admitted to the Pantheon of great writers, this was because despite the range of her work she never adopted the conventions of realism. Indeed, Sand displayed a consistent tendency to envisage social and philosophical issues through the narrative lens of romance.

In the course of the nineteenth century, then, romance became a feminized and a denigrated genre. In his 1895 journal, Jules Renard encapsulated in a rhetorical question the sense that no author who wished to be taken seriously could possibly align himself with the genre of the love story: 'Qui de nous oserait écrire un roman avec ces mots vidés de leur sens "Je t'aime" et "amour"?' (Constans 1999: 173).[6] As we have seen, the devaluation of romance was closely connected with the ideology of gender, but it was also determined by developments in the publishing trade, and by the complex question of the writer's social status in a market economy. As the market for and production of literature expanded in the nineteenth century, due to technological developments in printing and communications, and to the growth of retailing and that of literacy, so the demand for and the number of professional authors increased. Writers became more dependent on the market, rather than on the direct or indirect patronage of rich individuals or institutions. But in a market economy, as Pierre Bourdieu argues, Art defines itself precisely by its transcendence of the market, and those who aspire to the status of artists disdain the market as the arbiter of aesthetic quality. Indeed, the quality of a work of art may well be defined

---

[6] 'Which of us would dare to write a novel containing those words now bereft of meaning "I love you" and "love"?'

as being in inverse proportion to its marketability. Bourdieu traces how, in late nineteenth-century France, the author could gain social and cultural 'legitimacy' (recognition, status) according to three competing and hierarchized principles. Most prestigious was consecration by the literary community itself, by fellow producers; second came legitimacy bestowed by the dominant class in the form of success in a cultured 'literary' market and the awarding of public honours; last and certainly least came consecration from a mass popular audience, or commercial success (Bourdieu 1993: 50–1). Romance fiction, from the eighteenth century on, never ceased to be a widely read and popular genre, gradually extending its reading public as serialized *feuilletons* and cheap mass-produced novel series entered the market. It was politic for serious writers who aspired to the highest form of legitimacy to distance themselves from romance as a genre, and (as we shall see below) romance's lack of legitimacy remained constant throughout the twentieth century.

By the end of the nineteenth century, fiction whose narrative and thematic core was romantic love was firmly associated with women. Women readers were castigated for indulging in such self-indulgent fantasy ('rien ne les intéresse, pourrait-on presque dire, que par quelque rapport visible ou caché avec l'amour,'[7] sighed Professor Henri Marion in a Sorbonne lecture series (1892–4) entitled 'Psychologie de la femme' (Marion 1900: 110)), and women writers were criticized for the narrow, repetitive range of their concerns, in terms still current well into the twentieth century.[8] According to the scientific authorities of the day, irrationality and an excess of emotion were innate female qualities, and proved that the allocation of the public sphere to men, the private and domestic sphere to women, merely conformed to the natural order. Women's liking for romance was condemned, but condemned with condescending affection: a preoccupation with men and marriage was, after all, part of women's charm, and it confirmed male superiority. Throughout the twentieth century too, popular romantic fiction has consistently attracted more disdain than any other popular genre,[9] and

---

[7] 'one could almost say that nothing interests them unless it has some visible or hidden connection with love.'

[8] The critic Jean Larnac, in his 1929 survey of the history of women's writing in France, professed conclusions very close to the dominant discourse of the late nineteenth century: 'Pendant que son compagnon se tourne vers le dehors, l'objet, elle reste repliée sur elle-même, le sujet. L'homme écoute les rumeurs du monde. La femme entend les rumeurs de son être.' 'While her [male] companion turns outwards towards the object, she remains turned in on herself, the subject. Man listens to the sound of the world. Woman hears only the sound of her own being' (Larnac 1929: 269).

[9] 'Le roman sentimental moderne, type Harlequin, est sans doute actuellement le type de littérature populaire ayant le moins de raison d'accéder à une forme ou une autre de légitimité' ('The modern romantic novel of the Mills and Boon sort is currently the type of popular literature least

'serious' women writers, as Colette wryly acknowledges in the quotation at the start of this chapter, have often been tainted by association with a despised and feminine genre.

A sound feminist response to this is to dispute the identification of women's literature with romance. Because the reduction of all women's writing to the love story has been used to belittle and patronize, it is crucial to point out that, both generically and thematically, women's writing across the centuries has in reality been extremely diverse.[10] But having established this, we also have to acknowledge that the centrality of romance to female writing and reading is not solely a matter of hostile critical distortion. Many women writers, the canonized and the forgotten alike, do display a preference for the love plot as their primary narrative form, and romance has indisputably remained the most popular type of fiction for women readers, in France as elsewhere, throughout the nineteenth and twentieth centuries and up to the present day, with Harlequin-France, the largest publisher of popular romances, still bringing out over 500 new titles and selling twelve million books each year.[11] Although across the centuries the love story is one of the most recurrently used and intimately affecting narratives for both sexes, in the late nineteenth and still more in the twentieth century it comes to be—and not only in the patriarchal imagination—a genre favoured by women, both as producers and as consumers of fiction. Two questions arise from this. One is why this should be the case; if we reject the essentialist view, how do we explain the consistent connection between women and romance? The other is: does a taste for romance need justification? Is romance the inward-looking, regressive and formulaic narrative form that its detractors imply, or is it a genre that offers more liberating and creative possibilities?

Why women like romance—and should they?

An explanation of why women read and write romance must start from the social and material conditions of their lives, which have clearly predisposed them (us) towards a concern with personal and domestic

---

likely to achieve any form of legitimacy') (Péquignot 1997: 65). 'Serious' bookshops in France often have sections devoted to detective fiction, horror, science fiction, but almost never to romantic fiction.

[10] For the diversity of women's writing in nineteenth- and twentieth-century France, see Holmes 1996; Stephens 2000; Finch 2000.

[11] See below, Ch. 6.

relationships. Beauvoir's sharp dissection of romance in *Le Deuxième Sexe* debunks the idea that women are naturally inclined to prioritize love, and establishes instead a causal link between social dependence and emotional over-investment. 'En vérité, ce n'est pas d'une loi de la nature qu'il s'agit. C'est la différence de leur situation qui se reflète dans la conception que l'homme et la femme se font de l'amour' (Beauvoir 1976: 547).[12] If women have tended to see love and courtship as the essential dramas of life, and to favour stories that do the same, this is because economic, legal, and social dependence have meant that the choice of a partner has determined the security and happiness of women's lives to a much greater extent than those of men. The priority accorded by women in nineteenth- and twentieth-century societies to the choice of a mate and the quality of intimate relationships is closely connected to their restriction to the domestic, private sphere, and their subjection to the authority of father, then husband. It is not by chance that the production of cheap mass romantic fiction coincides with the thorough domestication of women. In France, as we have seen above, the separation of spheres by gender, and the cult of female domesticity, were propagated with a new intensity from the beginning of the nineteenth century. Napoleon's supremely patriarchal legal code (the *Code Napoléon*) enshrined the subjugation of women in law in 1804, and a gradual move from home-based to factory production in the second half of the century strengthened the ideology and (for most people) the lived reality of a gender-based division of labour and of space. The serialization of novels in the popular press (the *roman-feuilleton*) started in 1836, and very soon the *feuilleton* became synonymous with 'women's stories', and with romances, which by the end of the century were also being produced in cheap collections. Though the proportion of female authors remained low in France and does so to the present day,[13] the romantic novel was (and still is) one genre where women could find opportunities for publication since, as Bourdieu shows, it is the popular novel that is 'abandoned to writers issuing from dominated classes and women writers' (Bourdieu 1993: 190). It is the subordinate status of women that has determined their intense interest in the script of courtship and marriage, both as readers and as writers, and the romance novel has

---

[12] 'The fact is that we have nothing to do here with laws of nature. It is the difference in their situations that is reflected in the difference men and women show in conceptions of love' (Beauvoir 1972: 653).

[13] It is hard to give firm figures for this, since those that exist are contradictory. See Dudovitz 1990: 76–7. All literary historians are agreed, however, that women made up a small proportion of the overall number of authors in the nineteenth century, and recent figures published at the start of the twenty-first century set the proportion women/men at 30%/70%. (See Morello and Rodgers 2002: 9.)

provided a shape for the representation and the exploration of female experience.

What the socio-historical argument fails to explain, however, is the consistent popularity of the romance in the later twentieth century, despite a dramatic improvement in women's status and social opportunities, and a decline in the social and material necessity of marriage. There is no doubt that the genre has changed and adapted with the times, but nonetheless the basic narrative structure and the thematic focus on—in the vast majority of cases—heterosexual love remain constant. If we agree with Beauvoir that women's greater (or men's lesser) interest in romance is not determined by any 'law of nature', but by a difference of 'situation', then we need to look not just at the different material and social conditions of men's and women's lives, but also at how subjectivity and emotional identity are gendered in infancy and childhood. The part that gender plays in the construction of the self is clearly shaped by prevailing, and evolving, social practices and ideologies, but it takes time for social change (for example economic and legal reforms) to translate into the intimacy of family relationships. If, throughout a century of rapid social change, far more women than men have remained predisposed to choose stories in which love and the couple are central, then it may be useful to turn to a psychoanalytical perspective on the formation of female and male subjectivities in childhood. Although Freud's theories tend to ignore the socio-historical specificity of gender roles and childcare arrangements, and to universalize the socially contingent, they nonetheless provide the first serious investigation of how adult emotions and sexuality are shaped by experience in infancy, and they posit a gendered difference in that experience. Later feminist writers (notably, for the purposes of this argument, Dorothy Dinnerstein, Nancy Chodorow, and Jessica Benjamin) have drawn on Freud's legacy to theorize how, in patriarchal cultures, men and women develop with somewhat different emotional identities.

For Freud, the relationship of an infant with its parents forms the bedrock of emotional life for people of both sexes. Freud posited a close connection between adult desire and the unconscious memory of the first, symbiotically close bond with the mother: the extreme pleasure of love satisfied and reciprocated returns us to that infant experience of bliss, and if the pain of love lost or withheld in adulthood can sometimes seem disproportionately intense, this is because it reawakens echoes of the first separation.[14] Separation is nonetheless necessary to becoming a

---

[14] In *Fragments d'un discours amoureux*, Barthes refers repeatedly to the way in which separation from a loved one is lived through the memory of early maternal absence. A patient acceptance

functioning individual, and brings its own rewards, but here development diverges according to gender. Both girl and boy infants (provided they are not the victims of sustained neglect or abuse) experience the same early feelings of sensual plenitude, but the need to recognize the difference between self and other, and to assert the self as separate from the mother, is lived out differently by each sex. For Freud, the boy child relinquishes the joy of maternal identification to gain the greater good of acquiring masculinity, through the Oedipal drama of rivalry and identification with the father. The girl, though, confronts the difficulty that her adult role model is the mother, the very figure from whom she must separate. Her achievement of selfhood will involve a contradictory play of rejection and internalization of the mother, and will demand a difficult repression of the wish to identify with the father ('penis-envy'). Thus male and female subjectivities are differently constituted.

Post-Freudian feminist theorists agree that sexual love holds a unique fascination and promise for people of both sexes because it 'resonates', as Dorothy Dinnerstein put it, 'more literally than any other part of experience, with the massive orienting passions that first take shape in pre-verbal, pre-rational human infancy' (Dinnerstein 1977: 15). But they also de-naturalize what in Freud seems to be a necessary and universal process, and point out the historical and social determinants of this particular configuration of early development. It is in the patriarchal family that the mother is reduced to the selfless source of inchoate bliss, the object of infantile drives who must be left behind for the self to be formed, and that the father represents the adventure, excitement, and autonomy to which the emerging infant self dimly aspires. And this cultural devaluation of the mother, and overvaluation of the father, produces not just sexual difference, but also what Benjamin terms 'fault lines' (Benjamin 1988: 76) in both masculine and feminine identity. The masculine fault line arises from the necessary and radical repudiation of the first close relationship with the mother, the over-emphasis on separation and self-sufficiency driven by the fear of being reabsorbed, which produces a tendency to control affective relationships by an emphasis on rationality or by the exercise of domination. The girl's fault line, conversely, is more likely to be the opposite of this: uncertainty about her own separateness as a person, with a resulting emphasis on the self-in-relation rather than the autonomous self; idealization of the father or of father figures, since they represent what she can only partially aspire

---

of separation is described thus: 'J'agis en sujet bien sévré; je sais me nourrir, *en attendant*, d'autres choses que du sein maternel' ('I behave as a properly weaned subject; I can find nourishment, *in the meanwhile*, elsewhere than at the maternal breast') (Barthes 1977: 20).

to, and an incapacity to exert sexual agency. The connection between this and gendered reading practices is not hard to see. Freud and the Freudians acknowledge the initial bisexuality of all human beings, so that there is no suggestion here of an absolute divide between the sexes: men also like to read about love. But in patriarchal cultures, it is not surprising that a genre devoted to the narrative quest for a passionately intimate relationship with an adored Other, often at the cost of some loss of personal agency, should also be a 'feminine' genre.

Indeed Janice Radway, author of an ethnographically researched and persuasively argued study of popular romance in 1980s North America, draws on Nancy Chodorow's work to read the romance as a pleasurable re-enactment of the girl's Oedipal drama, with a happy ending. In the 'best' romances, as defined by Radway's representative group of readers, the heroine normally begins the story alone, separated from friends and family, almost invariably motherless, in a situation that echoes the child's attempts to seek individuation and emerge from the initial fusion of self and mother. In this solitude there is both a sense of emptiness, and a sense of adventure as the heroine tries to establish her autonomy through the 'masculine' routes of work and independence, identifying (as it were) with the father. But this attempt at separation will be rewarded not with social success or power, but rather with the love of the ideal partner who defines the heroine's identity as essentially that of a self-in-relation, and who simultaneously returns to her the joy of the lost maternal bond. Radway sees the tall, broad-chested heroes of popular romance not just as idealized objects of erotic desire, but also as maternal figures who offer the nurturing warmth that adult women mostly find themselves dispensing rather than receiving: they provide 'the reestablishment of that original, blissful symbiotic union between mother and child' which is really 'the goal of all romances despite their apparent preoccupation with heterosexual love and marriage' (Radway 1987: 156).

A post-Freudian reading of the romance then explains its attraction for women readers by the fact that it offers an imaginary replaying of the fundamental drama of female selfhood. The necessity for separation is represented through the heroine's initial solitude, but unlike the heroes of popular male genres (for example the lone detective of *noir* fiction), the selfhood achieved by the heroine is very much defined by her relationship with another: it is by loving and being loved that she achieves a happy ending. The idealized hero is both the father whose approval confers a sense of achieved identity, and the lost mother returned in a socially acceptable adult form. This kind of reading goes some way to explaining the ubiquity and consistency of the genre's success, and provides a useful perspective on the evolution of the popular romance in the twentieth century.

However, to see the romance genre as simply an endless replaying of formative childhood experience is problematic in a number of ways. The feminine identity produced by Freud's psycho-drama, even in its critical feminist version, can still be seen as a subjugated identity, premised on the identification of mother with a private, domestic, and finally claustrophobic world, and of father with the 'world out there' with its potential for self-discovery and creativity. Moreover, the ideal conclusion of the Freudian narrative, like the classic happy ending of the romance, demands that its heroine accept her own place within this gendered and inexorably heterosexual distribution of roles, and renounce further adventuring in favour of herself becoming a wife and mother. If the genre offers no more than a pleasurable confirmation of the rightness of this pattern, and of its capacity to provide women with happiness, then it seems to be (as some of its feminist critics have claimed) irremediably reactionary—an 'outil prodigieux, bon marché' ('a prodigiously effective and cheap tool', Coquillat 1988: 5) wielded in the anti-feminist cause. And this view in turn means the acceptance of a very negative assessment of past and present readers of romance. Harlequin-France calculate that around 20 per cent of the female population of France read their books in any given year. Since Harlequin are by no means alone in the popular romance market, and since I want to argue for an extension of the category 'romance' well beyond the mass-marketed product with which it has become virtually synonymous, the total proportion, even at the start of the twenty-first century, is clearly much higher. Are we to see all these female readers, and their predecessors across the century, as deluded, mystified, or masochistically colluding in their own subjection?

The argument for a close connection between the apparently inexhaustible pleasure of romance, and the female reader's formative Oedipal drama, is a persuasive one, but the vast range of romantic fiction cannot be reduced to a single, reactionary set of meanings. Despite Freud's assumption—unsurprising in the context of his day—that the healthiest outcome of a woman's emotional development was her acceptance of male authority and motherhood, his theories in fact provide the basis for a much more open-ended story. Freud posits an initial bisexuality common to both sexes, and identifies, in the theory of women's 'castration', the 'psychic cost to women of entering a culture in which our subordination is a *sine qua non*' (Hamer 1990: 135). Renunciation of her own phallic position in favour of being loved by the phallic father/lover may be the girl's most approved trajectory, but it is by no means the only logical possibility. As Janice Radway's work suggests, the appeal of the romance lies not just in its depiction of a final, rewarded surrender, but also in its acknowledgement of that 'pre-castrated' self who is at once nostalgic for the mother as primary love-object, and fully engaged in the self-invention that separation allows. Typically, the romance heroine begins her story in some sense alone and separated from a familiar world: she is the seeker, the agent of the narrative quest, discovering new realities—in the early twentieth-century popular romance, for example, loss of family fortune often forces her into paid employment far from home, frequently in exotic locations. The encounter with the hero is itself a challenging encounter with the unknown: if to win him means, at one level, renunciation of the quest, it also means the satisfaction of intensely felt desire. The function of the mass-market romance is to provide an enjoyable fantasy, therefore it offers its readers the imaginary pleasure of a perfect convergence between the selfish imperative towards emotional and erotic fulfilment, and the social imperative to take one's place in the gendered social order. Other forms of romance offer no utopian resolution, but address the potential conflict between desire and social acceptance directly, answering the genre's central question—can these two mutually desiring people find lasting happiness together?—with a qualified 'yes' or even with a clear 'no'. Romance provides a narrative form in which to address the difficult reconciliation of personal desire with social imperatives, and the particular forms that this takes for women.

Feminist reworkings of psychoanalytic theory have contested some of its more historically inflected assumptions, in ways that again suggest the possibility of more varied narratives, both lived and fictional. Dinnerstein, Chodorow, and Benjamin argue, for example, that the Freudian identification of the mother with an undifferentiated unity that must be left behind for individuation to occur, and of the father with escape and adventure, is strongly shaped by the patriarchal culture of its time, hence contingent rather than essential. Benjamin's argument in particular insists on the inter-subjectivity of what is more often characterized as a fused, symbiotic relationship between baby and mother. Rather than being fixated on the breast as object, she argues, the infant almost immediately takes pleasure in recognition of the mother, and in the interplay of looks, smiles, voices. The mother (before the father) 'embodies something of the not-me' (Benjamin 1988: 24), and the relationship with her brings not only the joy of total safety, of belonging, but also 'the joy and urgency of discovering the external, independent reality of another person' (ibid.: 44). If this first relationship is itself incipiently social, then it becomes possible to acknowledge the contradictory but equally powerful desires for, on the one hand, the security of belonging and, on the other, the excitement of freedom and agency, without tying them so firmly to gender. The romance might resonate with formative emotional experience, yet contest the necessary assignment of seductive otherness to the father's realm, and identificatory fusion to the mother's. Often, for the romance to end happily, the hero/father must be revealed or taught to possess a 'maternal' capacity for tenderness and intimacy; through secondary female characters, or through the heroine herself, a female capacity for adventurous self-assertion is claimed and approved. Thus it is not always only men who embody the excitement of difference in romance, and although it is heterosexual romance that dominates the field, the genre's codes and structures extend easily to love stories between women. The pleasures of romance are illuminated by a psycho-analytic reading, but the genre does not merely replay, but also contests and reworks, the classically gendered version of the Oedipal narrative.

Romance, then, despite its association with mindless sentimentality, deals with serious ethical questions: how to reconcile the fierce egoism of sexual and emotional drives with social responsibility, how to nego-tiate the boundaries between self and other, between loving desire and possessive control, between fascination with and fear of difference. It is the relevance of these issues to most readers' lives that produces, in part, the pleasure of reading. But that pleasure resides equally in the fact that romance is the genre in which women have been able to write and read about sex, in a century when—until relatively recently—erotic writing was predominantly male, and the taboos surrounding explicit discussion of sex were considerably stronger for women. The very structure of the romance lends it erotic potential: the first encounter with the loved one arouses desire; the body of the narrative plays with this desire, in some cases endlessly deferring its satisfaction, in others partially fulfilling and thereby heightening it, until the climax of either perfect union, or loss and separation. As Catherine Belsey points out, from the mass-market romance to the most formally sophisticated, what these texts have in common is that 'by evading, by teasing, they elicit the desire of the reader, thus demonstrating the degree to which desire is an effect of the signifier' (Belsey 1994: 19). From the Belle Époque seamstress snatch-ing a few minutes to read the latest episode of her romantic serial, to the feminist academic reading a critically lauded twenty-first-century love story, the romance reader finds not only her head but also her senses engaged, as the very bodily experience of desire is—obliquely and metaphorically, or directly and explicitly—evoked, and mirrored in the urgent, sensuous experience of reading itself. Across the century, romantic fiction, along with women's magazines (in which romance has generally featured), has been the principal forum—public, popular, and socially inclusive—in which women have collectively explored and enjoyed their sexuality, and attempted to define what constitutes good sex from a woman's point of view.[15] Avis Lewallen's half-jokey description of one American romantic blockbuster as 'pornography for women' has some relevance for the entire genre (Lewallen 1988).

Many feminist critics (for example Greer 1970; Firestone 1972; Coquillat 1988) have deplored women's taste for romance as a form of false consciousness, and seen the genre—at least in its popular form—as the opium of the mystified female masses. Others (for example Modleski 1984; Radway 1987; Constans 1999) have sought to explain what positive pleasures women find there, and explored the reasons why its readers have experienced romance as enabling rather than mystifying, empowering rather than undermining. The dangers of romance as a genre that insists on the inexorable centrality of love—in most cases heterosexual love—to women's lives demand serious consideration. But this book considers romance above all, despite its hazards, as a narrative form chosen by women writers and readers, across classes and across three centuries, not only for its capacity to provide pleasurable fantasy, but also for its ability to reflect and reflect on their lives. Romantic fiction represents a largely female space, an 'entre-femmes' ('amongst-women', Irigaray 1986), in which stories are told in order to make sense of experience, in which fears are identified and dreams indulged, dangers are confronted and extremes of happiness imagined.

---

[15] Several feminist commentators on romance have pointed out that the plot structure of the popular romance, where most of the narrative deals with anticipation rather than sex itself, 'may well correspond to many women's experience of sex as better in anticipation than in action' (Jones 1986: 200).

2 Passion, Piety, and the New Woman: Romantic Fiction at the Belle Époque

The legacy of Sand

George Sand, the only French woman novelist of the nineteenth century to achieve canonical status, died in 1876. A lifelong republican and a feminist, Sand lived to see only the first six years of France's third and most durable republican regime, with the hopes that it offered for women's emancipation. Sand's last novels, written in the 1860s and 1870s, were largely romances: stories of the mutual attraction between a man and a woman, of the adventures they enjoy and the obstacles they overcome on their journey towards a happy ending in each other's arms. Yet, though their plots placed them squarely within the genre of romance, these novels also dealt with a range of wider issues: the conflict between Catholic and secular moralities in *Mademoiselle la Quintinie* (1863), the ethics of science and colonization in *Laura ou voyage dans le cristal* (1863), the intellectual equality of women in *Mademoiselle Merquem* (1868), and, in each of the late novels, the question of what makes a man a suitable and desirable partner for an intelligent, independent woman.

Sand was the most significant model of literary success for the next generation of women writers, and her late work foreshadowed in a number of ways the development of the romance over the period 1880–1914, retrospectively characterized as the Belle Époque. Sand's romances entertain, withholding and gradually revealing narrative information, delaying the conclusion through a series of often melodramatic peripeteia. The Belle Époque romance would respond above all to the massive demand for good, exciting stories, in an age of near universal literacy and expansion of the press. Sand's love stories are also openly ideological—they moralize. The Belle Époque romance would develop in politically opposed directions, Catholic and conservative on the one hand, feminist and liberal on the other, but each of these would make the romance the vehicle of a clear ideological message. Like the novels of Sand, romances at the Belle Époque often make the relationship between heterosexual love and feminism a central issue. And just as Sand's work was denigrated, both in her lifetime and posthumously, for its feminine narcissism and espousal of a degraded genre ('Toutes ses œuvres furent des histoires d'amour qu'elle nourrit de ses propres sentiments',[1] wrote Jean Larnac in 1929: 212), so romance writers would continue to be seen as sub-literary, because of their emphasis on the 'feminine' domain of emotion, and of their association with the merely popular.

Women and popular fiction in the new Republic

Sand's novels of the 1860s imagine an idealized, egalitarian relationship between a woman and a man, and also recognize the social obstacles that situate such an outcome in the realm of the ideal. The gender inequalities Sand portrays were not about to evaporate with the arrival of the Third Republic, but the new regime would nonetheless change the conditions of women's lives. There was of course no neat divide between life under the Second Empire (1851–70), and under the Third Republic (1870–1940), but there are good reasons to see the Belle Époque as a key period in the conflict over women's rights and identity, and as a time of significant advances in women's education. The 1850s and 1860s had already seen a revival of feminist activity, and female literacy (like male literacy but slightly more slowly) rose steadily as the century advanced. What changed under the new Republic, despite the continuing exclusion of women from most of the rights of a citizen, and despite the remarkable similarity between republican views on women's subordinate role and those of the right-wing opposition,[2] was the fact that this regime publicly proclaimed its commitment to the principles of liberty, equality, and human rights. The blatant contradiction between the founding beliefs of the Republic, and its discriminatory practices, fuelled and provided a language for feminist protest. Moreover, the new regime's leaders were anxious to produce new generations of Frenchmen loyal to the Republic, as well as suitably trained to provide the labour for the country's economic development. For that, they also needed generations of good republican wives and mothers, and from the early 1880s, the French state began to provide primary education to the age of 12 for both sexes, and secondary education in sex-segregated grammar schools (*lycées*) for the daughters of the bourgeoisie. Women's place in and right to education were officially recognized.

Modernization took place slowly in France, but this was also a period when new technologies had a marked impact on the shape of every-day life, at least in towns and cities, and women's spatial and social

---

[1] 'All her works were love stories that she based upon her own emotions.'
[2] See Holmes 1996: ch. 1, 'Women in French society 1848–1914', esp. pp. 10–16.

mobility—consequently, perhaps, their sense of their own possibilities—began to increase. Trains, tramways, bicycles made independent travel more possible, and the accelerated development of the retail trade gave urban women legitimate reasons to move round alone or with female friends, as well as inviting them to enjoy the agency, and the limited but real power, of the consumer. The high proportion of French women in employment (38.9 per cent of the total female population in 1906 (McMillan 2000: 161)) were mainly agricultural or industrial workers, with a significant number also in domestic service, but the numbers working in commerce, public service, and the liberal professions expanded steadily between the 1890s and 1914, with the growth of retailing, the tertiary sector, the civil service, and female education. This is the age of the 'femme nouvelle' or New Woman, partly the mythical creation of journalists and anxious misogynists, but partly rooted in the changing reality of at least some women's lives.[3]

An important element of the new modernity was the expansion in publishing, driven by a combination of increased literacy, the Third Republic's relaxation of censorship laws (the 1881 law on freedom of the press), and new technologies that steadily reduced the costs of paper and printing (Leroy and Bertrand-Sabiani 1998: 16, 19). The appetite for news, *faits divers*, and fiction extended across all classes, and entrepreneurial publishers could make a fortune by commissioning, packaging, and marketing stories in ways that appealed to a mass audience. Since the 1830s, most daily newspapers had promoted reader loyalty by including a serialized novel or *feuilleton*, and this continued, with the whole range of dailies from the serious *Le Journal* to the downmarket *Le Petit Parisien* publishing novels that would later appear in volume form. Entrepreneurial publishers such as Émile Dentu, Arthème Fayard, Alphonse Lemerre, and Ferenzci also promoted new ways of packaging and marketing stories, from publication in instalments ('fascicules'), with each episode costing relatively little but a strong motivation for further purchases, to the 'petites collections', which targeted different types of reader through pricing, presentation, and publicity, aiming for a sort of brand loyalty. Dentu's *Nouvelle Bibliothèque Choisie* (New Selected Library), for example, appeared from the 1880s, offering the work of popular authors in an 'elegant and portable' format, at 1 franc for each (roughly 300 page) volume—a substantial cost when the average daily pay for a woman worker in Paris in the 1890s was 3 francs a day (McMillan 2000: 167). By 1905, Fayard's *Le Livre Populaire* collection was

---

[3] See Holmes and Tarr 2005 for a much fuller account of changes in women's lives and senses of identity at the Belle Époque. See also Roberts 2002.

retailing works by known, popular authors at 65 centimes per volume, and the 1914 Ferenczi series *Le Petit Livre*, clearly aimed at the lower socio-economic end of the market, offered small, 80–100-page novels at around 35 centimes.[4]

In this lively, expanding market for popular fiction, women were the primary consumers. As Anne-Marie Thiesse's research has shown, the popular *feuilletons*, unlike those in the more prestigious newspapers, made their address to a female readership clear: the stories revolved around female characters, incorporated domestic, emotional dramas that were identified with the feminine sphere, and emphasized their appeal to 'feminine' emotion in their titles and in publicity studded with words such as 'passion', 'poignant', 'émouvant' (touching) (Thiesse 1984). The format itself fitted the pattern of women's lives, as would the soap opera many years later: the episodic structure matched the interrupted rhythms of motherhood and domestic work; the gripping narrative highs and lows broke the monotony of repetitious labour; the stories provided material for discussion with other women, feeding into the pleasures of female sociability (Thiesse 1984: 21). Thiesse's interviewees, recalling working-class childhoods around 1900, were unanimous in their identification of the *feuilleton* with mothers, not fathers (ibid.: 20). Some women applied domestic skills to create a low-cost, personally produced book, snipping the episodes out and sewing them together in a cover sometimes provided by the newspaper. The same process could be applied to the *fascicules*.

Love, desire, romance, and marriage were the central components of a fiction designed primarily to address the lives and dreams of women readers. However, from a commercial point of view, the wider the stories' appeal the better, and most serialized novels mixed romance with other elements such as mystery, adventure, and crime. Moreover, both *feuilletons* and *fascicules* demanded novels of substantial length, as the system of paying authors by the line confirmed, and maintaining the reader's curiosity demanded more than one source of narrative suspense. Until around 1910, the romance plot rarely stood alone, but rather was woven into a dense, multi-stranded narrative, which appealed to several dimensions of (particularly but not solely female) experience. Xavier de Montépin's hugely successful *La Porteuse de pain* (The Bread Carrier, 1884), like Charles Mérouvel's equally popular *Chaste et flétrie* (Chaste and Branded, 1889), both placed a female protagonist at the centre of the story, and followed her though a series of trials and tribulations until finally all was resolved in a happy conclusion—but these were narratives driven less by romantic love than by false accusations of crime, of which

---

[4] Information from publishers' catalogues held in the Bibliothèque nationale de France.

the heroine had to be proved innocent so that her role as mother, and as guardian of morality, could be restored. The prolific novelist Émile Richebourg (1833–98) became a millionaire thanks to the sales of his fast-moving, colourful tales of love and passion, of cynical adventurers (and adventuresses), concealed illegitimate births, fortunes made and lost, crime and repentance. *Une haine de femme* (A Woman's Hatred, 1899) for example, reveals beneath the virginal beauty of the young Valentine Merson a ruthless fortune hunter, who deserts her sincere and ardent lover to marry an American millionaire, and passes off the child she is carrying as his. The plot shifts between Paris and New York as the real father seeks his lost child; stolen letters are used to blackmail Valentine, who by now has fallen in love with her stepson; the pages are turned because the reader wants to know will Valentine be unmasked? Will the Comte de Valmont (any reference to *Les Liaisons dangereuses* seems unintentional) regain his daughter? Can Valentine's love for her stepson be sincere? Commercial good sense, as well as Richebourg's fertile imagination, dictated that the answer to these questions could only be found by purchasing volume ii, *Les Hontes de l'amour* (The Shame(s) of Love).

Richebourg's recipe, mingling exotically wealthy locations with domestic family dramas, and violence and suspense with intimate emotions, made him 'le conteur préféré des midinettes' (Olivier-Martin 1980: 184).[5] Several other writers found a path to commercial success with stories that mixed mystery and passion, adventure and desire, and many of these were women for whom (as the number of male pen-names confirms) it remained harder to get published, and harder to be taken seriously by editors and critics. Pierre Ninous (1845–1907), prolific author of titles such as *Cœur brisé* (1890) and *Les Deux Aimées* (1902), also wrote under the name Paul d'Aigremont, but was in reality a woman, Jeanne Thérèse Lapeyrière. Marie-Louise Gagneur (1832–1902), publishing under her own name, continued a career begun under the Second Republic and managed to combine militant feminism and anticlericalism with great popularity as a *feuilletonniste* (for example *Les Crimes de l'amour*, 1874; *Le Supplice de l'amant*, 1888). Georges Maldague (1867–1938), in reality Josephine, had a long and successful career publishing novels such as *Rose sauvage* (1886), *Le Mal d'amour* (1888), *Trahison d'amour* (1910). Daniel Lesueur, née Jeanne Loiseau (1860–1921), was the author both of feminist-inclined *romans à idées* such as *Nietzschéenne* (1908) and of colourful, moving novels of love and adventure first published in the mass-circulation popular press (*Calvaire*

---

[5] 'the shopgirls' favourite storyteller'.

de femme, 1897; *Le Masque d'amour*, 1904—each of these subsequently published in two lengthy volumes).[6]

These widely read novels bear the signs of fiction written for a mass audience with limited education, limited leisure, and a desire above all for the vicarious pleasures of sensation, emotional intensity, variety of experience. Stock characters recur from one novel to the next, across the work of most of the authors in the field: from the scheming adventuress to the chaste but spirited heroine, from the sly villain, often of mixed race, to the strong, handsome hero. Characterization is generally explicit and definitive, without room for much internal contradiction, or for development.[7] The transparency of signs is another very evident mark of the popular: the pathetic fallacy is a commonplace, so that the reader is secure in their translation of a storm as the harbinger of violent events, and blue skies as signifiers of at least a temporary happiness. Moral or emotional events always produce physical effects: thus in volume ii of Lesueur's *Calvaire de femme*, the innocent young Bérengère, denied the right to marry the man she loves, almost dies of an unnamed illness; in *Le Masque d'amour*, the pretty but mean-spirited Françoise is physically altered by jealousy of her more beautiful cousin: 'les fossettes s'allongeaient en rides' (Lesueur 1904: 281).[8] Such devices produce a relaxing and reassuring ease of interpretation, or what Jean-Claude Vareille defines as the pleasures of effective 'écriture stéréotypique' (stereotypical writing): 'rien qui s'écarte du chemin, une avance assurée, expérimentée maintes et maintes fois. La sécurité, l'ordre, le repos de l'esprit, la tranquillité que procure le *déjà vu*' (Vareille 1994: 299).[9]

At the same time, to see all the genuinely popular novels of this period as stultifyingly formulaic would be to misrepresent them. They are works of considerable craftsmanship in the way they manipulate the genre to produce volume after volume of page-turning, moving, often thrilling narrative. Many of them are unafraid to tackle quite complex issues, both emotional and political. Richebourg paints a deft portrait

---

[6] P. Ninous: Broken Heart (1890), The Two Beloveds (1902); M. L. Gagneur: The Crimes of Love (1874), The Lover's Torment (1888); G. Maldague: Wild Rose (1886), The Pain of Love (1888), Love's Betrayal (1910); D. Lesueur: The Nietzschean Woman (1908), A Woman's Suffering (1897), The Mask of Love (1904).

[7] Richebourg, for example, directly addresses the reader to insist on the dangerously volatile nature of Éléna, the sly, jealous 'créole' in *Une haine de femme*: 'Nous le répétons, Éléna avait la même nature que son père et rien ne pouvait empêcher qu'il ne se fît en elle un débordement de violentes passions' ('Let me repeat, Éléna had the same nature as her father and nothing could prevent the upsurge of her violent emotions') (Richebourg 1899a: 202).

[8] 'Her dimples lengthened into wrinkles.'

[9] 'no diversions from the path, a steady progression that has been tried and tested again and again. Security, order, rest for the mind, the tranquillity of the familiar.'

of fin-de-siècle marriage as an inter-sex transaction exchanging money (his) for sex and beauty (hers). Gagneur and Lesueur depict the rights and wrongs of divorce legislation around the time of the new divorce law (1884). Lesueur's popular *feuilletons* provide fast-moving, densely plotted narratives full of suspense and extreme emotion, but it is there rather than in her *romans à idées* that she addresses, for example, the complex feelings of a young adult son faced with evidence of his mother's still active sexuality (*Le Masque d'amour*, i: *Le Marquis de Valcor*), and builds into the plot a lively, part-satirical portrait of the parliamentary conflict between royalists and republicans (in the same novel). These are not writers who patronize their readers, and both the skill and quality of many of the texts, and their high sales in volume form (often evidenced by repeated reprintings[10]), suggest a cross-class readership rather than a strictly segregated one.

This was certainly the case with perhaps the most commercially successful romance of the entire period, Georges Ohnet's *Le Maître de Forges* (1882).[11] Ohnet (1848–1918) was another of the best-selling popular authors of the age, critically denigrated for his romance-centred plots (Todd 1994: 22), but nonetheless widely read for that. With *Le Maître de Forges*, he seems to have captured with particular acuity the spirit of the times. Philippe Derblay is the ideal republican hero, a handsome, competent, virtuous engineer. He falls in love with Claire de Beaulieu, spirited daughter of the aristocratic family whose inherited estate adjoins the land he has acquired by hard work and good management. Claire, on the rebound from her desertion by a fickle, shallow cousin of her own class, Gaston de Bligny, accepts his proposal as a means to take her revenge on Gaston. Realizing that she has deceived him, Philippe maintains the façade of a happy marriage but withdraws emotionally from the wife he loves. Over the rest of the novel, as rivals compete for the affections of both partners, and a series of events display Philippe's integrity, constancy, and charm, Claire gradually falls in love, until in a dramatic dénouement she interposes herself in a duel between her husband and Gaston. Wounded in the hand, she wins Philippe back and the two exchange 'leur premier baiser d'amour' (Ohnet 1882: 237).[12] Claire's sentimental education serves to endorse the dominant values of the new regime, for through her the Republic's aristocratic opponents

---

[10] The Bibliothèque nationale catalogue shows that much of the work of Richebourg, Ninous, Gagneur, Maldague, Lesueur was reprinted over and over again, not only within the period dealt with here but also after the 1914–18 war. Richebourg's *La Dame voilée* (1877) was still being republished in 1950.

[11] The novel went through 250 editions between 1882 and 1900.

[12] 'their first loving kiss'.

are represented as vain, superficial, and anachronistic, their survival dependent on adaptation to the age of the republican bourgeoisie; at the same time patriarchy is endorsed, as an assertive heroine comes to learn that respect for one's husband brings happiness. Yet a woman reader can also find considerable pleasure here. Strong, handsome Philippe, graphically described from Claire's point of view, provides the vicarious delight of a faithful, adoring love. And if Claire's 'éducation sentimentale' means learning to relinquish the arrogance of her class, social privilege has also made her a confident, forthright heroine whose initiative and physical courage finally save the day. The reader who identifies with Claire finds herself rewarded at last with the reconciliation of desire, love, security, and family in that last passionate kiss.

Ohnet's novels are perfect examples of a fiction that combines romance with topical realism, and the pleasure of escapism—for few readers would have direct experience of such leisured and elegant lives—with the evocation of contemporary issues, thus appealing to a wide readership across classes, and to some extent too across the sexes. The beginning of the twentieth century saw a gradual specialization of the popular market that announced the direction romance would take after the First World War. The first Delly romances, in which every textual element is subordinated to the love story, appeared in 1900.[13] By around 1910, the German publisher Eichler had launched a series of cheap translated novels, sold in instalments at the very low price of 10 to 20 centimes, which included collections labelled 'romans d'amour' bearing titles such as *Un cœur de vierge* (A Virgin's Heart) and *Douleurs d'amour* (The Pains of Love) (Constans 1990: 23). By 1913, Ferenczi was publishing collections of 'petits livres' unmistakably aimed at a female readership, and marketed on the basis of their adherence to the romance formula rather than on that of the authors' reputation: in the catalogue that lists *Elle l'aimait trop* (She Loved Him Too Much), *Rien que nous deux* (Just the Two of Us), *Parce qu'elle l'aimait* (Because She Loved Him), no names of authors appear. For most of the Belle Époque period, however, romance was interwoven with other sources of reading pleasure, and the individual author remained an important guarantor of quality.

The moral romance

If *Le Maitre de Forges* was one of the most widely read books of its age, this was in part because it so neatly captured an ideological conflict that

---

[13] Delly romances dominated the French market for the first three-quarters of the twentieth century. They are discussed below, Ch. 3.

shaped the collective consciousness of the years 1880–1910. The novel pitted the values of the secular, rationalist, republican state against those of a Catholic, conservative, anti-democratic opposition, and showed the triumph of the former as inevitable. The conservatives only gradually relinquished their hope of overturning the Third Republic: if the *ralliement* of 1892 marked the Catholic Church's official acceptance of the regime, and the intention of the clergy to work within its structures, the Dreyfus affair of the late 1890s revived the full bitterness of the conflict. Though Left and Right, republicans and conservatives, shared the conviction that women were naturally subordinate to men's needs, they opposed each other in a battle for influence over women's hearts and minds. The Church was jealous of its traditional role as the educator of girls and the confessor and confidant of women, whilst the Republic sought through education to mould new generations of proudly secular, pro-republican women who would transmit their loyalties to their sons and daughters. What women read in their leisure time was one dimension of this struggle.

Conservative Catholic opinion recognized the role played by popular fiction in shaping female mentalities. Several of the best-selling authors of the day were overtly pro-republican—including Marie-Louise Gagneur, Pierre Ninous, Georges Ohnet—but the problem lay beyond the explicit views of certain writers. Romance, that central element of almost all the popular stories in circulation, tended as a genre to place the emphasis on love as personal fulfilment rather than as the realization of the divine will, or the means to found a Christian family. And the pleasure of reading much popular fiction lay in giving oneself up to unrestrained emotion and imagined sensation: most popular *feuilletons* and low-priced book collections or 'petits livres' belonged to what one contemporary film critic, writing of pornography, horror, and melodrama in cinema, has termed 'body genres'—that is, genres the success of which can be measured by the audience's bodily response of arousal, fear, or tears (Williams 1991). The indulgence of the senses and the emotions, albeit vicarious, ran counter to the self-discipline, chastity, and devotion to family prescribed by the Church as proper feminine behaviour. As one parish priest put it in 1912, working-class girls who buy themselves a cheap romance 'au titre alléchant' ('with an alluring title') on a Saturday evening will tend to spend Sunday

étendues sur un lit, à parcourir avidement ces pages licencieuses. Elles négligent pour cette lecture, et le soin de leur toilette, et une promenade salutaire, et l'assistance aux offices. Le lendemain, à l'atelier, elles ont un long sujet de conversation dans le récit de leurs impressions qu'elles transmettent à leurs jeunes compagnes, atteintes elles-mêmes de cette manière par le mauvais livre.[14] (Leroy and Bertrand-Sabiani 1998: 115)

Printed fiction had, however, become one of the principal forms of popular entertainment, particularly among young women, and to preach against it was unlikely to turn the tide. A more effective strategy, and one that achieved considerable success in France, was to provide an alternative kind of fiction—one that would support rather than undermine the Catholic, family-oriented values of the Church and of a large body of conservative opinion. Central to this campaign—though it seems to have been a broad campaign of many converging initiatives, rather than a coordinated or centralized one—was the fiction-based weekly (by 1894 twice weekly) *Les Veillées des chaumières*, founded in 1877, whose very title, evoking storytelling by the cottage fireside, suggests nostalgia for the threatened values of a traditional rural society. *Les Veillées* provided a diet of serialized fiction, all of it, as the publicity promised, 'de saines et intéressantes lectures' ('wholesome and interesting reading'). Subscribers (5 centimes per copy and 5 francs for a year's subscription) could take advantage of special offers once the serials were published in volume form, or (from 1881) purchase the annual 'almanachs' or volumes of stories, for themselves or as gifts.

> Rien de plus charmant à offrir que ces petits volumes illustrés; rien de plus amusant mais aussi rien de plus moral que les nombreuses nouvelles qu'ils renferment. L'almanach est le plus merveilleux agent de propagande qui se puisse trouver.[15]

The serialized novels, by a variety of authors including (regularly) Paul Féval, Raoul de Navery, Zénaïde Fleuriot, Marie Maréchal, provide many of the standard pleasures of popular fiction: narrative suspense, displacement to exotic settings (Scotland, Russia, and medieval France are particularly favoured), ease of interpretation thanks to an omniscient narrative voice and a transparently coded use of settings, weather, and characters' appearance. Romance is a central component, but hero and heroine are always—at least by the happy dénouement—devout

---

[14] 'lying on their bed avidly devouring its licentious pages. Reading makes them neglect care of their clothes and person, and takes the place of a healthy walk and attendance at church. The next day, in the workshop, they give their young workmates a long account of the story they have read, thus infecting them too with the evil effects of a bad book.' Speech by the curé de Serges, 28 Oct. 1912.

[15] 'Nothing could be more charming than these small illustrated volumes; nothing could be more entertaining, but also more moral than the many stories they contain. The almanach is the most marvellous agent of propaganda one could wish to find.' 'Propaganda' here seems to carry no negative connotations. The advertisement appears in *Les Veillées* regularly from 1881.

Christians, and their union takes the form of marriage and the foundation of a family. The pre-publicity for Marie Maréchal's *Le Mariage de Nancy*, set in the still recent Franco–Prussian war, promises an exciting but thoroughly proper love story: 'et, comme toujours, à côté de la petite fée...il y a le prince Charmant: ici, il nous apparaît sous les traits d'un brave et jeune officier français, le type du chrétien et du chevalier' (28 Feb. 1878).[16]

Perhaps the most prolific and well known of *Les Veillées*'s authors was Maryan, pen-name of Marie Cadiou (1847–1927). Maryan published at least a hundred novels between 1877 and her death, many of them serialized in *Les Veillées* then put out in book form by their publisher, Blériot; others appearing in, for example, Firmin-Didot's series *Bibliothèque des mères de famille* (The Mother of the Family's Library), which also promised reading matter suitable for good Christian readers. Maryan, like her liberal republican counterparts, is a skilful storyteller whose narrative techniques are both functional and flexible. Appearances and clothing (a good woman dresses simply, the style of her outfit 'et surtout la coupe, dénota(nt) ce souci d'une femme comme il faut de ne pas attirer l'attention'[17] (Maryan 1903: 6)) always signify character; a sort of pathetic fallacy operates whereby emotional states translate directly into physical symptoms; an omniscient narrator directs the reader's sympathies clearly, though leaving room for a variety of characters' viewpoints through shifting focalization. These techniques are used in the service of a moralizing mission. In *Une dette d'honneur* (A Debt of Honour, serialized in *Les Veillées* in 1885), a young woman denies herself love until she has rehabilitated the family name by paying off a large debt, and is then rewarded with romantic and marital happiness. In *Anne de Valmoët*, an older woman's story of unhappy marriage and loneliness is echoed and reversed by that of her young ward, an emancipated young woman who learns the value of family, security, and the love of an honest man. ' "J'ai été folle et présomptueuse" ', admits Anne to her new husband. ' "Maintenant j'ai soif de me laisser conduire et guider"... Le bras puissant de Georges se glissa avec un tendre respect autour de sa taille frêle, et elle sentit sa vie soutenue et protégée' (Maryan 1890: 250–1).[18] In *Mariage moderne* (1903), it is the husband who learns, through the events

---

[16] 'and, as always, beside the fairytale heroine there is the Prince Charming: here, he appears in the guise of a brave young French officer, the perfect example of a Christian and a gentleman.'

[17] 'and above all the cut, displaying the respectable woman's reluctance to draw attention to herself.'

[18] ' "I have been silly and presumptuous... Now I long to let myself be led and guided." Georges's strong arm encircled her slim waist with respectful tenderness, and she felt that her life was now supported and protected.'

of the narrative, to love and respect his young wife and find happiness within the family.

Though the romance plot of meeting, overcoming obstacles, and final union underpins most of Maryan's work, her dénouements significantly take the form not of a passionate embrace of the couple at last alone, but rather of a collective scene in which the couple are clearly part of a family. Thus Élisabeth and Félicien in *Les Chemins de la vie* (The Roads of Life, *Les Veillées*, 1882–3) renounce urban living and personal ambition to end the novel back in the family home, in a rural landscape glittering with snow that signifies both the solidity and the bright happiness of their future together: ' "Dieu nous a enlevés tous deux aux routes brillantes pour nous réunir ici . . . et nous rendre heureux" ', says Élisabeth, 'cachant son visage rougissant sur l'épaule de sa tante' (Maryan 1882: 328).[19] This combination of piety and passion would be one of the main trends of French romantic fiction in the twentieth century.

The feminist romance

Moral romances often featured strong, competent heroines, but their stories could only conclude happily in the arms of a husband whose authority they acknowledged, just as they accepted the supreme authority of a very patriarchal deity and his male representatives on earth. Though implicitly opposed to the anticlerical Republic, the moral values these novels defended were very much the dominant values of the age, for if the Republic disputed the authority of God and Church, it replaced them with an equally patriarchal state, and agreed entirely on the husband's authority within marriage. The 1804 Civil Code, despite four changes of regime, remained firmly in place. The Code defined women as legal minors, and enshrined the authority of the husband and father as the central principle of domestic law. A married woman owed obedience to her husband (Article 213), could not work, open a bank account, or dispose of her own earnings without his consent; she had no independent legal existence but was defined solely in relation to her spouse. Until 1884 divorce remained illegal, and the new law excluded the grounds of mutual consent, and made it harder for the wife than the husband to obtain a divorce on grounds of adultery, since her infidelity was far more threatening to the institution of marriage. In response to feminist campaigning, some of the Code's worst excesses were removed: in 1881

---

[19] ' "God has taken us from the brilliant roads of life to reunite us here . . . and make us happy" . . . hiding her blushing face against her aunt's shoulder.'

a married woman gained the right to open a savings account, and in 1907 a wife in paid employment could dispose of her own salary. Marriage remained, nonetheless, a contract based on male authority over women and children.

If progress on women's rights was slow, feminist ideas were very much in the air. The range of groups campaigning for the suffrage, social and educational reform, and revision of the *Code Civil* extended from the right-wing Catholic Le Féminisme Chrétien, founded by Marie Maugeret in 1897, to the socialist-anarchist Ligue des Femmes led by the ex-Communarde Louise Michel (1880), with the majority situated in the moderate republican centre. Feminist congresses were held regularly, giving rise to press coverage that was on the whole sardonically hostile, but that spread awareness of the phenomenon of women's militancy. Though a distinctly Parisian and minority movement, French feminism grew throughout the Belle Époque, and by 1914 could claim a total membership of well over 100,000 (Waelti-Walters and Hause 1994: 6, 167). The movement also had its press, with many organizations publishing a weekly or monthly paper, and the remarkable *La Fronde* appearing daily from 9 December 1897 to 1 October 1903. Owned and edited by the glamorous and enterprising Marguerite Durand, *La Fronde* was staffed entirely by women, from the journalists to the typesetters, and combined eloquently argued feminism with coverage of parliamentary debates, legal affairs, finance and the stock market, and domestic issues (in a column entitled 'le Home'). Page 3 normally carried a short story or serialized novel, always by a woman author, beginning with Daniel Lesueur's *Lèvres closes* in 1897.

La Fronde demonstrated the existence of an educated female readership eager for articles and stories that addressed the contemporary world from a woman's perspective. Mainly middle-class, these readers (we can surmise) included the new generation of female teachers created by the Republic, and some working-class women with an interest in feminism. For the six years of its existence, the newspaper provided an important forum in which feminist women writers could find their public. The titles of the *feuilletons* published there reveal an at first surprising similarity to the fiction of the mainstream press: words signifying or associated with love recur again and again (*Chemin d'amour* (The Road to Love), *Calvaire d'amour* (Love's Torment), *Au-delà de l'amour* (Beyond Love)—another of Lesueur's—, *Un Cœur ailé* (A Winged Heart), and so on).[20] But the strong romance component in feminist fiction is less surprising than it seems. Most of the novelists writing for *La Fronde* were professional

---

[20] Leroy and Bertrand-Sabiani (1998) provide a complete list of *La Fronde*'s *feuilletons*, 108.

writers trying to make a living in a competitive market, and publishing their work in volume form with mainstream publishers. They needed to appeal to an existing market, to combine their commitment to feminist principles with the offer of a type of entertainment that would be recognized by potential readers. Romance was the most tried and tested of popular genres. Nor was the emphasis on love merely a pragmatic response to an increasingly market-driven world. One burning question for the period's 'New Women', and one that had little place on the agendas of feminist congresses, was how to reconcile emancipation and love, being independent and being desirable, in a society that equated female seductiveness with fragility, innocence of the public world, and acceptance of male authority. *La Fronde*, combining home and beauty columns with high-quality political reportage, led by an editor who displayed a striking mix of theatrical seductiveness and canny political skill, was precisely the forum where the emotional implications of feminism could be discussed. The feminist novel found its place there, but publishers also recognized the market for a fiction that combined familiar pleasures with the topical debate on women's role. Writers like Marie-Louise Compain, Daniel Lesueur,[21] Gabrielle Reval, Camille Pert, and Marcelle Tinayre wrote and published New Woman romances, in which the central question of whether and how the couple could find happiness together was inextricably linked to another question: can a woman fall in love with a man yet keep her freedom?

The two examples of the feminist romance I propose to discuss here give opposing responses to this question, for if there was general consensus on the urgent nature of the problem, there was less agreement on the answer. Camille Pert (pen-name of Louise Hortense Grillet, 1865–1952) was a prolific author of feminist novels, most of them with 'amour' in the title (for example *Amoureuses* (Women in Love, 1895), *La Loi de l'amour* (The Law of Love, 1903), *L'Amour vengeur* (Avenging Love, 1906)). *Leur égale* (Men's Equal, 1899), as the title suggests, is a novel of ideas with an explicit thesis, but it is also a love story that imagines the joy of a passionate love between two equals, before concluding on the bleak note of its impossibility in fin-de-siècle French society. Thérèse is a highly educated young woman who has inherited her grandfather's publishing firm, and who thus has some standing in the very masculine world of work. Hard-working, content with her life, and determined never to marry and thus risk her freedom, Thérèse falls intensely in love with her cousin Adrien, a handsome, intelligent, but fast-living army officer. With Thérèse's free consent, the two become lovers, and an idyllic period

---

[21] See also Holmes 2005b and 2005c.

of mutual desire and love ensues. Pert emphasizes the fluidity of their roles, as Adrien chooses kitchen equipment for the little flat they rent in the bustling, newly developed Barbès area of Paris, and Thérèse reflects with amusement that 'C'est lui la femme et moi l'homme' (69);[22] this absence of rigid gender demarcation allows them to be at once lovers and friends, and both are profoundly happy. Adrien tries to explain how their relationship differs from those he has known before: 'Tu n'es pas quelqu'un d'autre: tu es moi...nous sommes un...suprêmement fondus ensemble' (82).[23]

The narrator, however, has already sounded a note of warning about the couple's subjection to 'l'antique mythe' of love, each of their minds 'soudain fermé à la réflexion, à l'analyse, à l'expérience déjà acquise' (74).[24] Reality catches up with them. Thérèse intervenes to save Adrien from being ruined by his debts, providing him with employment in her firm. Despite his love for her, he feels humiliated by this, and the prejudices of a deeply sexist society resurface, leading him to reject her in favour of a girl much closer to the feminine ideal of the day. Germaine is uneducated, frivolous, her only ambition to make a good marriage, a 'puerile, fausse poupée!' (180),[25] as Thérèse bitterly reflects, but such a woman reassures Adrien's sense of his own superiority, and Germaine is willing to accept her own subordination in exchange for the status and security of marriage. One of the novel's strengths is the characterization of Adrien not just as a blinkered, selfish individual, but also as a sensitive lover who sincerely regrets the loss of 'cette sensation de confiance dans l'intimité, d'estime, de camaraderie intelligente et dévouée'[26] (210) that he has known with Thérèse, and recognizes his own weakness in being unable to defy the internalized values of a patriarchal culture. The love story ends unhappily, as after one last night together, its emotional bleakness figured by the wintry snow that covers the city, Adrien marries Germaine and a colder, wiser Thérèse returns to a celibate life, editing a new feminist journal *La Femme moderne*. The novel sketches a dream of heterosexual love that combines sexual passion with friendship and intellectual companionship, but declares it an impossibility, at least for the current generation.

Marcelle Tinayre's *La Rebelle* (1905) was perhaps the best known of feminist romances. Tinayre (1871–1948), one of the most successful women writers of her generation, was the author of a dozen novels

---

22 'He's the woman and I'm the man.'
23 'You are not someone else: you're myself...we are one...completely fused together.'
24 'suddenly closed to reflection, analysis, and the wisdom acquired by experience'.
25 'a false, childish doll'.
26 'That feeling of intimate confidence, esteem, intelligent and devoted comradeship'.

between 1897 and 1914, a widely published journalist who also wrote for *La Fronde*, the subject of a bio-critical study published in 1909 in the series Les Célébrités d'Aujourd'hui.[27] Tinayre's novels are well-crafted stories that combine the theme of love with serious exploration of other topical issues—most famously, of the opposition between a puritanical form of Christianity and a secular culture, upon which love founders in the much praised *La Maison du péché* (The House of Sin, 1902). With *La Rebelle*, she created a New Woman heroine and provided her with a male partner sympathetic to the feminist cause as well as deeply in love with her, suggesting, however, that even with the ideal hero, the feminist heroine of romance struggles to combine love and independence.

Josanne starts the novel 'seule dans la rue, seule dans la vie' ('alone in the street, alone in life', 2), a solitude that represents both the traditional void in the life of a romance heroine destined to fill that space with the right man, and an indication to the reader that this is an emancipated, independent woman. Her solitude is emotional rather than literal, for she is unhappily married to a bad-tempered hypochondriac, and is also the mistress of the attractive but superficial Maurice, the father of her child: both men are clearly inadequate partners. Josanne supports her family by working for a women's magazine, *Le Monde féminin*. She is a moral heroine, not in conventional terms, but in those of a modern feminist morality: she is a good mother, a nurturing wife, but one who refuses to sacrifice herself to a tyrannical husband, and feels no guilt about her adulterous relationship because it is motivated by love. Her solidarity with other women is exercised through her work for the magazine. In the book's opening scene, waiting for Maurice in the rain, Josanne chances to pick up a book on women that seems to describe precisely her own situation, and that sings the praises of a new type of equal, companionate marriage. The book's author is a man, Noël Delyle, and the rest of the novel will trace Josanne's relationship—first as reader to author, then as friend, then as lover—with this wise feminist man, concluding in true romance style with their mutual happiness as they set out on a life together.

La Rebelle is in most senses an effective fusion of happy love story and progressive politics. Like Pert, Tinayre employs a third-person, omniscient narrative voice, but privileges her heroine's point of view by focalizing the fictional world mainly from her perspective. The reader is invited to identify with Josanne's growing attraction to Noël, and at the same time with her feminist values. In a manner typical of later, mass-market romances, Josanne further invites the reader's identification by her valorization of the ordinary: she is very pretty, but in a manner that is typical rather than exceptional: 'son joli visage . . . Joli? Qui sait? . . . Un visage de moderne Parisienne' (Tinayre 1905: 39).[28] Her everyday domestic concerns run alongside her activities as a feminist journalist: her relative poverty means that she must display some ingenuity to feed herself and her family well, and to dress attractively, and the novel lingers on these feats of feminine *débrouillardise* or practical inventiveness. Noël, for the most part viewed externally, is a romantic hero redefined for a feminist audience: set against the foils of the bullying, physically unappealing husband, and the vain, shallow Maurice, his intellectual and moral qualities promise that mix of intimacy and comradeship that Thérèse and Adrien glimpsed in *Leur égale*. At the same time, he exerts a strong sensual appeal, betraying 'une espèce de violence latente qu'il surveillait et réprimait' (148),[29] which suggests his capacity both for sexual passion and for protective strength, just as his 'regard clair, aigu, glacé . . . qui entra en elle du premier coup'[30] (137) signifies both potency and emotional understanding. Desire is signalled as soon as the two meet, and its satisfaction delayed as they contend with the obstacles to their happy union: above all, Noël must learn to live with his jealousy of Josanne's past, and overcome the deeply ingrained reflex of the sexual double standard. Thus the romantic happy ending depends on the acceptance of feminist principles.

Yet Tinayre's depiction of the couple's final happiness concedes considerably more to the genre's traditional values than does Pert's desolate acceptance of defeat. This is a novel that is, on the whole, at pains to present male domination and female submission not as the result of natural laws, but as historically and socially constructed. Yet the portrayal of a passionate and lasting heterosexual union seems to require the sudden incursion of a very different discourse of eternal truths and natural sexual difference. Josanne tries to distinguish between her wish for social emancipation, and the profound desire to accept Noël's mastery at the intimate level of their relationship: 'Mais la rebelle s'est rebellée contre la société injuste, et non pas contre la nature. Elle ne s'est pas rebellée contre la loi éternelle de l'amour' (305),[31] she tells her feminist friends. Without relinquishing her claim to social, intellectual, and legal equality, Josanne finds that love produces a desire for submission, and a pleasurable sense of Noël's mastery: 'Mon maître! Mon maître

---

[28] 'Her pretty face . . . Pretty? Who can say? . . . The face of a modern Parisian woman.'
[29] 'A sort of latent violence that he kept under careful control'.
[30] 'clear, cold, sharp gaze . . . which went straight inside her'.
[31] 'But the rebel rebelled against an unjust society, not against nature. She did not rebel against the eternal law of love.'

chéri!...Je n'ai pas d'autre volonté que la vôtre...Je ne suis qu'une chose, une très petite chose, dans vos chères mains' (305).[32] Writing for an audience emotionally and sexually shaped—like the author and her heroine—by a culture of polarized gender identities, Tinayre finds it impossible to portray heterosexual love that transcends entirely the domination/submission scenario which informs her society's view of sexual relations. By separating social equality from the couple's intimate relationship, she provides a happy feminist dénouement that acknowledges the contradiction between rational political thought, and the awkward obduracy of emotional and sexual desire. In *La Rebelle*, the feminist problem of reconciling love and freedom is not just a matter of educating men, of a transitional generation contending with a still powerfully misogynist culture, as it is in *Leur égale*. Tinayre's best-selling novel implicitly acknowledges that the problem is also one of reshaping female desire, of imagining new forms of erotic and emotional relations with men, outside deeply ingrained structures of power.[33]

Colette's romance diptych: *La Vagabonde* and *L'Entrave*

Colette's subsequent celebrity and literary status have meant that she is rarely discussed in relation to other women writers of her generation. But she too was the product of the new state education for girls, and her early career in Paris coincided with the widespread sense of a difficult, contested shift in gender roles and relations. Claudine, the immensely popular heroine of Colette's first five novels (published under the name of Willy, her husband), displayed an assertive sexuality, an irreverence for authority, and an energetic sense of adventure that connected with the notion of the New Woman, despite the complete lack of interest in feminism as a movement that Claudine shared with her creator. In 1910 and 1913, now divorced from Willy and publishing under her own name, Colette produced two novels that have much in common with the feminist romances of the period. *La Vagabonde* and its sequel *L'Entrave* (literally 'The Shackle', also translated as 'The Captive'), represent alternative versions of the romance plot with opposing conclusions: in the first, Renée Néré meets and falls in love with Max, but finally (like Pert's heroine) renounces love in favour of freedom; in the second, the same heroine falls in love with Jean, and ends the novel (like Tinayre's

---

[32] 'My master! My beloved master!... I have no will other than yours...I am only a thing, a very small thing in your dear hands.'

[33] This argument is developed in relation to a range of Tinayre novels in Holmes (1998).

'rebel') with their relationship as the centre of her life, 'ralentie, adoucie, changée...à jamais amarrée' (Colette 1986a: 463).[34] Both novels are concerned above all with the possibility, for a woman, of combining passionate heterosexual love with personal freedom, of reconciling the desire for relationship with the need to assert and express the self, in a culture that equates men's love with domination, and women's with submission. Both novels also conform to the genre's evaluation of love as a transcendent value: to relinquish the joy of reciprocal desire and tenderness demands courage and the absolute conviction that the cost of love is unacceptably high.

In these senses, then, Colette's pair of romances are close to those of her feminist contemporaries. Colette wrote not only out of a passion for language—what Julia Kristeva terms 'la volupté extrême qui n'est autre que celle de nommer'[35] (Kristeva 2002: 349)—but also, like Pert, or Tinayre, or Lesueur, out of the need to make a living. If her early career was propelled and controlled by Willy, that literary entrepreneur of the Belle Époque, her success also helped her to live independently after their separation, and she remained a widely published, widely read, and popular author as well as a critically acclaimed one. In other words, Colette belongs not alone on a pedestal, but alongside those women writers of her generation who combined the popular with the ideologically progressive. At the same time, her novels display a characteristic inventiveness and subtlety that sets them apart from even the best of the others' work. Colette not only uses the very topical genre of the romance of (feminist) ideas, she also reworks and transforms it.

The narrator-heroine of *La Vagabonde*, the writer and music-hall dancer Renée Néré, begins the novel in good romance fashion solitary, lonely, and defensively wary of men after an unhappy first love. But if she recognizes the difficulties of living as a single working woman ('la bête noire, la terreur et la paria des propriétaires' (Colette 1984: 1071)),[36] she also glories in her independence: 'Je gagne ma vie, cela est un fait. A mes bonnes heures, je me dis et me redis, joyeusement, que je gagne ma vie.' (1084–5),[37] enjoying the scarcely gendered camaraderie of the music-hall, returning gradually, as the novel progresses, to her passion for writing. The appearance of the tall dark handsome admirer, Max, at first offers little threat, for Renée's emotions are still numbed by the pain of her divorce and the sheer hard work of survival. But his persistence

---

[34] 'at a slower, gentler pace than my old one...anchored for ever' (Colette 1964: 158).
[35] 'The extreme sensual delight which is that of naming the world.'
[36] 'the landlord's abomination, outcast, and terror all rolled into one' (Colette 1960: 9)
[37] 'On my good days I joyfully say over and over again to myself that I earn my living' (ibid.: 24).

pays off: gradually, as the cold winter of the opening section turns to spring, Renée also thaws, and desire floods in. Colette depicts sexual desire vividly, sensuously, and as a mortal danger for Renée's freedom. Like Tinayre's heroine, but more self-critically, Renée finds that desire falls at once into a ready-made script of submission and domination, that wanting Max means experiencing herself both as a child in search of security ('l'enfant abandoñée qui tremble en moi, faible, nerveuse, prompte à tendre les bras, à implorer: "ne me laissez pas seule!" ' (1218)),[38] and as the submissive object of his pleasure. The relations of power between them are also played out in terms of specularity, of who looks and who is looked at. Renée rediscovers the pleasure of having a spectator in her life, 'un avide spectateur de ma vie et de ma personne' (1147–8),[39] whose fascinated attention embellishes her sense of self—but to be the subject of the gaze is also a form of power, and to grant that prerogative to another is to risk loss of one's own subjecthood: 'Il m'éveille d'un regard, et je cesse de m'appartenir s'il pose sa bouche sur la mienne? Alors c'est mon ennemi, c'est le pillard qui me vole à moi-même!' (1226).[40]

Thanks to her career as a dancer and mime, which carries Renée away from Max on a journey that returns to her the joy of an immediate, solitary engagement with the world, 'le plaisir de vivre, de contempler, de respirer profondément' (1213),[41] she is able to resist the intense desire for self-abandonment, security, tenderness that have taken her into Max's arms. The novel ends with Renée opting for 'vagabondage' rather than marriage to Max; if the desolation of renouncing love's warmth is signified by the cold, bleak dawn of the final scene, Renée's final solitude nonetheless (unlike that of Thérèse in *Leur égale*) constitutes a quietly triumphant dénouement, albeit one that reverses the traditional happy ending of the romance. The novel suggests a radical incompatibility between heterosexual love and personal fulfilment, but Renée's experience of love has enriched her and returned to her—through the reawakening of her senses, through the letters she writes to explain her feelings to Max—the joy of that 'jeu périlleux et décevant, pour saisir et fixer'[42] (1074) that is writing. The first-person narration makes possible a self-reflexivity quite absent from the other feminist romances: here the text itself is the

---

[38] 'the lost child . . . who trembles inside me, weak and nervous and ready to stretch out her arms and implore: "Don't leave me alone!" ' (ibid.: 173).

[39] 'an eager spectator of my life and person' (ibid.: 95).

[40] 'A look of his can rouse me and I cease to belong to myself if he puts his mouth on mine? In that case he is my enemy, he is the thief who steals me from myself' (ibid.: 183).

[41] 'the joy of living, contemplating, and breathing deeply' (ibid.: 168).

[42] 'the perilous and elusive task of seizing and pinning down' (ibid.: 13).

evidence both of the value of love, and of a female creativity that needs, at this point in history, to reject love. *La Vagabonde* mourns the loss of romantic love, but offers in its place the courageous pleasure of solitary engagement with the world, and of expressing that world in language: 'la volupté extrême de nommer'. In a valedictory passage of internal monologue, Renée acknowledges Max as the good romantic hero, and refuses his love in the name of the more urgent imperative to know, see, and give form to experience without the intermediary of a male other.

> Tu es bon, et tu prétendais, de la meilleure foi du monde, m'apporter le bonheur, car tu m'as vue dénuée et solitaire. Mais tu avais compté sans mon orgueil de pauvresse: les plus beaux pays de la terre, je refuse de les contempler, tout petits, au miroir amoureux de ton regard'[43] (1231–2)

La Vagabonde gives full weight to those desires that fuel the romance: the desire for material and emotional security, for fulfilled, reciprocal sensuality, for the enhanced sense of self that comes from loving and the sustained experience of being loved—but finally disputes their supremacy in women's lives. In the sequel novel, *L'Entrave* (1913), Colette has Renée reverse this decision and live a second romance through to its classic happy ending. Renée is now financially independent thanks to a legacy, has given up the music-hall, and is leading a leisured, rather purposeless life moving between the Côte d'Azur, Switzerland, and Paris. Thus she starts the novel in a state of celibacy, solitude, and unfocused expectation that imply to the reader the imminence of love. The single bed 'dont mon parfum ne masque pas tout à fait la chaste odeur de chlore' (347),[44] the visit to her ex-stage partner only to find herself replaced and redundant, the restless wandering so different from the energetic and purposeful *vagabondage*—all of these are signs of a vacuum that prepare for the revelation of Jean's desire for Renée, and her answering desire. The process of mutual seduction takes up the whole of the first and largest section of the narrative; the question then becomes one of the relationship between desire and love. Renée at first resists the commitment and the intense intimacy Jean seeks, refusing (in a very Colettian reversal of the gender norms) the 'grands transports' of 'l'Amour' (413), and defending the 'nothing' so categorically condemned by those who

---

[43] 'You are good and, with the best faith in the world, you meant to bring me happiness, since you saw me deprived and solitary. But you counted without my beggar-woman's pride: I refuse to see the most beautiful countries of the world microscopically reflected in the amorous mirror of your eyes' (ibid.: 191).

[44] 'sheets whose chaste smell of chlorine is not wholly disguised by my perfume' (Colette 1964: 27).

declare themselves for 'all or nothing' in love: 'Eh! Eh! Un joli rien, bien présenté, c'est déjà quelque chose' (411).[45] But Jean's departure, when he can no longer bear the provisional, uncertain nature of their relationship, makes Renée realize what she has lost. The novel ends with Renée opting for love over freedom, accepting (in true romance fashion) that self-fulfilment lies not in adventure but in the gift of self to the chosen lover.

> Sans force pour mentir, je me mis dans ses bras, et je fermai les yeux pour qu'il ne vît pas que c'était mon âme que je lui donnais.
>   ...
>   Je le seconde, mais en arrière de lui, ralentie, adoucie, changée. Il me semble, à le voir s'élancer sur la vie, qu'il a pris ma place, qu'il est l'avide vagabond et que je le regarde, à jamais amarrée.[46] (463)

As the Colette novel that comes closest to a classic romance plot, and has its heroine freely choose that shackled, secondary role she had so eloquently rejected in *La Vagabonde*, *L'Entrave* has never been a critical or a feminist favourite.[47] Colette herself was the first to malign it: 'J'ai fini *L'Entrave*. J'exulte de soulagement, mais je la vomis et je la méprise' (Colette 1961: 96).[48] Like its prequel, the novel has a strong autobiographical dimension, and Colette's own circumstances at the time of writing, very much in love with Henri de Jouvenel and about to give birth, were not irrelevant. But *L'Entrave* can be defended on grounds other than the biographical: for the precise sensuality of its depiction of sexual desire, allied with a close exploration of the emotions that desire contains; for the way it deals, lightly but seriously, with the ethics of self/other relations; for the questions it implies about the relationship between sex, gender, and power.

The romance narrative is always, implicitly or explicitly, a narrative of desire and its delayed fulfilment, hence a form of erotic writing. Colette charts Renée's growing attraction to Jean through the attention she pays to his body, particularly the mouth 'rasée, gonflée, boudeuse, fine aux

---

[45] 'Well, well, a charming nothing, admirably presented, is anyway something' (ibid.: 98).

[46] 'Too exhausted to lie, I threw myself into his arms and I closed my eyes so that he should not see that it was my soul I was giving him' (ibid.: 157). 'I follow his example, but in his wake and at a slower, gentler pace than my old one. It seems to me, as I watch him launch out enthusiastically into life, that he has changed places with me; that he is the eager vagabond and that I am the one who gazes after him, anchored for ever' (158).

[47] Elaine Marks, for example, found the novel's very 'moral' conclusion 'not quite satisfying', and Renée's tone in the final passage 'that of a person newly converted, a pedantic, irritating tone' (Marks 1960: 98). Many subsequent critics have agreed with her.

[48] 'I have finished *L'Entrave*. I am triumphant with relief, but I loathe and despise it.' In a letter to Léon Hamel dated 16 Sept. 1913.

coins' (338);[49] when he first touches her, the gesture evokes the sexual union Renée desires—'Une main chaude et forte s'abat sur la mienne, l'enferme et l'épouse comme une coque vivante'[50] (361)—and makes it clear to the reader that desire is mutual. Sexual tension mounts as Renée resumes her restless wandering, Jean pursues her to Geneva, and at last kisses her, on the back of the neck, 'un bon baiser chaud, pas trop mordant, long, tranquille' (394),[51] described in close, ecstatic detail. The novel is more than halfway through when at last, by the last embers of a log fire in Jean's house, the two make love: Colette evokes with nice humour the problems that Belle Époque female clothing posed for spontaneous sex, but the scene is nonetheless erotic for that: 'que c'est doux, cette bouche nue, ces lèvres pleines qui résistent au baiser, elastiquement, qu'il faut écraser un peu pour rencontrer les dents' (405).[52] Colette's capacity to write desire and sexual pleasure from a woman's point of view is one of her great strengths as a writer, and L'Entrave, with its central focus on the process of seduction and the nature of sexual love, is one of her finer pieces of erotic writing.

As in La Vagabonde, Colette explores the different emotions contained within desire. On the veranda of the hotel in Geneva, transfixed by Jean's physical presence and aware of the imminence of their mutual declaration, Renée returns in imagination to the maternal house and garden, as yet scarcely a theme in Colette's work. The contrast between the dark night and the hotel's lights evokes the 'clarté rose et chaude d'une fenêtre illuminée' (388), which in turn signifies 'amour, amour abrité, foyer, isolement précieux et permis' (388).[53] Desire contains the longing for shelter, warmth, protection, even as it represents adventure, discovery of the unknown, self-assertion: 'la curiosité, le goût de l'intrigue et de l'aventure, l'envie qu'on me désire' (379),[54] forms of energy that Renée has lost as the novel opens, and that are reawakened by her attraction to Jean. Desire also responds to the desire of the other, for as Renée discovered in La Vagabonde, the fascinated gaze of the spectator confers value on the self and enhances one's sense of worth: leaving Jean to resume her wandering near the start of the novel, Renée regrets what

[49] 'the clean-shaven, sulky mouth, full-lipped but finely chiselled at the corners' (Colette 1964: 17).

[50] 'A warm, strong hand had pounced on mine, imprisoning it and enclosing it like a living shell' (ibid.: 41).

[51] 'A good kiss, not too devouring, warm, long and tranquil' (ibid.: 79).

[52] 'How sweet it was, that naked mouth on mine, those full lips that resisted the kiss and had to be crushed a little to make them part' (ibid.: 93).

[53] 'the warm rosy glow of a lighted window'; 'love, sheltered love, home, precious and lawful privacy' (ibid.: 73).

[54] 'my dormant curiosity, my taste for intrigue and adventure, the desire to be desired' (ibid.: 62).

she has left behind, for if she were there 'J'aurais . . . , pour donner du prix à chacun de mes gestes, de mes regards, à toutes me paroles, j'aurais le désir d'un homme' (373).[55]

To be the object of the other's passionate attention is one of the goals of desire. But in *L'Entrave* Colette develops *La Vagabonde*'s theme of the double-sided nature of this attention: to have a loving spectator in one's life valorizes the self, but also carries the risk of fixing an idealized, unchanging image of the self which must then be lived up to. The self constructed by the lover becomes a constraint, an imprisonment, 'la douce forme où tu m'as emprisonnée'; 'ton amour', thinks Renée, 'crée à chaque minute une femme plus belle et meilleure que moi, à laquelle tu me contrains de ressembler' (427).[56] Nor is this solely a question of gender; rather, the ethics of self/other relations hinge on the need to avoid objectification or reification of the other person, and to accord them instead the right to the 'evasive, stubborn otherness' (Bauman 2003: 9) of all human beings. The fettering of the other evoked by the novel's title can work in both directions, and Renée is aware that her perception of Jean limits and constrains him, struggling to remember that

Il y a un Jean qui n'est pas l'amant de Renée, un Jean qui n'est ni mystérieux, ni sensuellement inquiétant, un Jean qui ressemble, mûri, développé, . . . à un Jean tout petit dans le passé et que je n'aurai jamais connu.[57] (429)

Renée's final decision is in part an attempt to accept Jean's existence fully, independently of her own needs and emotions; to sacrifice self-assertion in the name of absolute tenderness for the other—what Jean's friend Masseau has expressed earlier in the novel by the following maxim: 'Si l'amour (. . .) que vous dédiez à votre amant l'engage envers vous, en quelque manière que ce soit, ce n'est plus le véritable amour' (454).[58]

If Colette places this ideal of love in the mouth of the ironic, opium-smoking, sexually indeterminate Masseau, thus at once proposing and undermining its validity, this may be because the self-sacrifice in love he recommends to Renée reproduces too neatly the unequal power relations enshrined in the marriage laws of the day. The problem with

---

[55] 'I should . . . have, to give value to every gesture, every glance, every word of mine, a man's desire' (ibid.: 55).

[56] 'the gentle shape in which you have imprisoned me'; 'your love creates a woman better and more beautiful than myself whom you force me to resemble' (ibid.: 116).

[57] 'There is a Jean who is not Renée's lover, a Jean who is neither mysterious nor sexually exciting. And that Jean . . . has matured and developed from the boy he was in the past and whom I never knew' (ibid.: 118).

[58] 'if the love you devote to your lover engages him in any way whatever towards you, it is no longer genuine love' (ibid.: 147).

the ending of *L'Entrave* is that Renée's choice to privilege Jean's needs and desires above her own maps uncomfortably onto the very male supremacy that the same heroine has radically contested in the previous novel—and the characterization of Renée does make the conclusion not just unexpected, but also to some extent implausible. But it is worth considering whether the choice she makes might be considered not as an acceptance of women's subordinate place, but rather as an extreme and ideal ethical choice, available regardless of sex. The novel's typically Colettian, consistent undermining of essentialized gender difference could support such an argument: Jean seductively mingles the most masculine strength with feminine softness, as in his 'menton . . . à la fois têtu et féminin . . .', his 'cou fort, mais noyé dans sa rondeur, sans muscles apparents' (338),[59] while Renée's financial independence, mobility, and practical competence often make her the dominant partner; secondary characters like Masseau and May also combine the attributes of each gender. The seductive strategies of each sex, like their psychology and basic drives, are here very similar, so that attraction is based on the fascinating otherness of the individual other, rather than on a form of difference that is only and essentially gendered. The symmetry of the dénouements of the two novels, with Renée playing first the vagabond, then the still centre content to await the vagabond's return, suggests the possible reversibility of roles, and undermines the determining role of sexual difference in the resolution of the romance plot.

Conclusion

Colette's pair of romances, with their radically opposed conclusions, rework the structures and themes of the romantic fiction that dominated female reading and writing practices at the Belle Époque. If the genre had such tremendous and generalized appeal to women readers, this is because it spoke of sexual as well as emotional desire, and of the difficult alignment of personal fulfilment with social imperatives, in a form that provided the escapism, the vicarious pleasure, and the satisfying shaping of reality offered by good fiction. Colette's novels represent a wise, witty, and explicit re-articulation of romance themes, and conclude the Belle Époque period with a dazzling confirmation of the genre's capacity to provide a compelling structure for the exploration not only of emotion, but also of ethics and ideology.

[59] 'chin . . . at once obstinate and feminine'; 'the neck . . . strong but so smoothly rounded that no muscles were visible' (ibid.: 17).

3 Reaction and Resistance: Romance in the 1930s and under the Occupation

War and its aftermath

The outbreak of war in 1914 made it difficult to pursue internal political conflicts, and most feminists, along with the majority of the population, rallied behind the flag. Although, at a practical level, the absence of most of the active male population opened up new areas of employment to women, their fulfilment of the traditional roles of nurturing mother, nurse, provider of emotional solace became all the more imperative as a generation of young men found themselves suddenly in the raw, brutal world of battlefield and trenches. Wartime fiction written by women contains many strong female characters, but on the whole 'for them, autonomy and self-determination [are] inseparable . . . from . . . maternal compassion and dedication' (Goldberg 1999: 2). Love is a central element of women's writing in the 1914–18 war, but the drama of meeting, desire, and its fulfilment takes second place to stories of painful separation from a beloved companion, or courageous sacrifice that alleviates the soldiers' suffering, or motherly devotion.[1]

The 1914–18 war meant suffering and loss for both sexes: 1.3 million young French men died, and a further 1.1 million were seriously disabled. The febrile, brittle gaiety of the post-war 'années folles' ('crazy years') was a reaction to this trauma, and seemed to signify too a radical change in relations between men and women. The image of the smoking, Charleston-dancing 'garçonne' ('tomboy' or in this context 'flapper') of the 1920s supports the view that the war, for all its destructive horror, liberated women from their corseted, chaperoned pre-war lives and from confinement to the domestic sphere. Victor Margueritte's 1922 novel *La Garçonne*, with its rebellious, outspoken, and sexually promiscuous heroine, at once crystallized and fuelled a widespread belief that the war had created a new generation of selfish, independent women whose

---

[1] See O'Brien 1996; Goldberg 1999. Marcelle Tinayre typifies the wartime shift in emphasis in women's writing: her 1915 novel *La Veillée des armes: le départ: août 1914* (*To Arms!*) emphasizes not romantic love, but the supportive, self-sacrificing duty of women on the home front. Colette's droll, poignant novella *Mitsou, ou comment l'esprit vient aux filles* (*Mitsou, or the Education of Young Women*, 1986b, first published in 1917) is a love story, and gently mocks the bombastic patriotism of the era, but its heroine's love for her soldier is also generous and concerned above all to answer his needs.

androgynously slim ideal of beauty expressed their permanent rejection of marriage and motherhood.

The sense of a shift in women's patterns of employment and behaviour had some substance, for the men's absence had accelerated women's move away from domestic service and into commercial and administrative work, and had given many the experience of new freedoms and responsibilities. But the figure of the 'garçonne' was more mythology than fact. Between 1918 and 1945, women's situation changed remarkably little in France, in terms of civil and political rights, rights within marriage, or socially permissible ways of living. The post-war backlash against working women was swift and effective, so that by 1926 the percentage of women at work outside the home was scarcely higher than in 1906 (Sullerot 1965: 421). The deaths of so many men meant that marriage was simply not a possibility for all women, but an independent life as a single woman remained difficult, both financially and socially. Motherhood was still the most valorized role for a woman, and in any case was difficult to plan or prevent, since the draconian pro-natalist law of 1920 criminalized not only abortion, but also the dissemination of information on contraception. The ideal life trajectory for most women, whatever other pleasures it might include, would follow the form of the happy romance: falling in love, a good marriage, children. The specialized series of short, formulaic 'romans d'amour' that had made their appearance just before the outbreak of war returned and flourished. Even Victor Margueritte, having thoroughly outraged much of the nation with the exploits of his 'garçonne', provided her with a romantically happy ending in the arms of a strong, understanding, and morally superior hero: 'Elle se sentait une pauvre chose, salie, diminuée. Et pourtant jamais elle n'avait eu un tel élan de tout l'être vers le besoin de croire et l'ivresse d'aimer' (Margueritte 1922: 293).[2] At least in popular and middlebrow fiction of the inter-war years, a woman's happiness was rarely represented in terms other than those of romance.

In the 1930s, the independent woman again became the fantasized source of the nation's ills. When the Depression hit France in the early 1930s, there were renewed calls for women to return to the home, on

---

[2] 'She felt herself to be a wretched thing, soiled and degraded. And yet she had never felt such a yearning of her whole being to believe in and enjoy the intoxication of love.' *La Garçonne*, which sold over a million copies in France between 1922 and 1929, and was translated into twelve languages, was the first in the trilogy *La Femme en chemin*. Volume ii, *Le Compagnon*, appeared in 1923 and *Le Couple* in 1924. Margueritte published a second trilogy, *Vers le bonheur*, between 1927 and 1930. Though they contain some hard-hitting criticism of women's lack of legal and contraceptive rights, and of male arrogance, both trilogies represent heterosexual love as a transcendent force and idealize the couple.

the grounds that the removal of women from paid employment would, at a stroke, 'diminuer le chômage, augmenter les salaires, faire croître la natalité, abaisser la mortalité infantile, améliorer la vie de famille' (Richet 1931).[3] The male-dominated trade unions were inclined to share the view that paid work was better left to men, and as in earlier periods, a broad consensus prevailed across the political spectrum on the question of women's social place. Throughout the 1920s and 1930s, repeated efforts were made to grant women the right to vote, but the Senate consistently rejected these, and even the supporters of the cause, such as the Socialist Party, tended to base their arguments on women's role as the 'gardiennes du foyer' (guardians of the home) who could bring to the national scene the domestic concerns of wives and mothers.[4] The broad Left, united in 1936 to form the Popular Front government, did at least offer an ideological basis for feminist claims, for their commitment to the principles of freedom and equality implied recognition of the need for struggle to ensure that these rights were extended to all human beings. Yet neither their discourse nor their practice on gender was markedly different from that of the Right.

When the defeat of 1940 ended the Republic and brought the deeply conservative Vichy government to power, Marshal Pétain's representation of the nation as a 'hierarchy of families', and of paternal authority as essential to the health of family and nation, was in line with the dominant discourse of the preceding years. Through speeches, propaganda, and legislation, the Vichy government strengthened the pro-natalist policies already in place, glorified motherhood within marriage as women's only proper destiny, and protected the authority of the husband and father even in his absence by, for example, passing a law that punished adultery with the wife of a prisoner of war with heavy fines or imprisonment (Fishman 1987: 187).

Thus, despite some progress in women's education, employment, and everyday social freedoms,[5] the three decades that separate the Belle Époque from the Liberation maintained a strongly androcentric model of society, repeatedly responded to domestic and international crisis with a reassertion of the absolute need for male authority, and ended with a radically male supremacist government in power. The consistent, if differently inflected, emphasis on women's domestic and maternal

---

[3] 'reduce unemployment, increase salaries, improve the birth rate, reduce infant mortality, and improve family life'.

[4] For example, in the Socialist Party (SFIO)'s presentation of their 1926 bill to Parliament.

[5] For example, the numbers of women in higher education remained low as a proportion of the whole, but increased steadily (Sullerot 1965: 432). Social mores relaxed to allow middle-class women much greater freedom of movement, behaviour, and casual contact with the opposite sex.

role was accompanied by an increased gendering of popular fiction. The 300- or 400-page volumes of a Richebourg, a Lesueur, or a Maryan, with their multi-stranded sub-plots and broad appeal, gave way to specialized collections, of which the 'romans d'amour' were far and away the highest sellers (Olivier-Martin 1980: 237). Ferenzci's *Le Petit Livre*, *Le Livre Épatant*, *Mon Livre Favori* competed with Tallandier's *Le Livre de Poche* and Rouff's *Mon Roman*, and the successful women's magazine *Petit Écho de la mode* set up its own romantic series, the twice-monthly *Collection Stella*. Although—as we shall see—the romance form could also be used to contest the prevailing emphasis on submissive love as the only path to female happiness, this is the period when women readers first consumed the formulaic romance in massive numbers. Among the army of authors needed to respond to this mass demand, one of the most consistently popular was the very conservative Delly.

Delly and the moral romance

Marie Petitjean de la Rosière (1875–1946), the daughter of a Catholic, military, bourgeois family, published her first romantic novels in the early 1900s. Her brother Frédéric (1876–1949) acted as her business manager, adviser, and general collaborator, and the pair adopted the joint pen-name of Delly. Publishing, on average, two novels a year, with most of these running into several editions and reprintings, the Petitjean de la Rosière soon became very wealthy, to the extent that in the late 1920s they were able to have a chateau built in Glatigny, near Versailles, and to live there in affluent seclusion for the rest of their lives. Marie Petitjean de la Rosière lived the sheltered, uneventful life of a respectable spinster, and spent it spinning romantic stories that captured the imagination of millions of readers, most of whose lives were undoubtedly very different from her own. From 1903 until the early 1940s, with a hiatus during the 1914–18 war, Delly brought out at least one new novel per year; reprints and re-editions meant that there were always numerous Delly novels in print, on sale, and in municipal libraries.[6] In the 1930s and 1940s, Delly was already a brand name, the guarantee of a page-turning, pleasurable read that was nonetheless entirely in line

---

[6] Richard Saint-Germain has compiled a detailed bibliography of Delly titles, reprints, and re-editions by different publishers (Bettinotti and Noizet 1995: 157–99). New titles appeared almost annually until the author's death; the novels also reappeared in new editions with great regularity, and some first appeared in volume form in the 1950s and 1960s. Strangely, the novels enjoyed the highest rate of republication between the mid-1960s and early 1980s.

with Catholic, conservative values. Published mainly in series such as Gautier-Languereau's *Bibliothèque de ma Fille* (My Daughter's Library), Plon's *Romans Pouvant Être Mis entre Toutes les Mains* (Novels Suitable for All), and Tallandier's *La Véritable Bibliothèque de la Famille* (The True Family Library), Delly adopted the mission of the moral romance, and made it into a commercial triumph.

Delly novels express the values of the conservative, Catholic French Right—values in accordance with which, under the Occupation, the Vichy regime would attempt to rebuild France. Anti-republican and anti-democratic, Delly's fictional world intertwines the hierarchies of class and sex, presenting both as natural and God-given. 'Dieu lui-même', says the heroine of *Comme un conte de fées*, 'a établi des rangs dans la société.' (62),[7] and plot and characterization consistently endorse this view. Typically, the aristocratic hero is a natural leader, handsome, highly intelligent, an alpha male with an unmistakable air of authority, like Lord Ralph Felborne with his 'physionomie d'un homme sachant se faire obéir' (*La Vengeance de Ralph*: 20).[8] The heroine is generally of the same elevated caste: she may first attract the hero's love when in the guise of a humble tutor's daughter (*Une misère dorée*), or that of an impoverished orphan (*La Biche au bois, VR, Le Repaire des fauves*), suggesting a democracy of the heart, but sure enough her aristocratic connections will be revealed before the novel ends. Her inborn nobility is signified by attributes different from, but complementary to, those of the hero: sharing his exceptional good looks and air of distinction, she is quiet and modest where he is authoritative, gentle where he is forceful, and instinctively pious. These qualities are the result of nature, not nurture, for they survive the separation from class of birth from which so many heroines—impoverished, orphaned, dispatched to boarding schools or distant relatives—suffer. The positive female qualities of piety and modesty may be found in more plebeian characters—for submissiveness is appropriate to both the dominated class and the dominated sex—but any will to self-assertion in a lower-class character

---

[7] 'God himself established the different ranks of society.' The Delly novels discussed are given their full title at the first mention; thereafter, titles are shortened to initials for page references. Since most Delly novels first appeared in serialized form, the details of which are unobtainable, and also went into many reprintings and re-editions, it is impossible in some cases to date them accurately. Dates of first publication in volume form are given (as far as possible) in the References. The novels cited are: *Comme un conte de fées* (*CCF*; Like a Fairy Tale); *La Vengeance de Ralph* (*VR*; The Vengeance of Ralph); *Une misère dorée* (*MD*; A Gilded Poverty); *La Biche au bois* (*BB*; The Doe in the Forest); *Les Deux Fraternités* (*DF*; The Two Fraternities); *Esclave . . . ou reine?* (*ER*; Slave . . . or Queen?); *Rue des Trois Grâces* (*RTG*; Three Graces Street); *La Douloureuse Victoire* (*DV*; Painful Victory); *Les Hiboux des roches rouges* (*HRR*; The Owls of Red Rock Castle); *Le Repaire des fauves* (*RF*; The Wild Beasts' Lair).

[8] 'The face of a man who knew how to make himself obeyed'.

of either sex is a sign of evil. Good working-class or peasant characters embrace their lowly place in the social order and welcome the patronage of the 'natural aristocracy' of their social betters; any contestation of social privilege is shown to be driven by envy and a lust for power.[9] Cross-class marriage is virtually unknown: the rules of endogamy, as one critic puts it, are always miraculously respected (Jumelais 1990: 178).

The representation of France, in the majority of the novels, as both rural and timeless chimes with the Vichyite emphasis on land and tradition. Delly plots are almost always set in the French provinces, where semi-feudal relations appear to prevail, or in some loosely defined, rural region of Eastern Europe where the feudal relations between landowner and peasants are presented as natural and right. Cities, and especially Paris, are the site of modernity and hence of moral danger. The time period is loosely 'the present', but is never identified by reference to historical events, nor by any specific details of clothing or style: social change is irrelevant to a philosophy of fixed, eternal values. The trenchant categorization of characters as good or bad, the melodramatic convergence of all narrative elements towards a single moral view of the world, are characteristic of texts designed for effortless reading, but they are also consonant with an authoritarian rather than a democratic philosophy.

Not all Delly novels follow the romance formula, but most do, tracing the development and the triumph of love between a man and a woman, and the resulting creation of a devoutly Catholic family. Even those novels whose plots are more varied maintain a central focus on love, and make love, marriage, and motherhood the only possible happy ending to a woman's story, at least in this life. Not surprisingly, Delly's gender politics have been the target of some feminist criticism. Michèle Coquillat accuses them of deifying male authority, idealizing female passivity and submission, and purveying a 'mythologie socio-patriarcale' (Coquillat 1988: 187) all the more dangerous for its pleasurable camouflage as fairytale fantasy. Jennifer Milligan seeks, and fails to find, any sign of 'incipient opposition' in Delly's romances: they do not 'offer any possibility of seditious readings' (Milligan 1996: 168), but rather reassure their readers of the rightness and inevitability of their own subordination. The extreme conservatism of Delly's vision of love and gender is undeniable, and certainly merits analysis. However, such analysis will lead us into a further and perhaps a more interesting question: why did so many women find pleasure in reading stories that seem to work against their interests both in terms of gender and—in most cases—in terms of social class?

---

[9] *Les Deux Fraternités*, a novel that mingles romance with a story of conflict between socialism and Catholicism, is the most extreme example of anti-Left propaganda I have found in Delly.

Like those of class, gender roles in Delly are fixed and essential, and happy love rewards only those who observe the codes of behaviour appropriate to their sex. The typical Delly hero is securely established in the world through heredity, land and possessions; his impact on the heroine—and the reader—arises not only from his extreme beauty, but also from his forcefulness, and an arrogance that carries the threat of brutality: 'La bouche était dure... un énigmatique regard, très froid, dédaigneux et sans douceur, mais fascinant par son étrangeté même et par l'intelligence rare qui s'y exprimait' (*Esclave... ou reine?*: 16).[10] The work of the narrative will be to explain his tyrannical behaviour both as the consequence of past emotional damage—a harsh, unchristian upbringing (Serge Ormanoff in *ER*, Harold Treswyll in *RF*) or betrayal by an evil woman (Ralph in *VR*)—and as the sign of his passionate love for the heroine. Though, in order for the happy ending to occur, his harshness must be moderated by the heroine's civilizing influence, it remains nonetheless the sign of his virility, an extreme form of 'natural' masculine authority. For, as Michèle Coquillat puts it, the true hero 'marque le monde de sa puissance et de son poids' (Coquillat 1988: 27).[11]

Not so the heroine, whose need to find her place in the world is signalled from the outset by her extreme youth—'C'était une créature délicieuse... elle sortait à peine de l'adolescence'[12] (*ER*: 2–3)—her fragile slenderness, and (in the majority of the novels) her motherless or orphaned state. There is no scope for bad behaviour on her part: she will be loved for her modesty, innocence, and reserve, and though the coded acknowledgement of female sexuality will be discussed below, at least on the surface of the text she will remain ignorant of desire. In winning the hero's love, her aim will be not just personal happiness, but the establishment of a family within which she will find her place as 'l'idéal de l'épouse chrétienne, de l'épouse dévouée' (*MD*: 182).[13]

Women who fail to observe this ideal of female identity provide much of the friction that drives the plots, and are inevitably punished. Whereas the heroine is always the passive, innocently unaware object of desire, the bad woman recognizes and expresses her own sexuality, and is willing to deploy sexual charm to reach her goals. She indicates an active will to seduce by the use of make-up, or by too low a neckline—thus Iris, the *femme fatale* of *Rue des Trois Grâces*, wears a dress 'un peu trop

---

[10] 'the mouth was harsh . . . the look in his eyes was enigmatic, very cold, contemptuous and hard, but fascinating in its strangeness, and in the exceptional intelligence it expressed.'

[11] 'his power and weight leave their mark on the world.'

[12] 'she was a delightful creature . . . scarcely out of adolescence.'

[13] 'the ideal of the Christian wife, the devoted wife'.

échancré pour le goût de Régis'[14] (*RTG*: 76)—or by look and gesture, like Myrrha Nadopoulo whose eyes 'noirs et expressifs, caressaient et provoquaient' (*BB*: 14).[15] Iris's cupidity and ambition lead her to complicity in a murder, and she ends the novel living alone in Paris, heading—in Delly terms—for eternal damnation. Myrrha attempts to murder the heroine, and is savaged to death by the hero's loyal dog. Floriane Jarlier in *La Douloureuse Victoire* is a more unusual case of Delly's demonization of the emancipated woman, for Floriane occupies the role of heroine, in as far as she is loved by and marries the hero. However her low-cut dress (27), heady perfume (35), and willingness to take the sexual initiative—the hero notes 'le vif désir qu'exprimait très simplement le regard to Mademoiselle Jarlier'[16] (26)—are the outward signs of her moral inadequacy. For Floriane has been brought up in a secular household, without religion or a proper ideal of the family. Although she is utterly devoted to the hero, Bruno, she is too worldly, too self-assertive, and insufficiently maternal (her neglect leads to the death of their child) to make a Delly hero happy. The once devout Bruno sacrifices his religion to his love for Floriane, but dies after a deathbed return to God in the arms of his mother, who is a mature version of the 'épouse idéale'. However loving, female characters in the 'New Woman' or 'garçonne' mould must always be punished, if only by loss of the hero.

The enormous popularity of Delly novels over generations of readers can be measured by their multiple re-editions and reprintings (*Entre deux âmes*, for example, first published in 1913, reached its 212th reprint by 1927 (Bettinotti and Noizet 1995: 11)), by their high borrowing rate in municipal libraries (Bettinotti 1995: 137), and by the fortune they made for their authors. The readership was such that it surely went well beyond the *bien-pensant*, middle-class Catholics who were the most obvious recipients of such novels: the evidence suggests that these romances appealed to a genuinely popular—and, we can safely assume, female—audience. And yet, even in an ideological climate where conservative views of gender were the norm, it is hard to imagine that Delly's endorsement of class privilege, exaggerated respect for male authority, and uncompromising insistence on women's domestic and maternal duties—at a period when over 30 per cent of the female population worked outside the home—were in themselves pleasurable for their working-and lower middle-class readers. These romances offered pleasures that analysis of their reactionary politics simply fails to see.

---

[14] 'a little too low-cut for Régis's taste'.
[15] 'her black, expressive eyes were caressing and provocative.'
[16] 'the intense desire in Mademoiselle Jarlier's eyes'.

What Delly novels provide is above all a representation of the reader's own everyday story in an enhanced and idealized form. Like the later Harlequin romances analysed by Janice Radway, they 'function as a symbolic display and explanation of a process commonly experienced by many women' (Radway 1987: 138), and do so in the form of a 'fairytale where a heroine's needs are adequately met' (ibid.: 93). Most Delly heroines start their story on the brink of adulthood, uncertain of their identity and future. In a society that made marriage and motherhood the only respected destinies for a woman, the standard path to adult status lay through marriage. In most Delly romances, the need to marry in order to find a viable place in the world is dramatized by the heroine's lack of a loving family or of a real home: Serena (*VR*) is an orphan ill at ease and badly treated in her guardian's house, Lise (*ER*) lives with a cold, distant stepmother, and has just lost her dearest friend.[17] Each heroine finds a future and an identity by falling in love and marrying, thus reproducing the probable or already realized destiny of most Delly readers, but doing so with fairytale perfection. The husband is often imposed rather than freely chosen, for example in novels like *La Biche au bois* or *Esclave...ou reine?*, where the dowryless young heroine is married off to a tyrannical aristocrat with little regard for her feelings. His apparent indifference to her wishes and his domineering manner signal the dangers of marriage, within a contract that allotted authority solely to the husband, but here ferocity will be reassuringly revealed to be the result of a curable emotional wound, and the mask of a passionate tenderness. Many of the heroines must also adapt to their new circumstances by learning the codes and skills of domestic life: how to manage a home, how to dress and behave in a new role and environment. When the home becomes a vast country house and estate staffed by servants, the social occasion an elegant soirée, and the heroine's success complete ('Lise eut ce soir-là un immense succès d'admiration et de sympathie' (*ER*: 121)),[18] the reader can at once recognize a common female experience of necessary adaptation, and enjoy the fantasy of glamorous surroundings and universal admiration. For most women, marriage involved tension between personal aspirations, and the social imperative to subordinate her pleasure to the good of husband and children. In the Delly romance, marriage becomes the magical reconciliation of personal desire and social duty: the heroine ends the novel passionately loved and in love, and respected by her new community.

---

[17] The Cinderella story is often very close in Delly. One of the novels is actually entitled *L'Héritage de Cendrillon* (Cinderella's Inheritance).

[18] 'That evening, Lise was a great success, eliciting the admiration and liking of all.'

Narrative point of view plays an important part in the reader's pleasure. Though a few novels adopt the point of view of the hero (for example *La Douloureuse Victoire*), the typical Delly romance encourages identification with the heroine by a third-person narration mainly focalized from her perspective. It is her journey from solitude to perfect happiness that drives the story, and her gradual recognition of the hero's true sentiments that produces the happy dénouement. However, Delly's narrative omniscience also allows for a slightly more complex relationship between reader and character. The reader at once identifies with the heroine, and is allowed to know more than she does. Focalization may switch briefly to the hero, revealing—before the heroine has read in his behaviour anything other than arrogance—his spontaneous recognition of her unique qualities. Thus the Prince de Wittengrätz is struck at their first meeting by the look in Lise's eyes: 'Quelle profonde, mystéreuse lumière s'en dégageait, le rendant si différent de tous ceux qu'il avait connus jusqu'ici' (*BB*: 51).[19] The hero may equally betrays signs of tenderness that the heroine fails to notice, because she is simply too innocent, or because she is herself too moved by his presence.

> ...comme l'angoisse obscurcissait ses yeux, elle ne vit pas l'expression étrange—mélange de douleur et de colère—qui traversait le regard de Serge, ni la pâleur qui couvrait son visage, ni le geste ébauché pour tendre les bras vers elle.[20] (*ER*: 141)

Delly offers the reader a sense of knowing complicity with the narrator, and the anticipated pleasure of a happy outcome. The heroine's recognition that she is intensely loved and desired may come only at the end of the story: the reader can both enjoy the tension and excitement of her quest and the dangers she encounters, and know that in this fictional world if not elsewhere, female virtue and courage will be rewarded with perfect love.

But the heroine also has to win this happiness against much opposition. A smooth passage to a perfect dénouement neither makes a good story nor acknowledges the reader's sense of a more complex, difficult world. Delly heroines reconcile their own desires with their social function as women under patriarchy, but they do so by confronting dangerous enemies. In the figures of jealous rivals, they meet raw, violent emotion:

---

[19] 'What a deep, mysterious light emanated from those eyes, making them so different from all those he had known up to now.'

[20] '... as anguish misted her eyes, she did not see the strange expression—a mixture of gentleness and anger—that crossed Serge's face, nor the way he paled, nor the interrupted move to reach out to her.'

the threat the rivals pose is physical and highly (melo)dramatic, for these angry women may attempt murder, as in *La Biche au bois* where Myrrha tries to knife Lilia, or *Esclave...ou reine?* where Varvara (also revealed to be a Bolshevik revolutionary!) literally throws Lise to the wolves that howl at the walls of her husband's estate. Delly's categorical rejection of rebellious women means that the rivals are always—and often brutally—punished, but their presence in the text gives colourful expression to those female passions (carnal desire, ambition, anger, jealousy) that the heroines appear to deny, even if only to demonstrate the need for their repression. These shameless, ruthlessly desiring 'bad girls' might be read as embodying all that 'phallic' energy that the heroine must repress, if her story is to end safely in the domestic and maternal realm of secure femininity. Narrative technique channels reader identification toward the virtuous heroine, but also invites enjoyment of her rivals' transgressively selfish pursuit of pleasure and power.

Delly romances are explicitly opposed to emancipated, openly pas- sionate women, but a significant element of reading pleasure depends on the presence of such women in the text. Similarly, they are explicitly pro-family in a way that would have warmed Pétain's heart, but the threat to individual happiness posed by the powerful patriarchal dynasty often plays an important part in the narrative. In *Une misère dorée,* Marysia comes to the Gothic château de Runsdorf as the tutor's daughter, and uncovers a history of murdered wives, and daughters driven insane by the brutal repression of any love that did not serve the dynastic interest. In doing so, she persuades the heir to the estate of the need for a more liberal view of family relations, and thus ensures her own happiness in marrying him. Hermine, heroine of *Les Hiboux des roches rouges,* resolves the mystery of another Gothic castle when she discovers that her father was murdered there, and her mother, as a witness to the murder, imprisoned in its cellars. The unquestioned authority of the head of the family has led to the concealment of the crime, and to Hermine's growing up as an orphan. By rescuing her imprisoned mother, and bringing to light the mystery of her own origins, Hermine puts an end to the damaging effects of the crime on the whole family, and makes possible her own happy marriage. These elements of violence, mystery, and adventure make for an emotionally varied, entertaining read—as, on a larger scale, did the generic mix of Belle Époque *feuilletons*—but they also acknowledge that the harmonization of individual desire with the social institution of the family is no easy matter.

Although Marysia and Hermine have all the marks of a true Delly heroine—they are very young, virginal, respectful of authority—the roles they play in solving the mysteries and bringing about the happy dénouement suggest a degree of agency. It is true that the novels demand identification with a heroine who never questions her destiny as obedient wife and devoted mother, and that this is part of the texts' deliberate function to confirm the rightness of patriarchal institutions. Nonetheless, like Janice Radway's sample of romance readers in the 1980s, mid-century Delly readers would certainly have found the story of a passive, wholly submissive heroine less than pleasurable: to elicit identification, the romance heroine must also appeal to the impulse towards individuation and independence. And pious and conformist as they are, Delly heroines are not weak women, but are strong-minded in the defence of their own integrity and values. The fact that these values are Catholic ones does not alter the fact that when male authority threatens their moral and spiritual freedom, they put up a fight. Marysia and Hermine uncover and thus put an end to years of oppressive tyranny that also threatened their futures. Faced with her new husband's refusal to let her attend mass, Lise

> se redressait devant lui, grandie soudain par l'indignation de la douleur, les yeux étincelants, belle d'une beauté surnaturelle de chrétienne intrépide . . . , une femme révoltée devant l'injustice, devant la tyrannie morale qui prétendait s'exercer sur elle.[21] (*ER*: 226)

Varvara, perceptive in her jealousy, compares Lise positively to Serge's submissive first wife, 'une pâte molle, une jolie statue sans intelligence que Serge n'avait jamais réellement aimée' (*ER*: 244).[22] Not only do heroines like Lise win their own right to practise their religion, they also educate their heroes to produce husbands who are not only loving, but also spiritually and morally in tune with their wives. Thus the domineering Prince de Wittengrätz is softened and humanized:

> Un grand amour avait eu raison de l'égoïsme, de l'ironie, du scepticisme, et celle qui l'inspirait étant une être d'élite, cet amour élevait l'âme de son mari, en faisant déjà un homme quelque peu différent.[23] (*BB*: 212)

The 'spectacularly masculine' (Radway 1987: 128) heroes of similar novels such as *Esclave . . . ou reine?*, *La Vengeance de Ralph*, and *Le Repaire des fauves* also change under the influence of gentle but uncompromising women, so that the heroine (and with her, vicariously, the reader) is

---

[21] 'stood up and faced him, made suddenly taller by indignation and pain, her eyes sparkling, lovely with the beauty of an intrepid Christian . . . a woman rebelling at injustice, and at the moral tyranny imposed upon her.'

[22] 'a shapeless dough, a pretty, stupid statue that Serge never really loved'.

[23] 'A great love had vanquished his selfishness, irony, and scepticism, and since she who had inspired it was an exceptional being, this love elevated his soul and made him a rather different man.'

rewarded with a husband who is not only rich, intelligent, loving, and exceptionally good-looking, but also shares her values.

If Delly novels offer an idealized reflection of women's own stories of love and marriage, then sex might be expected to play its part. Indeed, the romance has always provided a means for women to explore and enjoy fantasies of sexual desire. And yet with their Catholic emphasis on female purity, Delly novels tend to simply elide the heroine's sexual experience. One recurring plot line has the young heroine married off to the arrogant hero—who both attracts and alarms her—in the early pages, so that the discovery of mutual love happens within marriage, but the question of sexual relations between the couple is simply never raised. 'Chez Delly', in Coquillat's view, 'la femme ignore le désir' (Coquillat 1988: 91),[24] and certainly these texts allow for no explicit mention of the heroine's desire, or of any aspect of her sexual experience. However, sexuality is not entirely absent from Delly, even if it appears in coded form. As we have seen, the heroine's rival functions in a sense as her dark side or double, representing that female sexual energy that the characterization of the heroine herself denies. And the hero's focalization of the heroine, as Ellen Constans argues (Constans 1990: 118–26), is certainly charged with desire, even if any description of her body is limited to eyes ('quelle profonde, mystérieuse lumière s'en dégageait' (*BB*: 51)),[25] hair ('le flot soyeux et onduleux' (*VR*: 105)),[26] and abstract general qualities such as beauty, elegance, and 'souplesse' (suppleness). No Delly heroine consciously recognizes or expresses sexual desire, but her blushes (the hero's 'regard ému ... fit un peu rougir Hermine, sans qu'elle sût pourquoi' (*HRR*: 93)),[27] like her physical reactions to his touch ('Sa main, que venaient de toucher les lèvres de Ralph, frémissait' (*VR*: 57)),[28] indicate a sensual, bodily response to the hero's presence that is a recurring signifier of developing love. Beneath the 'cri du cœur' ('cry of the heart') of Delly novels, the reader is invited to hear a distinct 'cri du corps' ('cry of the body') (Constans 1990).

The scenario of enforced marriage to a handsome, dominating hero is a recurring one, in Delly as in other contemporary romance writers such as Max du Veuzit. This suggests that it held a strong appeal for readers, possibly because it addresses a simultaneous fear of and fascination with sex. The heroine is placed in enforced proximity to a man whom she finds

---

[24] 'In Delly, women simply do not experience desire.'
[25] 'what a deep, mysterious light emanated from them.'
[26] 'the silky, waving mass of it'.
[27] 'his tender look made Hermine redden slightly, without understanding why.'
[28] 'Her hand, which Ralph's lips had just touched, was trembling.'

increasingly attractive, and who (given contemporary marriage laws, as well as the laws of Catholic morality) has the right to her body. The unspoken fear underlying this situation is that of unwanted, coercive sex; in the case of the 'jeunes filles', to whom the moral romance series were specifically addressed, this fear may have been compounded by sexual ignorance. But the situation also carries an implicit erotic charge, for as we have seen, Delly heroes are always supremely desirable, and marriage makes sex between the couple the inevitable and legitimate outcome of their relations. Delly has oblique ways of signalling the heroine's sensual attraction towards the hero. In *Esclave . . . ou reine?*, Lise is allowed into Serge's private study to nurse him when he is wounded, and the description of the room is redolent with sensuality. Animal skins bring a 'note sauvage' (191) to the decor:

> Dans l'atmosphère chaude flottait une étrange senteur faite du parfum préféré du maître de céans, des émanations du cuir de Russie, de l'odeur des fines cigarettes turques, des exhalaison enivrantes s'échappant des gerbes de fleurs répandues partout.[29] (192)

The heady atmosphere suggests the possibility of a male otherness that is not alarmingly powerful, but rather intoxicatingly erotic, although the couple's mutual misunderstanding means that even such chaste physical contact as the novel allows (her head on his shoulder, a brief kiss) is delayed until the final chapter. As in almost all Delly romances, the novel's conclusion sees the resolution of the threat of sexual violence in a wholly idealized love and tenderness.

Delly novels are thoroughly reactionary in their values, and it would take a very determined reading against the grain of the text to find there any contestation of the dominant, androcentric ideology of the inter-war years and (still more) the Vichy regime. But this is not to say that their readers were simply stupid or mystified: the novels provided a colourful, agreeably glamorized account of what Janice Radway terms 'a woman's journey to female personhood *as that particular psychic configuration is constructed and realized within patriarchal culture*' (Radway 1987: 138). The idealization of marriage and motherhood, like the fantasised resolution of the problems they pose, works to encourage acceptance of women's secondary status and limited destiny. But within the limitations of the status quo, Delly romances offer imagined journeys to the successful reconciliation of personal autonomy and social role,

---

[29] 'In the warm atmosphere there floated a strange scent composed of the favourite perfume of the master of the house, the smell of Russian leather, the odour of fine Turkish cigarettes, and the intoxicating scent that came from the bunches of flowers that were scattered everywhere.'

images of a circumscribed but resolute female strength and integrity, and a safely disguised foray into the erotic.

Beyond Delly: Max du Veuzit, Collection Stella, and Magali

Throughout the inter-war years and on into the 1950s, the moral romance dominated the popular romance market in France. Delly was probably the best-known and most successful 'brand' of romance, but many other writers made a living, and sometimes a fortune, by the regular publication of romantic stories that subscribed to a conservative, and in most cases Catholic, ideology. Max du Veuzit (1876–1952), whose pen-name concealed a married woman and mother of three, Alphonsine Zéphirine Vasseur, achieved long-lasting commercial success with novels that are fundamentally similar to Delly's in plot and values, but that bring to the moral romance a lighter tone, a mildly ironic humour, and a degree of attention to a changing contemporary world.[30] Like Delly, du Veuzit was mainly published in series that offered a guarantee of conformity to respectable moral values, like the *Bibliothèque de ma Fille*. In 1928, the same series began publication of what was to be an epic, forty-volume amplification of the romance narrative: Berthe Bernage's *Brigitte* novels, with their unrelenting propaganda for marriage, wifely submission, and motherhood as the roads to female happiness.[31]

The moral romance also flourished in small-format, low-cost paperback series, published by women's magazines and sold mainly by subscription, such as the *Petit Écho de la mode*'s Collection Stella—'collection idéale des romans pour la famille et la jeune fille par sa qualité morale et sa qualité littéraire'[32]—and *Foyer-Revue*'s fortnightly collection *Foyer-Roman*. Such series employed a large number of authors, of whom a majority (and given the continuing fashion for male pen-names, possibly a larger majority than the lists reveal) were women.

Few of these authors became well known in their own right, and the consistency of plotting, style, and values suggests that the series laid down guidelines for their contributors. In a variety of settings and periods, the neatly crafted plots weave endless colourful variations on the love story,

---

[30] In *Nuit nuptiale*, for example, like most du Veuzit novels impossible to date because of multiple reprintings and re-editions, the 'reluctant bride' plot results from a drunken prank in an American bar, during which a slightly tipsy heroine finds herself legally married to an arrogant, inebriated hero. Such behaviour would be unimaginable in a Delly heroine.

[31] See Cosnier 1999: 241–54.

[32] 'A collection of novels ideal for the family and for young girls, thanks to both their moral and literary qualities'.

each narrative impelled towards the inevitable conclusion of shared emotional bliss, or—in a minority of cases—the suspension of that bliss through the hero's death, with the hope of a reunion in heaven.[33] If there is a difference between the formulaic, multi-authored collections and the novels of Delly and du Veuzit, it lies in the nature of the obstacles to love that delay the inevitable dénouement. Whereas the subscription series tend to make these obstacles external (war, family opposition, rivals), Delly and du Veuzit make the moral and spiritual conflict between hero and heroine central to the drama, so that the happy ending depends on its resolution. As we have seen, this both produces an undercurrent of eroticism, and foregrounds the strength beneath the heroine's demure passivity. This adept combination of conservative moralizing and asser-tion of women's moral agency helps to explain the particular success of the sub-genre's 'star' authors. They most perfectly fulfilled the mission of the moral romance: to discourage transgression by glamorizing the restricted destiny allotted to women, but to do so by indulging their read-ers' dreams of being at once passionately loved and socially respected, cherished both as sexual beings and as women of integrity.

The success of Delly and Max du Veuzit lasted throughout the inter-war period and indeed on into the 1980s, but by the 1930s a younger gen-eration of romance writers were also finding a large readership among their contemporaries. Of those, perhaps the most widely known and read was Magali, or Jeanne Philbert (1898–1986). Magali's entertaining novels maintained the basic formula of the moral romance, in that her young, virginal heroines inevitably found their happy ending in marriage and the prospect of future maternity. Tallandier soon recruited her for their *Collection Blanche* (White Collection) and their Family Library, where her novels appeared alongside those of Delly and du Veuzit. However, Tallandier also astutely placed some Magali romances in the *Collection Bleue*, which explicitly targeted a younger, more self-consciously 'mod-ern' readership: this collection was to be the 'vraie bibliothèque de la jeune française ardente, moderne et honnête aujourd'hui', though it also promised novels that would be 'sains, moraux, bienfaisants'.[34]

---

[33] For example, *Le Mariage de Rose Duprey* by G. d'Arvor (1925) is a love story between a handsome smuggler and the customs officer's daughter, set in the Napoleonic wars; *Lucile et le mariage* (Pierre Alciette, 1930) has an impoverished, orphaned—but nobly born—girl win the love of a rich aristocrat, in contemporary Paris; *La Malle des Îles* (J. Grandchamp, 1931) is set in colonial Algeria and France, and takes the couple to a happy union before the First World War intervenes. After the hero's death, the heroine becomes a missionary nun and lives in anticipation of a reunion with her lover in heaven.

[34] 'the library for the passionate, modern, honest young French woman of today'—'decent, moral, uplifting'.

Magali's own life was distinctly less sheltered and more adventurous than those of the unmarried, reclusive Delly, or the family-oriented du Veuzit. Orphaned early, like most of her heroines, she left the kindly aunts who brought her up to travel to Algeria, as a teacher, at the age of 17. In 1922 she gave birth to an illegitimate daughter, Anne. In 1926 she married the writer and journalist Marcel Idiers, serving her literary apprenticeship by acting as ghost-writer to an indolent, exploitative husband. Magali soon left Idiers and became a successful journalist and novelist in her own right. When war broke out in 1939, she volunteered as a driver, then under the Occupation became part of the Resistance network Berthaux, near Toulouse, establishing a small publishing house—the Éditions Chantal—which published romances and children's fiction as a cover for its clandestine output of pro-Resistance material. Post-war, she was the first winner of the Prix Littéraire Max du Veuzit, awarded by the Société des Gens de Lettres for the highest-selling works of romantic fiction. Her fiction reflects the independence and energy of its author, for despite the relentless dynamic of the romance plot, Magali's stories place love within the broader context of women's lives, and suggest that marriage, whilst a narrative necessity, is not the only possible form of female happiness. As one heroine says: 'Je sais que je risque fort de rester vieille fille. Eh bien, je serai une vieille fille qui travaille et qui lutte, comme les autres' (Magali 1931: 20).[35]

The heroine of *Le Jardin de l'enchantement* (1931 and a *Collection Bleue* novel) is—like so many romance heroines—orphaned at an early age, but Muriel is a self-reliant modern girl who takes her fate into her own hands, and sets off south to begin a new life with an aunt she scarcely knows. When she finds that the aunt has mysteriously disappeared—thus providing an additional narrative strand of quest for her whereabouts—Muriel sets up home in her abandoned cottage, and takes employment as the 'English' companion to the daughter of a nouveau riche family, comically portrayed and entirely taken in by Muriel's masquerading as an English native. Magali's narrative voice is sometimes lightly ironic and self-referential: despite her independence, Muriel dreams of a hero very like the hero of the conventional romance, 'comme le héros de son livre de prix: noble seigneur', with an 'allure conquérante', 'un visage impénétrable et des yeux pleins de mystère' (27).[36] But the man in whose arms she ends the story, despite conforming

---

[35] 'I know I'm in serious danger of remaining an old maid. Well, if I do, I'll just be an old maid who works and fights on like the rest of them.'

[36] 'like the hero of the book she was given as a prize', 'a noble lord with a conquering air, an impenetrable expression and eyes full of mystery'.

to the genre's preference for aristocratic heroes with a 'lueur railleuse' ('mocking light', 145) in their eyes, is also a kind, gentle young man, who turns out to be the author of Muriel's favourite poetry which he publishes under the female pen-name 'Roselyne'. The wealth, good looks, and authority of idealized masculinity are here combined with a very 'feminine' empathy: the readers of 'Roselyne' all believe the poetic voice to be that of a woman, and Muriel feels that the poet shares her emotions. Gender boundaries are less fixed than in Delly, and the happy ending celebrates mutual love and liking rather than the formation of a new family unit. Magali does not share the family ethic of the moral romance, nor its piety.

Un baiser sur la route (A Kiss on the Road) was published in 1942, under the Occupation, in Tallandier's Family Library collection. While it is certainly not a Resistance novel, nor overtly subversive of the Vichy regime's intensely conservative morality, nor does it support Vichy's patriarchal model of family and social relations. Florine—'vingt-deux ans, du courage, de l'optimisme et une immense bonne volonté'[37] (23)—is another independent, self-supporting heroine, in peacetime a fashion designer with a specialism in women's sportswear. The story begins in 1940, during the exodus south before the German invasion; Florine is a volunteer driver and carer in a home for refugee children. She first meets the hero when he brings his little son to the home, as he himself sets off to join his regiment. The kiss on the cheek with which he leaves her is one of gratitude and comradely affection, but it also carries an undercurrent of desire: 'deux mains solides étreignaient ses épaules, un baiser brûla sa joue' (20).[38] The couple's first meeting establishes both sensual attraction, and a shared adult responsibility at this time of crisis.

Florine drives the children south, and finds a refuge for them all with a household of eccentric old sisters, who are locked in a long-standing feud with the neighbouring family of equally eccentric, curmudgeonly old brothers. Florine forms a friendship with the gardener's niece—class frontiers are also distinctly less rigid than in Delly—and between them the two young women help to manage the property, try to end the bitter hostility between the two households, and re-educate the overprotected, prematurely middle-aged Georges (son of one of Florine's hosts) with whom Vivette is in love. In other words, Florine's story has dimensions other than the romantic. Nonetheless, this is a romance, and the reappearance of Daniel, the hero, both solves the mystery of the feud—with a touch of magical coincidence, he turns out to

---

[37] 'Twenty-two years old, courageous, optimistic, and full of good will'.
[38] 'two firm hands held her shoulders, and a kiss burned her cheek.'

be the estranged nephew of the sisters, and to have intensified the feud some years previously by eloping with the daughter of the enemy family—and produces the happy dénouement. The mother of Daniel's son is conveniently dead, and Daniel asks Florine to marry him. Mutual sexual attraction is more explicitly evoked than in the moral romance: 'Elle ne pouvait détacher son regard de ce visage ciselé d'ombre, à qui la passion prêtait une violence contenue' (243),[39] and Magali makes her happy ending dependent on Daniel's acceptance of Florine as an equal and an adult: 'je ne suis plus une enfant. Les années d'épreuve m'ont mûrie,' says Florine, and Daniel replies, 'Je le sais et c'est cela que j'aime en vous' (244).[40] It is Florine who insists that they stay in France and take over Daniel's family estate, defining their future life together in words that discreetly evoke a national return to the values denied by Vichy. The novel closes as Florine looks forward to 'l'immense orgueil d'être l'instigateur de cette richesse, de cette renaissance, dans une vie libre, sous un ciel libre' (254).[41]

Magali's novels maintain the basic pleasures of the moral romance: her heroines win respect through their virtue whilst being passionately loved and desired by men whom, in their turn, they find supremely lovable. Mutual love and marriage remain the goal and the sole happy dénouement of the plot. But her heroines are grown-up, emancipated young women who expect to be treated as equals, and for whom life is profoundly enhanced by, but not reducible to, heterosexual love. Magali's use of the Editions Chantal as a cover for Resistance activities made romance the ally of Resistance rather than Vichyite reaction. Her novels too propose a discreet refutation of the values of the moral romance: here the self-assertive woman is not the demonized rival but the heroine, and only the hero who can recognize a woman as an equal gets the girl.

Romance and Resistance writing

In the moral romance, love is universally and eternally the most perfect form of female self-realization, a constant ideal scarcely inflected by historical change or cultural difference. The shock of defeat and occupation in 1940 brought the realities of time, place, and history sharply into focus:

---

[39] 'She couldn't take her eyes off that face sculpted by shadow, to which passion lent a contained violence.'

[40] 'I'm not a child any longer. These years of hardship have made me grow up.'

[41] 'the immense pride of being the creator of this wealth, this renaissance, in a life of freedom, beneath a sky of freedom'.

if Delly's world of timeless values continued to offer escape from the real, Magali made the chaos and despair of 1940 a significant element of her story, and discreetly proposed the romantic happy end as an image of the nation's future return to freedom. Magali's caution was strategic: since her romance writing served as a cover for Resistance activities, any hint of subversive attitudes had to be camouflaged within the familiar discourse of the genre. For those writers who made literature itself a weapon of resistance, publishing and distributing their work through the clandestine press, the contestation of Nazi and collaborationist values needed no such textual concealment. Romantic love plays its part in Resistance fiction, and particularly that of female authors, not as an unchanging human truth, but as an emotion the meaning and value of which are subject to the imperatives of history.

In some clandestine fiction, as in Aragon's Resistance poetry,[42] love becomes an affirmation of that respect for and care of the other which is denied and persecuted by Nazism and by Vichy. Édith Thomas (1909–70), a left-wing writer and journalist before the war, wrote stories under the pen-name Auxois for publication by the underground Éditions de Minuit. The *Contes d'Auxois* (first published in 1943) are a series of very short stories (six to eight small pages), all set in the present of the Occupation, among ordinary people who find themselves, in one way or another, resisting. *Les Moules et le professeur* (The Professor and the Mussels) narrates a morning in the life of an elderly couple in a cold, hungry Paris beset by shortages. The Professor leaves his study, and his work on Homer and Virgil, to scour the shops for food, but returns disconsolate and empty-handed, to accept a warm drink into which his wife slips the gift of a rare sugar cube. The story works by opposing to the deprivation of war both the stoicism and solidarity of the queuing women, which briefly cheers the old man, and the discreet but passionate tenderness between himself and his wife. A story of oppression and material misery ends on a note of elation: 'Il savait qu'elle s'en privait pour lui. Il regarda son sourire secret, dont il connaissait la tendresse. Oui, la vie était une aventure merveilleuse' (Thomas 1944: 13).[43] In *La Relève*, Robert receives the letter conscripting him to the Service du Travail Obligatoire, Vichy's scheme to send French workers to Germany. His choice is between obedience, or going into hiding. The decision is made when he returns

---

[42] Some of Louis Aragon's most famous Resistance poetry celebrates his love of 'Elsa'; the poem 'Les Yeux d'Elsa', for example, makes her eyes an emblem of freedom and resistance. Aragon was the husband of Elsa Triolet—see below.

[43] 'He knew that she did without so that he could have more. He looked at her secret smile, whose tenderness he knew so well. Yes, life was a wonderful adventure.'

home to his lover Simone, and her quiet certainty that he must not go. Robert recognizes the inseparability of his love for Simone, and his new sense of collective moral responsibility: 'tout était confondu en elle. Il savait que depuis qu'il la connaissait, il était devenu meilleur... Plus conscient, comme s'il était personnellement responsable de tout' (21).[44] Simone will hide him, refusing his labour to the enemy, and enabling him to join the Resistance. Love is at once a refuge—the couple's discussion takes place in bed, bodies entwined—and a stimulus to positive action. It represents a counter-value to the brutal philosophy of those in power.

But if love is on the side of Resistance, love's selfish desire for the presence and safety of the loved one can also conflict with the demands of the collective struggle. Simone's concealment of Robert fuses her personal and political desires, for she keeps him close as well as preventing his potential contribution to the German war effort, but she acknowledges that 'Quant il faudra sortir les fusils et les mitraillettes, alors, va, je ne te retiendrai plus' (22).[45] In Thomas's stories, recognition of the need for armed action is shadowed by the terror of losing a beloved man. Alice, in the story *F.T.P.*, acts as the liaison between her husband and the other members of a local Resistance group who are planning to blow up a German train. As they await the train, Alice waits at home in a state of painful anxiety, and reflects on the incompatibility between her romantic desires—'avoir un mari qu'on aime, et l'aimer jusqu'à la fin'[46]—and the harsh reality of the times: 'il n'y a pas de bonheur, même le plus simple, même le plus humble, *actuellement* sans mensonge et sans égoïsme' (56).[47] *Veillée* is similarly focalized from the perspective of a woman in love, who simultaneously loathes and accepts the war's disruption of the expected pattern of the romance narrative. 'Et pourquoi faut-il que ce soit moi qui l'aime à en perdre la raison, à l'attendre éveillée toute la nuit?' (27).[48]

In perhaps the most famous example of clandestine Resistance fiction *Le Silence de la mer* (1942), Vercors (Jean Bruller, 1902–91) uses the love story to show the impossibility, under the Occupation, of a love that transcends history and politics. The love that develops between the young German officer, von Ebrennac, and the niece of the Frenchman in whose

---

[44] 'everything came together in her. He knew that since he had known her, he had become a better man... More aware, as if he were personally responsible for everything.'

[45] 'When it's time for the rifles and machine-guns to come out, then I won't hold you back.'

[46] 'To have a man you love, and love him till the end'.

[47] 'as things are, there can be no happiness, not even the most simple, undemanding happiness, that doesn't also mean lies and selfishness.'

[48] 'Why has it got to be me who loves him enough to lose my reason, enough to wait up for him all night, wide awake?'

house he is billeted can never be lived out, nor even spoken. Although as an individual von Ebrennac has all the qualities of the romantic hero—he is handsome, intelligent, cultured, and well intentioned—he remains objectively an agent of Nazi Germany, and as such must be resisted. When he himself discovers the full horror of the ideology he serves, he can only concur in the impossibility of any attachment between himself and the French woman. Von Ebrennac at first naively likens Franco-German relations to those of Beauty and the Beast, but the fairy tale's romantic ending has no place here. The story's dénouement lies not in the couple's union, but in a declaration of love that can only be made because it is also a farewell. Until then, the niece has refused to say a single word to the German; as he leaves for the Eastern front, and probable death, she utters a single, whispered 'Adieu'. Von Ebrennac's smile means that this one exchange represents confirmation of a mutual love that the situation renders unlivable, and all but unspeakable. Irène Némirovsky, in a novel written in 1941–2 shortly before she was transported to Auschwitz, but only rediscovered and published in 2004, depicts a similarly intense and impossible love between a billeted German officer and his French host. In Némirovsky's story, love is admitted and expressed, and brings a lasting enrichment to Lucile's hitherto narrow, closeted life. Nonetheless, the lovers' attempt to 'oublier tout ce qui n'était pas eux-mêmes'[49] (Némirovsky 2004: 371) is doomed to failure, and Bruno departs for the Russian front and probable death.

Elsa Triolet's *Les Amants d'Avignon* (1943), originally published by the Éditions de Minuit and later the first story in Triolet's Goncourt prize-winning collection *Le Premier Accroc coûte 200 francs*, is the Resistance story that most explicitly addresses the relationship between romantic love and commitment to the collective cause. First, Triolet establishes her heroine as a typical, ordinary young woman by making her an avid consumer of romantic fictions. Juliette could be seen as a prototypical romance reader: single, she supports herself and her family by working as a shorthand typist, but dreams of another life of perfect love, 'aimer quelqu'un de beau . . . Il y aurait de la musique, des chansons' (Triolet 1945: 44).[50] But this pretty, dreamy young woman, 'séduisante comme une dactylo de cinéma' (29),[51] is also an intrepid Resistance agent, whom the reader next encounters staying in an icy, rat-infested ruin of a farmhouse as she checks possible hiding places for resisters on the run, and risking her life by carrying messages between Resistance groups

---

[49] 'forget everything that was not themselves'.
[50] 'to love someone handsome . . . There would be music, and songs.'
[51] 'as seductive as a typist in the movies'.

in different cities. Juliette's conflation of the ordinary feminine with active commitment extends the image of Resistance beyond the heroic male figure of the *maquisard*, and simultaneously gives the lie to Vichy's dogma of an incompatibility between 'natural' femininity and political activity.

But *Les Amants d'Avignon* does not only use romance as a means of characterizing Juliette as the ordinary heroine. Juliette's dreams of love adopt the common currency of her culture: the love songs of Piaf, the films of Charles Boyer, women's magazine stories. They have the banality and vagueness of mass-produced fantasies: 'il y aurait de la musique, des chansons . . .', and they bear no relation to Juliette's lived experience of a single love affair which ended only in 'honte et mépris' ('shame and contempt', 37). Yet the story accords to romance a positive function, as the repository of counter-values under an oppressive regime, and as an expression—however banal its form—of authentic emotion.

As in Thomas's stories, the society created by the Occupation is here characterized by extreme sensory and emotional deprivation: by cold, hunger, darkness, shortages, separation from loved ones, cruelty, and mutual suspicion. It is the very antithesis of Pétain's image of the nation as a great family reunited in traditional values. Against this bleak world, Triolet sets the magical interlude of Juliette's encounter with Célestin in Avignon. Célestin is a Resistance leader, and Juliette is sent to warn him of the imminent arrest of some of his men, whose lives she therefore saves. Within the twenty-fours that they have together, Juliette proposes the enactment of a romantic dream: 'on va jouer comme si on s'aimait' ('we'll act as if we were in love', 71). Célestin joins in the game wholeheartedly, and the episode takes on the perfection, and the sense of inevitability, of a good dream. Avignon is a city 'tissée de légendes' ('woven of legends', 70), the city of love where Petrarch met Laura, sparkling with light in the icy sunshine as the couple stroll its streets, their arms around each other, and climb to the top of the fortress from where they look out over a luminous landscape. 'L'air, les pierres, le soleil, cette herbe sous leurs pieds, le vent, n'essayaient même plus de paraître inoffensifs, ils avouaient leur pouvoir magique, ils les tenaient, les possédaient' (75).[52] It is Christmas Day, a feast day outside normal time, and also Juliette's day, since her surname is 'Noël'. Célestin, whose very name 'connotes light and space' (Atack 1990: 240), has the beauty and courage of a romantic hero—'Une tête d'archange, sombre, déchu' ('the head of an archangel, sombre, fallen', 70). Everything contrasts with the France of darkness, fear, and

---

[52] 'The air, the stones, the sun, the grass beneath their feet, the wind, no longer even pretended to be neutral, they admitted that they had magic power, and that they held and possessed the lovers.'

lack that lies beyond the dream: the sunlight, the relative abundance of a special Christmas dinner in a warm, festive-looking restaurant, the physical intimacy and openly declared emotion between the couple.

Love here transforms the world, but it is a fantasized, pretend love, framed by the self-awareness of an agreed 'as if'. It is a space of dream, swiftly ended by Célestin's sudden need to depart on Resistance business, and by the sound of heavy boots marching down the city streets: 'Une ville allemande, qu'Avignon' ('A German city, was Avignon', 85). In occupied France, the story suggests, love can only be a utopian dream of desire and belonging, within a bleak and broken world. But the assertion and the survival of that dream is important: it sustains Juliette and Célestin in their struggle, and offers the reader an alternative model of human relations to counter the domination/oppression model of Nazism, and Vichy's subjection of female desire to the needs of family and nation. It is the story of love that counts, however difficult it may be to translate into reality. Thus Juliette and Célestin are moved by the inscriptions on the fortress walls, traces left by a pair of lovers which form an elliptically narrated tale of passionate, mutual love sustained across the years: 'Ils sont venus', 'Ils sont revenus 24-7-31. Son cœur est toujours tremblant devant elle', '1937—il est vieux. Elle est belle. Ils sont venus' (77–8).[53] This story comes to represent the unrealized possibility of their own relationship: when Juliette and Célestin meet again, briefly, he evokes what might have been with the echoed words 'Elle est venue', 'Seigneur, éternisez l'amour qu'il a pour elle' (115).[54]

Juliette ends the story still engaged in the Resistance struggle, but taking temporary refuge in her dreams. Juliette, Triolet's 'fille comme une autre' ('girl like any other', 13), is also the common reader, who knows the difference between life-sustaining fiction, and the necessities of living, but who sacrifices neither.

Conclusion

The romantic fiction that dominated the market in mid-century France was largely conservative in intention, providing, as it did, the fantasized reconciliation of women's subjective desires with the circumscribed destinies allotted to them in a society that remained (particularly under Vichy) strongly patriarchal. If women consumed the Delly-style moral

---

[53] 'They returned, 24-7-31. His heart still trembles before her.' '1937—he is old. She is beautiful. They came.'

[54] 'She came.' 'Lord, make his love for her eternal.'

romance in such large numbers, this reflected the genre's capacity to replay—enjoyably—a process of identity formation and social adaptation familiar to most readers, to represent these in agreeably idealized form, and to give due weight—albeit in coded form—to women's 'phallic' desires for self-assertion and sexual agency, even if the happy ending implies their necessary sublimation into wifely and maternal devotion. That the romance does not necessarily conform to a conservative agenda is confirmed by its deployment in the Resistance cause. In Resistance fiction, love signifies not the primrose path that leads inexorably to women's subordination, nor even the assertion of selfish freedom against that fate, but rather a model of self/other relations that at once accepts and transcends each partner's difference or 'otherness'. In this, the romance could articulate resistance to the ideologies of Nazism and of the Vichyite Right.

4 Love in a Brave New World: Romance in the 1950s

In November 1945, in a newly liberated France, *Elle* magazine made its first appearance with the headline: 'FRANCE RECORD DU MONDE DE DÉPUTÉES. 32/575 À LA CONSTITUANTE'. French women had voted for the first time, and *Elle* celebrated the election of a small but world record breaking number of women MPs to the Constituent Assembly of the Fourth Republic. In that same first edition, Paul Géraldy asked: 'La femme doit-elle sacrifier ses préférences politiques à l'homme qu'elle aime?' ('Should a woman sacrifice her own political views to the man she loves?'), and concluded that she definitely should not, even though, he suggested, women in love would tend to share their lover's convictions.[1] The serialized book was Colette's latest, *L'Étoile Vesper*, with its celebration of female creativity and presentation of motherhood as merely one of its many forms. The short story was an adapted translation of an American romance, in which a soldier and a woman doctor meet at a railway station, and each pretends to already know the other in order to start a conversation, and thus pursue their immediate, mutual attraction. *Elle*'s early fiction contained a lot of returning soldiers and women who engage with them on equal terms, just as the articles often focused on women resisters, and on practical strategies for coping in a country just emerging from chaos. Françoise Giroud, at the start of what was to be a long and glorious career in journalism, exhorted women to use their right to vote (30 Apr. 1946), and sang the praises of work outside the home as a source of personal fulfilment: 'Travailler, ce n'est pas seulement gagner sa vie. C'est ouvrir une porte sur le monde, un monde multiple qui vous appartiendra si vous lui tendez la main' (8 Oct. 1946).[2]

The tone is confidently opposed to Vichy's preaching of submissive, domesticated femininity. But even by 1946, a competing discourse can also be traced in what soon became France's most popular women's weekly, at least among younger middle-class women. Marcelle Ségal's advice column '*Elle* et vous' ('*Elle* and you') focused relentlessly on

---

[1] Géraldy, romantic poet and playwright, figures in Camille Laurens's 2003 novel *L'Amour, roman*. See chapter 6, n. 21.

[2] 'Working does not simply mean earning a living. It means opening a door onto the world, a rich, varied world that will belong to you if you just reach out a hand.'

the importance of marriage to a woman's happiness. In February 1948, a series of articles by one Dr Clifford Adams, an 'expert' from the University of Pennsylvania, explained to readers 'Comment trouver un mari ... et le garder' ('How to find a husband ... and keep him'), recommending avoidance of the 'seven capital sins of the married woman' which included trying to change a husband rather than accept him as he was, and refusing his sexual advances. André Maurois offered a 'cours de bonheur conjugal' ('a course in conjugal happiness') in the spring of 1950, and with the exception of another serialized Colette book (*Le Fanal bleu* in 1949), *Elle*'s fictional component turned solely to romance. Women had emerged from the war more independent, able to vote, and equipped for paid employment, but they were also being told quite clearly, by the magazine that aimed to reflect a flatteringly positive image of its readers, that to be part of a happy heterosexual couple must be every woman's aspiration, and that the couple's happiness depended primarily on her.

The Liberation had brought important advances for gender equality: the vote, a formal declaration of the principle of women's equality in the constitution of the new Republic, and a degree of recognition for women's role in the Resistance, to which was attributed de Gaulle's decision in favour of female suffrage. However, the dominant image of the Resistance remained that of the (largely male) Free French, and the armed *maquisards*: out of the 1,030 Croix de la Libération that honoured the heroes of the Resistance, only six were awarded to women, four of these posthumously (Duchen 1994: 12). The public humiliation of women suspected of having had sexual relations with the occupying forces reasserted the sexual double standard, since, as Claire Duchen points out, a much more accommodating view was taken of male prisoners of war who had had relations with German women (Duchen 1994: 16). The law continued to limit the rights of married women, giving the husband rights over his wife's assets, and allowing him to refuse her the right to work if he deemed this to be against the family interest. A strong—and understandable—urge to normalize life after five years of conflict and turbulence, combined with an optimistic will to regenerate the nation, produced a pervasive emphasis on family and motherhood. Laws were already in place to dissuade women from preventing pregnancy through contraception or abortion; these were supplemented by a strategy of persuasion, as the state began to offer loans for young married couples, 'to encourage the establishment of young and fertile households' (the Minister for Public Health and Population, quoted in Duchen 1994: 31), and the system of family allowances, later to be mercilessly satirized by Christiane Rochefort in *Les Petits Enfants du siècle* (Children of the Century, 1961), encouraged large families by offering financial rewards for each additional child born. Between 1946 and 1950, the marriage rate rose to become the highest France had ever known, and the birth rate rose in its wake.

Reconstruction, initially supported by aid from the USA, meant the rapid modernization of the French economy, and the beginnings of a new commercial culture that aimed, through the production and marketing of an endless stream of new merchandise, to maximize consumption. The couple and the nuclear—as opposed to the extended—family represented the optimal consumer unit, not only because small, separate households meant more sales of domestic goods, but also because the ideal of a stylish, happy, and affluently modern family worked to encourage the acquisition of commodities associated with this image, from home furnishings to off-the-peg fashions, high-tech kitchen equipment to beauty products. Kristin Ross sees a new ideology of love and conjugality as central to the reordering of French society in the 1950s and 1960s. As the demands of a more centrally planned, industrialized economy led to an exodus from rural France towards the cities, and to greater social and geographical mobility, the old, stable model of the family living in one place for generations gave way to a more fragmented pattern. The couple became both 'the standard-bearer of the state-led modernization effort' and 'the bearer of all affective values as well' (Ross 1995: 126). Celebrity couples such as Yves Montand and Simone Signoret, Françoise Giroud and Jean-Jacques Servan-Schreiber, Brigitte Bardot and Roger Vadim,[3] featured prominently in the media of the 1950s and 1960s, and particularly in those magazines that addressed a readership that was, or aspired to be, up-to-date and in tune with modernity, notably *Paris-Match* (founded 1949) and *Elle*. The new model couple was composed of a virile, high-achieving man and a beautiful, elegant woman, whose informed and energetic engagement with the world outside the home did not prevent her from being the guardian of the couple's happiness, and of their domestic perfection. *Elle*'s mission was precisely the reconciliation of a newly energized, 'modern' image of the feminine with the traditional ideal of a man-centred, domestically skilled angel of the house.

Elle projected an image of the modern French woman as stylish, cultured, and competent, but also suggested that her self-fulfilment

---

[3] The Vadim–Bardot courtship and marriage (1951/2) featured prominently in *Paris-Match*, and encapsulated a certain ideal of modern romance, with Vadim portrayed as the handsome, intrepid young journalist and Bardot as the perfectly feminine, innocent bride who was nonetheless a modern girl with a career. After Vadim, Bardot formed a series of 'perfect couples' with glamorous men, amongst them Jean-Louis Trintignant, Sacha Distel, and her second husband Jacques Charrier.

remained inseparable from her role as a devoted wife and mother. 'Point de bonheur, semble-t-il', wrote the editors in 1948, 'hors des sentiers traditionnels du mariage et de la maternité.'[4] Delly's novels supported exactly the same conclusion, and the popular romances of the inter-war period continued to achieve high sales figures, with Delly, Max du Veuzit, and Magali continuing to dominate the popular market alongside the new comic-style romance magazines such as *Confidences* (1946) and *Nous deux* (1947), the latter, like *Elle*, reaching regular sales of over a million in the course of the 1950s (Bonvoisin and Maignien 1986: 23–4). At the literary end of the market, despite the dominance of the often opaque anti-narratives of the *nouveau roman*, love stories remained central to the work of many women writers, though often with a strongly critical charge. Marguerite Duras's 1958 *Moderato cantabile* is a passionate love story, but it portrays love as a violent, essentially extra-social emotion utterly incompatible with its heroine's affluent, conventionally gendered marriage.[5] By the late 1950s and early 1960s, other women authors were attracting large readerships with novels that satirized the prevailing emphasis on conjugality and consumption as the twin paths to female happiness. In Elsa Triolet's 1959 *Roses à crédit* (Roses on Credit), the heroine experiences an equal passion for the man she marries, and for the cornucopia of domestic and beauty products that her married affluence makes available to her. Neither brings lasting happiness. In Christiane Rochefort's *Les Petits Enfants du siècle* (1961), working-class women sacrifice their health and last vestiges of freedom to give birth to child after child, thus qualifying for the family allowances that will fund the purchase of more and more consumer goods. Rochefort's rebellious young narrator, Josyane, holds out against this fate until finally romantic love defeats her, and she settles for marriage, maternity, and a well-equipped apartment. In the same author's *Les Stances à Sophie* (1963), the romantic 'couple' is comically exposed as a myth that serves both to subordinate women and to fuel the consumption of beauty products, home furnishings, and the developing leisure industry.

---

[4] 'Happiness, it would seem, can only be found along the traditional paths of marriage and motherhood.' In 1948 readers were invited to send in the love letters 'they had never dared to write', as the basis for a survey of the intimate life of couples. The conclusions of this survey were categorically pro-marriage, contrasting 'les cris d'angoisse de l'amour dit libre' ('the cries of anguish of so-called free love') with 'le chant serein de l'épouse comblée' ('the serene song of the fulfilled wife') (6 Apr. 1948).

[5] Flora Larsson demonstrates the recurring presence of the romance narrative in Duras's novels of this period in Larsson 1990.

Beauvoir's critique of romance

But well before the dangers of romance had become a theme of feminist-inclined fiction, Simone de Beauvoir produced a telling critique of romantic love as a form of peculiarly feminine bad faith and self-delusion. In *Le Deuxième Sexe* (1949), Beauvoir devotes a chapter to 'L'Amoureuse' (The Woman in Love), defining the woman who makes love for a man the central purpose and meaning of her life as a woman in flight from her own freedom, and doomed to dissatisfaction and a sense of emptiness. The thesis of *Le Deuxième Sexe*, that in most forms of human civilization men have abrogated the position of subject and defined women as their 'Other', applies to centuries of world history, but it also has an acute relevance to the post-war years when it was written and published. Beauvoir is writing of her own times when she identifies the contradictory discourse of an officially egalitarian society that continues to define one sex in terms of the needs and desires of the other:

> Il y a dans l'attitude des hommes d'aujourd'hui une duplicité qui crée chez la femme un déchirement douloureux: ils acceptent dans une assez grande mesure que la femme soit une semblable, une égale; et cependant ils continuent à exiger qu'elle demeure l'inessentiel.[6] (Beauvoir 1976: i. 394)

Le Deuxième Sexe propounds a firmly social constructionist view of gender. If romantic love occupies so much more central a place in women's lives and culture than in those of men, it is not because of any innate emotional difference between the sexes, but because women find themselves dependent on winning and keeping a man, not just to have a respected place in society, but also for their own internalized sense of worth. Beauvoir's argument is that the comprehensive 'Othering' of women translates both into the material reality of financial dependence, and into women's incapacity to experience themselves as independent, whole subjects. One way of achieving a sense of self-worth is to ally oneself with a being who is socially valorized, and to see oneself through his approving eyes: 'ce que rêvera la femme qui n'a pas étouffé sa revendication d'être humain, c'est de dépasser son être vers un de ces êtres supérieurs, c'est de s'unir, se confondre avec le sujet souverain' (ii. 547).[7] Man, the sovereign subject, can confer value by loving and

---

[6] 'The men of today show a certain duplicity of attitude which is painfully lacerating to women; they are willing on the whole to accept woman as a fellow being, an equal; but they still require her to remain the inessential' (Beauvoir 1972: 291).

[7] 'The woman who has not repressed her claim to humanity will dream of transcending her being towards one of these superior beings, of amalgamating herself with the sovereign subject' (ibid.: 653).

desiring a woman, his approbation transforming her body, her past, her very self into something wonderful and unique: 'son pour-autrui se confond avec son être même' (580).[8] Beauvoir's 'amoureuse' presages Jessica Benjamin's female masochist who 'search(es) for recognition through an other who is powerful enough to bestow this recognition' (Benjamin 1988: 56).

Though Beauvoir does not address the connection between the female temptation to live only 'pour-autrui', and women's taste for romantic fiction, the implied narrative of the woman-in-love's story corresponds to that of the popular romance. Beauvoir's 'amoureuse' needs a man who fulfils the role of 'sovereign subject'; in order to bestow value on her life, he must adequately represent the male sex, be someone in whom 'se résume l'essence de l'homme' ('is represented the essence of manhood', 1976: ii. 548). Delly novels and their like—their popularity undiminished in the post-war period—provided idealized heroes, physically strong, intellectually powerful, and without any of the undignified human flaws that could reduce their power to guarantee the exceptional status of the heroine. Through the hero's desiring gaze, the heroine—and with her, in suspended disbelief, the reader—is transformed from a young, unconfident girl, uncertain of her own identity, to an adored, socially and emotionally secure woman. The *roman d'amour* makes a woman's total self-investment in love into a story with a happy ending. Beauvoir's story, however, continues past the formation of the couple, and demonstrates the fragility of an identity sustained only by the desire and approval of a single, privileged other. A man's greater social freedom, together with the hegemonic view of male sexuality as naturally promiscuous, make his fidelity uncertain. Moreover, the emotional dependence of the woman-in-love, and her need for her partner to maintain his status as representative of powerful masculinity, make her a demanding companion: in constant need of reassurance that his love is for ever, and unforgiving of his weaknesses, her demands may precipitate the end of the affair. And without love, the woman-in-love—as Beauvoir was to illustrate in her 1967 stories *Monologue* and *La Femme rompue*— discovers that she is no one, or that she no longer knows who she is. Writing from within a culture that continued to make women both dependent on and responsible for the heterosexual couple, and that in the pages of *Elle* and elsewhere insisted on the centrality of durable romantic love to women's happiness and status, Beauvoir analysed love as a dangerous form of alienation for women, and as a serious threat to their integrity and happiness.

---

[8] 'her *pour-autrui*, relation to others, is confused with her very being' (ibid.: 678). 'Relation to others' might be better translated 'being-for-others'.

However, it is not love itself that is condemned in 'L'Amoureuse', but rather love as it is lived out within a situation of inequality, where women are the 'second sex'. Towards the end of her chapter, Beauvoir envisages an authentic form of romantic love, in which each partner would experience her- or himself as both subject and object, as the active agent of desire and its passive recipient, and loving the other would be, for each, a form of self-discovery and self-affirmation. Love in this case could mean a shared 'révélation de soi-même par le don de soi et enrichissement de l'univers' (579).[9] Like the authors of the Belle Époque feminist romance, Beauvoir sees authentic, mutually enriching heterosexual love as incompatible with female dependence, but as an ideal to be glimpsed, imagined, and struggled for.[10] In the novel she began writing soon after publication of *Le Deuxième Sexe*, *Les Mandarins*, she explored love between men and women both in its destructive, alienated form, and in its potential for transcendence.

Les Mandarins

Published in 1954, winner of that year's Prix Goncourt, *Les Mandarins* is a novel firmly located in its time. Drawing extensively on Beauvoir's own life in the late 1940s, it tells the story of a group of left-wing Parisian intellectuals, as they emerge from the Occupation into what at first seems to be a brave new post-war world. However, the joy of the Liberation is soon darkened by the onset of the Cold War, the growing evidence of Stalin's atrocities in the USSR, and the intensifying realization that the Allied liberators are themselves oppressors in other parts of the world. Composition of the novel immediately followed that of *Le Deuxième Sexe*, and the novel intertwines themes of gender, heterosexual relations, and personal ethics with those of political commitment and the role of the intellectual. The frank treatment of sexual love, from both a female and a male perspective, confirmed Beauvoir's reputation as a morally dangerous writer. The novel was placed on the Catholic Church's index of forbidden books in 1956, and in the same year the translation into English omitted or toned down the erotic scenes to avoid shocking American readers (Klaw 1995: 197). In Henri-Georges Clouzot's 1960 film *La Vérité*, the prosecution lawyer at the heroine's trial for murder demonstrates the

---

[9] 'revelation of self by the gift of self and enrichment of the world' (ibid.: 677).

[10] There is no logical reason why Beauvoir's model of authentic love should be restricted to heterosexual relations, but her argument here relates specifically to love between women and men.

fundamental immorality of the accused by revealing that she was once caught in possession of *Les Mandarins*.[11]

Set in the highly educated, cosmopolitan milieu of the Paris intelligentsia, the novel depicts a world where women frequently work (the characters include a female psychiatrist and journalist, as well as clothes designers, singers, and actresses), enjoy a considerable degree of social and sexual freedom, and have some involvement in politics. Nonetheless, the genders are strongly differentiated, to reflect not Beauvoir's ideal but what she perceived as the reality: 'j'ai décrit les femmes telles que, en général, je les voyais, telles que je les vois encore...Aucune, d'un point de vue féministe, ne peut être considérée comme une "héroïne positive"' (Beauvoir 1963: 286).[12] The political side of the plot—the difficult choices between writing and political activism as the proper function of a left-wing intellectual, and between loyalty to or denunciation of the USSR at a time of Cold War—are the domain of the male characters, the middle-aged Robert and the younger Henri. Love relationships have only a relative importance for these two. Robert leads a self-contained life, enriched by the presence of his wife Anne, and by the occasional passing sexual encounter, but essentially independent of these. Henri's story is more concerned with the pleasures and responsibilities of relationships, but he leaves women when their needs or demands encroach on his freedom as a writer and political journalist, ending the novel in a marriage to Robert's daughter that is protective, comradely, and compatible with his political activities, rather than passionate. The women's stories, on the other hand, are essentially concerned with love: Paule's drama is that of the 'woman-in-love' who exists entirely through her lover, Henri, and falls apart when he leaves her; Anne's secure, warm, but no longer sexual relationship with Robert is threatened by her passionate affair with an American writer, and she must choose between her well-established life in Paris, and romance at the cost of exile in the USA.

As Elizabeth Fallaize's study of the novel shows, if men are identified here with a reasoned, self-preserving, relative view of love, and women with a more passionate, risky, absolutist emotional stance, the narrative logic of the book favours the former (Fallaize 1988: 105–15). Passionate romantic love fails, in each case, to produce lasting happiness or a livable relationship, whereas the couples based on rational compatibility and the

---

[11] The sequence is partly comic, since the heroine—played by the by now iconic Brigitte Bardot—replies that it was a disappointingly dry read, but Clouzot could clearly depend on the public's familiarity with Beauvoir's reputation.

[12] 'I described women just as, in general, I saw them, and as I still see them ... None of them could be considered from a feminist point of view as a "positive heroine".'

self-sufficiency of the male partner (Robert, Henri) end the novel with the promise of a durable, enabling companionship that can also support each partner's engagement in the social world beyond the home. Nonetheless, the novel does not present the desire for romantic love as merely a form of feminine false consciousness: its dangers are effectively dramatized, but the masculine model of love based on reasoned preference does not, in the end, emerge as adequate.

It is in the character of Paule, Beauvoir's 'amoureuse' in fictional form, that the risks of heterosexual love for a woman are most vividly dramatized. As Henri's mistress for the past ten years, she has invested everything in her relationship, giving up her career as a singer, and finding her own sense of self-worth in being the lover of a man who embodies her culture's ideal of masculinity. In post-Liberation France, Henri represents the quintessence of appealing virility: he is an ex-Resistance leader, a successful novelist, a handsome, charismatic political journalist. His initial passion for Paule gave her a confident sense of 'le miracle d'être elle-même' ('the miracle of being herself', Beauvoir 1954: 80), but as the signs of Henri's increasing detachment multiply, Paule tries with growing desperation to assert her indispensability and the absolute, irreducible nature of their love: 'Il y a un seul Henri, et moi je serai toujours moi, le temps n'y peut rien, . . . fondamentalement, nous sommes un seul être' (177–8).[13] Deliberately deluding herself rather than face the void of life without Henri, Paule alienates him all the more, and spirals towards insanity.

The scenes of Paule's humiliation are painful to read. What to her is the abandoned sexual behaviour of a woman in love, when focalized by a detached, dispassionate Henri becomes a repugnant display of self-abjection:

La tête renversée, les yeux clos, les dents nues, elle était si totalement donnée, si affreusement perdue qu'il eut envie de la gifler pour la ramener sur terre, de lui dire: C'est toi, c'est moi et nous faisons l'amour, c'est tout.[14] (26)

The novel alternates between an external narrative voice, focalized by Henri, and Anne as first-person, intradiegetic narrator. Since most of Paule's behaviour in the relationship is therefore given from Henri's

---

[13] 'There's only one Henri, and I shall always be I. Time is powerless to change it . . . fundamentally, we are one single being' (Beauvoir 1979: 239–40).

[14] 'With her head thrown back, her eyes closed, her mouth open and exposed, she was so abandoned to him, so terribly lost in the moment that he wanted to slap her to bring her back to earth, to tell her 'Look this is just you and me making love, that's all' (my translation—passage omitted from published translation).

perspective, the reader can hardly fail to share his irritation as she insists on continuing to centre her life on Henri's presence and his career, appointing herself the eternal guardian of what in reality is a love subject to time and change: 'je ne te laisserai pas trahir notre amour' ('I'm not going to let you betray our love', 82). And though Anne's perspective on Paule is that of a sympathetic friend, her embarrassed recoil from Paule's progressive loss of dignity and honesty further emphasizes the novel's condemnation of total self-investment in love as a path to female fulfilment. It is through Anne's compassionate but horrified eyes that we witness Paule's breakdown and hospitalization, and meet the embittered, posturing, woman with 'bovine eyes' (496) that the therapeutic 'cure' produces. Paule is only saved from complete narrative antipathy by Anne's recognition of the common and collective nature of her plight: without her belief in love, Anne reflects, Paule risks becoming, and indeed does become, 'comme moi, comme des millions d'autres: une femme qui attend de mourir sans plus savoir pourquoi elle vit' (420).[15]

Anne's partial identification with Paule is significant, but she is a much more positive and complex character. It is through Anne that the novel most radically addresses the ethics of self/other relations, and explores the possibility of a passionate love that respects both one's own and the other's freedom. Anne combines the traditional feminine roles of wife and mother with a successful career as a psychoanalyst and an informed, serious interest in politics. More than the other characters, she has found her faith in humanity shaken by the experience of the war and the Occupation: whereas Robert and Henri pragmatically accept the need to move on and build on the final victory over Nazism, Anne's sense of absolute grief and solitude ('je n'ai plus confiance, en rien'—'I no longer have faith, in anything', 44) affirms the ethical impossibility of reducing the suffering and death of others to the foundation for a better future. On a cycling holiday in the Vercors, the site of recent Resistance struggles, Anne, Robert, and Henri find themselves at a fête held in honour of the region's dead, which mingles celebration of freedom restored with matter-of-fact evocation of atrocities. It is Anne who responds by vomiting up the wine and food they have been invited to share. 'S'évanouir, pleurer, vomir, les femmes ont cette ressource: mais ça ne sert à rien non plus' (229):[16] her reaction is typically 'feminine', and of less practical value than the men's pragmatism, but it also affirms

---

[15] 'She'd be like myself, like millions of others: a woman waiting to die, no longer knowing why she's living' (Beauvoir 1979: 556).

[16] 'Fainting, weeping, vomiting—women have these expedients. But they, too, are useless' (ibid.: 307).

the irreducible horror of deliberately inflicted suffering and death, and dramatizes through the body the novel's consistent critique of human relations that instrumentalize the other.

Here vomiting expresses a moral repulsion for which Anne cannot find words. Her post-war sense of alienation takes the form, in part, of a loss of the vital connection between mind and body, most apparent in her lack of all sexual feeling. Robert's love for her has ceased to be sexual, and she inhabits a culture that excludes her almost middle-aged body (she is 40) from the category of the desirable. When she attempts to regain a sense of her own sexuality by agreeing to sleep with Scriassine, she experiences her body as an alien, separate entity: 'ce qui se passait là-bas me concernait si peu que si j'avais regardé, je me serais fait l'effet d'un voyeur' (74).[17] This sensation is reinforced by Scriassine's insistence on exacting from her a submissive, appreciative response to his sexual performance: any possibility of rediscovering a unified sense of self through sex is blocked by his observance of a gendered code of erotic behaviour based on male control and the objectification of the female body: '"As-tu du plaisir? Je veux que tu aies du plaisir." Sa voix s'irritait, elle exigeait des comptes' (74).[18] The Scriassine episode shows how in sex between a man and a woman, the man is socially empowered to allocate himself the position of subject of desire, whilst women are '(socially) pressure(d) to experience themselves erotically as non-subjects' (Fishwick 2002: 190). Anne's awkward, pleasureless intimacy with Scriassine dramatizes her general sense of disconnection from her world, but also shows how gendered power relations shape even the most private experience.

The depiction of both love and sex in the first third of the novel is decidedly negative, but in chapter 6 (of twelve) Beauvoir takes Anne to the USA and—drawing on her own passionate affair with the novelist Nelson Algren—has her rediscover sexual passion with the American writer Lewis Brogan. The Anne–Lewis story is strongly romantic, in the sense that it makes reciprocal love and desire the most extreme form of human fulfilment, and deploys with persuasive conviction many of the commonplaces of romance: Lewis immediately feels 'familiar' to Anne (306), as if their coming together was somehow predestined; the world feels well lost for love, 'Pour lui, pour moi, pour nous, rien n'existait que nous' ('For him, for me, for us, nothing existed but ourselves',

---

[17] 'what was happening down there had so little to do with me that if I had looked, I would have felt like a voyeur' (my translation—passage omitted from published translation).

[18] ' "Does that give you pleasure? I want you to feel pleasure". His voice was growing irritated; he was calling me to account' (my translation—as above).

427); they feel part of each other, 'Ce qu'il y a c'est que vous êtes un petit morceau de moi' ('The thing is, you've become a little piece of me', 433). The semantic and syntactical simplicity of such passages evokes those popular love songs that are the most common currency of twentieth-century romance. Some feminist critics have been taken aback by this indulgence in what they see as a dangerously mystifying myth of idealized love—Mary Evans, for example, finds the Anne–Lewis relationship 'astonishingly romantic' and 'conventional' (Evans 1985: 83)—but the romance plot of Les Mandarins is in fact entirely consonant with Beauvoir's definition in Le Deuxième Sexe of a hard-to-achieve but theoretically possible authentic form of heterosexual love, and rather than constituting an escapist interlude, in what is a serious political novel, I would argue that it contributes to the text's broader ethical project.

In the 'woman-in-love' chapter of Le Deuxième Sexe, Beauvoir argues that heterosexual love can only be lived as a positive, life-enhancing experience for a woman if she is firmly established as existing 'pour-soi', *for* herself, as a subject, 'ce qui impliquerait qu'elle possédât une indépendance économique, qu'elle se projetât vers des buts propres et se dépassât sans intermédiaires vers la collectivité' (Beauvoir 1976: ii. 506).[19] In Paris, Anne's brief liaison with Scriassine arose from his knowing her as Robert's wife, and took place at a time when she had lost all confidence in the value of her own work. She meets Lewis from a position of strength, as an independent, professionally and socially engaged subject: invited to the USA as a respected French psychoanalyst, she goes reluctantly, but soon finds herself revitalized by the excitement of a new country and by the sense that her work and ideas are taken seriously. Travelling independently, she takes control of her life again, and rediscovers the pleasure of desiring and being desired with one of her young hosts, Philipp (*sic*). It is Anne who actively instigates the meeting with Lewis, ringing him on the recommendation of a mutual friend, more or less inviting herself to Chicago, picking him up from his apartment despite his stated intention to collect her from her hotel. She also chooses to return for a second visit, admitting to herself with a touch of humorous self-derision that she might try out on him her newly restored capacity for desire: 'entre deux autres sourires, je me suis considérée avec scandale: je n'ai pas eu Philipp, alors je vais me jeter dans les bras de Brogan! Qu'est-ce que ces mœurs de femelle en chaleur?'

---

[19] 'this would imply that she had economic independence, that she moved towards ends of her own and transcended herself, without using man as an agent, towards the social whole' (Beauvoir 1972: 678).

(310).[20] It is Lewis who first falls in love, Lewis who seeks a permanent, committed, monogamous relationship, Lewis who is identified with the domestic spaces of apartments and cottages where they live together, whereas Anne is the more mobile and unsettled of the two. Gender roles are blurred by the particular situation of their encounter.

And under these conditions, Anne's sense of herself as whole, as at once desiring subject and desired body, returns. Rather than feel objectified by Lewis's desire, she feels it confer upon her body both definition and a beneficial power that is specifically feminine: 'Son désir me transfigurait. Moi qui depuis si longtemps n'avait plus de goût, plus de forme, je possédais de nouveau des seins, un ventre, un sexe, une chair; j'étais nourrissante comme le pain, odorante comme la terre' (319).[21] The self's alterity is here experienced positively. During the period of their happiness, each feels affirmed by the other, and their reciprocal passion also lights up the world beyond the couple, so that exploring Lewis's home town of Chicago, or travelling together to Mexico, are adventures enhanced by sharing the other's different perspective. It is that 'révélation de soi-même par le don de soi et enrichissement de l'univers'[22] (Beauvoir 1976: 505) described in *Le Deuxième Sexe*. Through Anne's narration, Beauvoir emphasizes the spontaneity and gratuitousness of their relations; Anne's status as foreigner and the provisional nature of her presence in the USA frees them from any framework of social expectation, family, or routine, and at first she experiences Lewis's words and gestures as pure, spontaneous gift, unconstrained by conventions or social norms. 'Il s'arrachait ses phrases avec hésitation et puis il me les jetait avec tant d'élan que j'avais chaque fois l'impression de recevoir un cadeau' (304).[23] At its best, their relationship transcends the gendered inequalities that made sex with Scriassine so unrewarding, and love in Paule's case so intensely damaging. It is a mutually enriching encounter in which each experiences both self and other as at once subject and object, and in which the other's desire and regard make each feel whole, and better able to enjoy and engage with the world beyond the couple. The happy phase of the Anne–Lewis relationship represents

---

[20] 'Between two other smiles, I looked inside myself and felt ashamed: I couldn't have Phillip, so I was going to throw myself into Brogan's arms. What about those morals of a bitch in heat?' (Beauvoir 1979: 412).

[21] 'His desire transformed me. I who for so long a time had been without taste, without form, again possessed breasts, a belly, [a sex—omitted], flesh; I was as nourishing as bread, as fragrant as earth' (Beauvoir 1979: 423).

[22] 'revelation of self by the gift of self and enrichment of the world' (ibid.: 677).

[23] 'He formed his sentences hesitantly and then threw them at me with such force that I felt as if I were receiving a present each time' (ibid.: 405).

the novel's implied ethic of self/other relations at the most intimate level.

However, neither the novel's feminist logic nor its political values can envisage a happy ending to a heterosexual, Franco-American romance set in the post-war years. Anne and Lewis meet from positions of relative equality, but Anne is soon aware of the impossibility of combining a future with Lewis with the retention of the identity and values that give her life meaning. Lewis does not envisage following her back to Paris, nor is he able to settle for the solution Anne proposes, that they spend a part of each year together and also maintain their separate lives. Thus to opt for love would mean leaving behind her family, profession, and place within the community of the French intellectual Left. Like Paule, she would depend entirely for her sense of self on her lover's support and desire. Moreover, although as the site of adventure and romance the USA here retains some of the glamour it held for post-war Europe, it also represents the selfishly materialist, aggressively imperialist model of society that Anne's circle devote their lives to combating. The American Left figures in the novel as weak, passive, and all too ready to compromise (534), so that a move from Paris to the USA would mean relinquishing any part in effective political opposition. 'L'amour', Anne recognizes, 'n'est pas tout' ('love is not everything', 435), and she continues to divide her time between France and the USA, life with Robert and life with Lewis, until Lewis withdraws his love rather than suffer any longer the pain of her absence and refusal of total commitment. Like Colette's 'vagabond' Renée Néré,[24] Anne chooses a bleak but self-determined life over the temptation of being sensually, comfortingly possessed by a beloved other.

The ending of La Vagabonde is shadowed by regret, but its dominant tone is nonetheless one of elation. The closing pages of Les Mandarins are decidedly more desolate. Whilst the validity of Anne's decision is made clear, through the cautionary tale of Paule's self-destruction, and through the novel's consistent ethical rejection of personal solutions that ignore the social and the collective, her final settling for the responsible, sober life she has made for herself seems—as Beauvoir acknowledged in La Force des choses—more like a defeat than a triumph.[25] Back in Paris after the final break with Lewis, Anne falls into a depression that erases all sense of meaning or purpose, and contemplates suicide. She recovers sufficiently to recognize that even in death, she has a responsibility to those closest to her: 'Je mourrai seule, pourtant ma mort ce sont les autres

---

[24] See above, Chapter 2.

[25] 'ressemble plutôt à une défaite qu'à un triomphe'. Also quoted in Fallaize 1988: 290.

qui la vivront' (578),[26] and decides to live for the sake of others, and in the hope of some future return of happiness. The novel nonetheless closes on a note of intensely painful loss.

Les Mandarins is clearly not simply a romance novel, but a novel of ideas and a vivid, detailed portrait of the intellectual and political life of an era. Beauvoir's achievement is to merge this 'masculine' genre with the 'feminine' genre of the love story, to the enrichment of both. The novel's commitment to a belief in personal freedom and responsibility underpins the depiction of love as a threat to the individual's self-determination, particularly in the case of women for whom dependence is socially encouraged. But, as in the romance, the experience of reciprocal, passionate love also represents a transcendent value, 'the most sublime of all human conditions' (Bauman 2003: 7), 'the palliative answer(s) to the blessing/curse of human individuality' (ibid.: 17). Hard to sustain as it is, the Anne–Lewis relationship in its warmth, its spontaneous recognition and acceptance of the other, and its suspension of each partner's solitude, adds colour and substance to the ideal of human relations that implicitly underlies the novel's political themes. Anne's final refusal to sacrifice all for love, hence her return to a life that is ethically unexceptionable but sensually and emotionally impoverished, confirms the novel's ethic of freedom and social responsibility—but it also leads to a longing for oblivion, and lacks any of that compensatory sense of new adventure that makes *La Vagabonde*, finally, an optimistic version of the feminist romance. Over all, *Les Mandarins* accepts the view which it identifies mainly with its male characters, that passion is an impossible basis for a purposeful, ethical existence; but what Fallaize terms the 'female aspiration to absolutes' (Fallaize 1988: 107) is too compelling a narrative thread to be neatly woven into a soberly pragmatic dénouement.

Françoise Sagan and the anti-romance

It was not Beauvoir's intention to situate herself within a tradition of women's writing; rather, in order to be taken seriously as a writer, she was at pains to 'plac(e) her work in an authorised, male tradition' (Fallaize 1988: 180), and to distance herself from what she identified as the 'housewife' literature associated with women.[27] Nonetheless, both her theoretical exploration of heterosexual love in *Le Deuxième Sexe*,

---

[26] 'I would die alone; yet it's the others who would live my death' (Beauvoir 1979: 761).

[27] In *Le Deuxième Sexe*, however, Beauvoir quotes many women writers including, extensively, Colette (the index of the English translation gives thirty-three references to Colette of which five are to *La Vagabonde*). Beauvoir's discourse represents the organizing, analytical voice while the women

and her critical yet sympathetic deployment of the romance plot in *Les Mandarins*, were important interventions in the predominantly female genre of romance, particularly at a period when women were at once more emancipated, and subject to a renewed social imperative towards marriage and motherhood, the latter reflected in the ubiquity of the love story in writing by and for women. From *Elle*, addressing a mainly middle-class, educated readership, to the easy-to-read photo-romances of *Nous deux*, from Beauvoir to Delly, much of women's writing and reading in 1950s France reflects on the possibility of reconciling desire with social responsibility, or imagines the utopian convergence of self-fulfilment with social acceptance through happy marriage.

In the same year that *Les Mandarins* won the Prix Goncourt (1954), a first novel by a 17-year-old, cleverly marketed by its publisher, caught the attention of both public and critics, and in May won the prestigious Prix des Critiques. Françoise Sagan's *Bonjour tristesse* rapidly became a bestseller in France and, after its translation in 1955, in the USA. The novel was more a family romance than a romance proper. Its 17-year-old heroine forms a happy couple with her widowed, playboy father Raymond, who shares with her his affluent, carefree, and pleasure-loving lifestyle. The third element in the triangle is Anne, a mature, intelligent woman whose proposed marriage to Raymond threatens the father–daughter bond. Despite a reluctant appreciation of the order and emotional depth that Anne represents, Cécile sets out to get rid of her, and succeeds more literally than she had consciously intended. The novel at once shocked and delighted readers with its representation of teenage girlhood as sexual, amoral, bent on pleasure and selfish comfort rather than on the search for True Love. *Bonjour tristesse* could be seen as in tune with the developing consumerism of the post-war period, as well as prescient of the relaxation of sexual mores that would be a phenomenon of the later 1960s. Slim, elegant, fond of fast cars and alcohol, Sagan's own persona soon merged with her fictional world in the public imagination, and she remained an iconic figure throughout the 1950s and 1960s and, to a lesser extent, up to her death in 2004. The succession of Sagan novels that followed the success of *Bonjour tristesse* belong more clearly to the genre of romance: slim, slight narratives of love and loss mainly set in the stylish milieu of the Parisian arts and media.[28]

quoted are used as evidence to support her argument, which creates a safe distance between the author herself and 'women writers'. Nonetheless, the book demonstrates the extent to which Beauvoir had read other female authors—and particularly Colette.

[28] 'Françoise Sagan writes romances, that is, novels whose narratives concern themselves with the coming together and/or breaking apart of that compelling entity "a man and a woman"' (Miller 1988: 16).

Sagan's universe is one of chic world-weariness, of cafés and soirées where journalists, theatre directors, models, and actresses congregate to flirt, talk, drink, and fall—in a desultory fashion—in love. Its appeal in the mid–1950s to 1960s surely lay in its capturing of an ambivalent mood of attraction and repulsion in the face of the affluent, fast-moving superficiality of the new consumerized France. Sagan's characters take for granted the material pleasures of speedy travel, holidays on the Côte d'Azur, leisure, and good food and drink, but they are also disoriented, aware—sometimes complacently, but sometimes painfully—that they live in a moral vacuum. The heroines of Sagan's second and third novels—*Un certain sourire* (A Certain Smile, 1956) and *Dans un mois, dans un an* (In a Month, in a Year, 1957)—share the social and sexual freedom of Cécile in *Bonjour tristesse*, but also her resigned, bittersweet sense that there is nothing meaningful to be done with this freedom. Each of them also falls in love, and struggles with the conflict between love and personal autonomy.

Sagan's world refuses transcendent values—it is a world without God, or absolute moral truths, or ultimate meaning—and freedom is the uncomfortable condition of her protagonists' existence rather than their goal. The influence of existentialism was soon noticed by critics, and fully acknowledged by Sagan herself both in interviews and within the novels themselves by, for example, having her heroine read Sartre's *L'Âge de raison* (Sagan 1956: 34),[29] though Sagan certainly does not share Sartre's sense of personal and political responsibility, nor his ethic of commitment. The impact of Beauvoir, whose much-discussed work Sagan must certainly have known, may be traced in the latter's rejection of normative models of female fulfilment: marriage and motherhood, the destiny of what one heroine dismissively calls 'la femme biblique et normale' (Sagan 1957: 95),[30] are simply not options that her characters consider. On the other hand, Beauvoir's preferred alternative of financial independence and socio-political *engagement* are quite alien to Sagan's early heroines, whose arena for thought and action extends no further than personal relationships and the leisure pursuits available to the affluent in a newly modernizing France.

In this world without illusions or absolutes, agreeable sexual encounters of a provisional kind ought logically to suffice, and to an extent they do. If Sagan's heroines, as some critics have claimed,[31] are implicitly on

---

[29] See Morello 1998: 75–85, for discussion of the influence of Sartre and Beauvoir on Sagan's work. *L'Âge de raison* subsequently influenced Sagan's narrative technique in *Dans un mois, dans un an*.

[30] 'The biblical, normal woman'.

[31] See Miller 1991: 392; Morello 1998: 85–9.

the side of feminism and help to lay the foundations for the post-1968 women's movement, it is mainly because of their casual assumption of their own sexual freedom, and the value they attach to solitude and self-determination. In a sense the ideal relationship is that proposed to Dominique, the student heroine of *Un certain sourire*, by Luc, a seductive, married, older man who honestly, and without any pretence of romance, offers 'une aventure sans lendemain et sans sentimentalité' (Sagan 1956: 79),[32] in which mutual desire and interest will allow each to suspend briefly the *ennui* that is their habitual state, without any implications for the rest of their lives. Dominique accepts. In *Dans un mois, dans un an*, Josée first takes Jacques home with her simply to indulge a casual attraction: 'Il était assez beau mais vulgaire et sans intérêt' (Sagan 1957: 16),[33] and later spends three days in a hotel with her ex-lover Bernard more out of a disinclination to disappoint him—for he still loves her—than out of love or passion: 'Un vrai bonheur, une fausse histoire d'amour' ('A real happiness, a false love story', Sagan 1957: 105). These anti-sentimental heroines[34] treat sex and love in much the same way as do Sagan's male characters: the connection between the two is far from essential, and love is acknowledged to be random, transitory, and a threat to that purposeless yet precious state of solitary independence to which her heroines always return. Though Dominique, despite her best efforts, falls in love with Luc, the 'certain smile' with which she ends her story marks the end of that love and her pleasure—albeit a pleasure tinged with resignation—in solitude regained, emotional detachment recovered.

> **Je ne m'empêchai pas de sourire, je ne pouvais pas. A nouveau, je le savais, j'étais seule . . . Seule. Seule. Mais enfin, quoi? J'étais une femme qui avait aimé un homme. C'était une histoire simple; il n'y avait pas de quoi faire des grimaces.[35] (125)**

Josée ends her story in love with Jacques, but lucidly acknowledging the truth of Bernard's prophecy: 'Un jour vous ne l'aimerez plus . . . et un jour je ne vous aimerai sans doute plus non plus. Et nous serons à nouveau seuls et ce sera pareil' (188).[36] Sagan's love stories are the antithesis of

---

[32] 'an adventure without any tomorrow and without sentimentality'.

[33] 'He was quite handsome, but slightly coarse and not very interesting.'

[34] Susan Weiner links Sagan to other women writers of the same generation (Françoise Mallet-Joris, Michèle Perrein) under the category 'novels of anti-sentiment' (Weiner 1993: 95); Nathalie Morello also refers to Sagan's novels of the 1950s as 'anti-sentimental novels' (Morello 1998: 81).

[35] 'I didn't stop myself from smiling—I couldn't. Once again, I knew, I was alone . . . Alone. Alone. And so what? So I was a woman who had loved a man. It was a simple story; nothing to get upset about.'

[36] 'One day you won't be in love with him any more . . . and one day no doubt I won't love you any more either. And we'll be alone again and it will be exactly the same.'

the classical romance script, in which solitude is finally exchanged for happiness in the arms of the one true lover.

Yet Sagan's narratives depend for their momentum on the intrusion into this dispassionate world of an awkward intensity of emotion, of sentiments that disturb the 'civilized, adult, reasonable' (Sagan 1956: 87) tenor of its relationships. It is Dominique's falling in love with Luc that provides the novel's tension and shape, though faced with his resolute return to his wife she soon regains her equilibrium. *Dans un mois, dans un an* weaves together the stories of eight characters linked by criss-crossing lines of desire, but the narrative is propelled by their several experiences of involuntary, intense, and often unreciprocated love. Josée finds herself searching the Latin Quarter for Jacques in a desperate need to have him with her 'Même pour être battue ou repoussée' ('Even if it was to be beaten or rejected', Sagan 1957: 129). Bernard's compelling desire for Josée briefly reorients his life, and both the young Édouard and the ageing Alain Maligrasse fall obsessively, hopelessly in love with Béatrice. Love, in Sagan, as opposed to simple desire, means wanting to be with the other person even if this brings no gratification, experiencing a need for their presence, and longing for the breaking down of those boundaries of the self which, in their normal, out-of-love state, her characters value so highly. Dominique reassures herself that 'Nous nous plaisions, tout allait bien' ('We liked each other, it was all going well', Sagan 1956: 73), and struggles against the wish for Luc to make 'ce bouleversant effort qu'il faut accomplir pour aimer quelqu'un, le connaître, briser sa solitude' (73).[37] If the novels are, finally, anti-sentimental and anti-romance, their plots also depend on the recognition that desire cannot always be kept safely within the boundaries of self-interest, or lived with the elegant nonchalance that is the hallmark, and the charm, of Sagan's fictions.

When her main protagonists fall—temporarily—in love, they glimpse a mode of relationship that is less self-interested, more empathetic and attentive to the other, than the pleasant but provisional encounters that are the norm in their milieu. Sagan also sketches in a more generous, adult form of love in the characters of good older women, who, without falling into the despised category of the 'femme biblique et normale', represent some of the more traditional feminine virtues. Françoise, Luc's wife in *Un certain sourire*, Anne in *Bonjour tristesse*, and to some extent Fanny in *Dans un mois...*, are in some ways positive models of adult femininity: each combines a lucid but loyal, committed, and strongly

---

[37] 'that huge effort that it takes to love someone, to know them, and break through their solitude'.

sexual relationship with a man with interests and friendships of their own, and a generous, nurturing attitude to younger women, even when these are their rivals in love. But for each of these women, the attempt to live out a durable romance results in suffering and even, in Anne's case, death.[38] It is as if the ideal of fidelity and unselfishness that they represent has no place in a world of resigned meaninglessness and transient pleasures, and although they introduce into the novels a warmth and dignity lacking in most of the characters, they confirm rather than challenge the younger heroines' rejection of love as a possible road to self-fulfilment.

Sagan's portrayal of post-war society underlines its sense of pleasurable modernity, freedom from old moralities, but also its quietly desolate sense of an ethical void. Her young heroines assume a degree of social and sexual liberty that is new in women's writing, but their sphere of action remains the traditionally feminine domain of relationships and emotions. Male characters, similarly disaffected and similarly preoccupied by affairs of the heart, also have professions: they are businessmen, journalists, theatre directors, publishers, writers; the women, on the whole, are lovers or wives. We can see in this a reflection of 1950s France in which cultural mores, shaped in part by economic trends, did indeed emancipate women in significant ways, but did little—as yet—to shift male domination of the public world. Sagan's heroines demonstrate their capacity to adopt masculine models of detachment and independent living, but still find themselves largely confined to the private sphere. However, whilst the novels observe this gendered social division, they offer no explicit critique of it. Rather, Sagan is concerned with the emotional rewards and costs of new forms of female selfhood. If her love stories are read as Oedipal dramas or 'family romances',[39] what we find are heroines who successfully reject maternal models to identify strongly with father figures who represent excitement, engagement in the public world, a glamorous freedom and detachment. Rather than move on from the 'phallic' stage by sublimating 'masculine' desires in 'feminine' love and motherhood, as Freud would have it, Sagan's early heroines adopt self-sufficiency and acceptance of the provisional, finally uncommitted nature of relationship as the long-term basis for their lives. The reward is that 'certaine forme de liberté' ('certain form of freedom', Sagan 1956: 54), that avoidance of deadening routine and a traditional female destiny, that Luc promises Dominique. The cost is that 'tristesse' that closes and

---

[38] In the 1969 novel *Un peu de soleil dans l'eau froide* Nathalie is another example of the mature, strong, loving woman destroyed by a cynically frivolous culture that has no place for her.

[39] Judith Miller (1988) defines Sagan's early novels as 'perversions of the family romance' (16).

defines the story of Sagan's first heroine, and characterizes the emotional tenor of her successors.

Feminist critics have suggested, interestingly, that Sagan's fiction stages the struggle between the existentialist ideal of the autonomous self, and a distinctively feminine 'intuitive sense that autonomy is not the desired state' (St-Onge 1984: 10).[40] Her heroines aspire to the self-determination and self-sufficiency that for Sartre and Beauvoir means a proper acceptance of one's own inalienable freedom, but—as with Beauvoir's fictional heroines—the recurring inclination to love and be loved betrays the inadequacy of independence without emotional bonds. Yet the only available models of the life lived through love are negative ones, for Sagan's 'good women', whilst morally admirable, are always rejected or destroyed. Neither the autonomous self nor the self-in-relation seems to be the solution, and Marian St-Onge is right to see in Sagan's novels 'a desire (largely unconscious, yet clearly expressed) for a different femininity, one which would comprehend identity in terms of both independence and relationship' (St-Onge 1984: 10). In this quest, the anti-romantic novelist is clearly working within the territory of romance.

Conclusion

From the point of view of French women, the 1950s were characterized by the tension between new political and cultural forms of emancipation, and a powerful social imperative towards domesticity and maternity. The dominant narrative of women's lives and fictions remained the heterosexual romance, fantasized pleasurably as reconciling female desire with social demands both in mass-market *romans d'amour* and in the spectrum of women's magazines that addressed readerships across the range of class and generation, and subjected to question and critique, but deployed nonetheless, in the best-selling work of women writers such as Beauvoir and Sagan. Romance functioned as a means of encouraging conformity, by imagining its possible pleasures, in an age of compulsory heterosexuality and maternity, but it also provided a way of exploring and affirming women's aspiration to self-fulfilment beyond permitted social roles. Most interestingly, perhaps, the continuing emphasis in women's writing on the significance of love relationships questions the desirability of simply emulating the era's dominant masculine ideal of selfhood.

---

[40] Apart from Marian St-Onge, Judith Miller (1988) and Nathalie Morello (1998) have discussed Sagan's work in terms of a gendered critique of the ideal of the autonomous self.

5 Romance after Feminism

Plus jamais ne nous marions
Non, non, non, non . . .
Leur amour c'est une prison (Song of the MLF)

(Let's not marry any more
No, no, no, no . . .
Their love is a prison)

The feminist movement that emerged from the upheavals of May 1968 utterly rejected heterosexual romance as women's natural and desirable destiny. This wave of feminism insisted on the inseparability of the personal and the political: its goals were not just equal pay and equal rights, but a profound transformation of a culture that it soon defined as patriarchal and androcentric, from the level of political institutions to that of intimate experience. Marriage was seen as the playing out, at a private level, of collective power relations between the sexes. In Beauvoirian terms, the husband in a couple assumed the privileged position of subject, while to be a wife meant to become his socially and sexually subordinate 'other'. From a Marxist perspective—and the early MLF (Mouvement pour la Libération de la Femme) was largely propelled by women already active in leftist groups—the family's role in the reproduction of labour made women a social group defined by domestic exploitation. The new feminism saw marriage as an alienated state for a woman: sleeping with the enemy, she was isolated from the rest of her sex and encouraged to see her dissatisfactions as mere personal failures. The MLF demonstration of 20 November 1971 chanced upon a white wedding, with its symbolic performance of the virgin bride's transferral from the control of father to that of husband, and invaded the church with shouts of 'Libérez la mariée!' ('Free the bride!'). The goal was not simply to reform the marriage contract. In fact, marriage in France had been gradually shifting towards a union of legally equal partners, and in June 1970 parental authority over children finally ceased to be the father's prerogative. Marriage remained, nonetheless, the institution that entrapped women into the abandonment of their own goals and interests in favour of domestic labour, often unwanted pregnancies, and a culturally accepted subordination to male authority that also legitimized domestic violence. Marriage was, in the words of one slogan, a 'piège à cons', which in French has the double meaning of a 'trap for fools' and, since the original meaning of 'con' is 'cunt', a trap for female sexuality.

It was clearly not marriage alone that came under attack, for the post-1968 feminists soon realized that the pervasive, internalized nature of socially constructed gender difference meant that all relations with men were going to be problematic. Feminism aimed at the liberation of men as well as women ('La femme ne se libérera qu'en libérant l'humanité entière; elle libérera l'homme de la nécessité d'une telle femme' ran one particularly messianic slogan (Anon. 1971)),[1] but in the shorter term it was essential for women to explore their situation without the dominating presence of male comrades. Women-only meetings and 'consciousness-raising' groups uncovered the extent to which habitual, blatant sexism (itself a new and potent concept) was as common amongst men of the Left, committed to the liberation of exploited peoples everywhere, as it was amongst the avowedly hierarchical Right. Married or cohabiting feminists often found themselves under attack and embarrassed by their allegiance to one of the oppressors. As some lesbian feminists pointed out, the logical conclusion of commitment to the cause was to love other women, rather than men. When the question 'Les femmes peuvent-elles encore aimer les hommes?' ('Can women still love men?') was posed in a 1971 special issue of *Tout!* (a radical publication committed to sexual liberation), the response was far from affirmative. If a new kind of heterosexual love between equals could be imagined in the future, women would first have to find their own 'totalité d'être humain' ('wholeness as human beings', Picq 1993: 108–9). The romance to which feminist women could really subscribe was the thrill of a newly discovered passion for other women, not as rivals or occasional companions whose lives were really centred elsewhere, but as companions whose warmth, humour, anger, and energy could be shared and directed to a common cause.

Heterosexual love was above all a danger. It could lead to pregnancy, often unwanted: the campaign for free and legal access to contraception and abortion was one of the central themes of the movement. It could produce a dreamy false consciousness in a woman, persuading her, against her own best interests, that to be with the beloved man was more important than anything else, and trapping her into domesticity, maternity, and emotional subjection. In the collectively and anonymously authored *Livre de l'oppression des femmes* (The Book of Women's Oppression), a

---

[1] 'Woman will only liberate herself by liberating the whole of humanity; she will liberate man from the need for such a woman' (i.e., a traditionally dependent woman).

voice that is almost certainly Christiane Rochefort's[2] analyses the way that men's 'love' reduces women to material and psychological dependence: 'il n'existe pas d'amour à l'intérieur de conditions d'oppression' ('love can not exist within oppressive relations', Anon. 1972: 74), she concludes.

From a lesbian perspective, this meant simply that authentic love relations were impossible within heterosexuality. A wider, more inclusive definition of human sexuality, and a liberalization of sexual mores, were central to the unwritten manifesto of May 1968. Lesbian women were as involved in the setting up of the Front Homosexuel d'Action Révolutionnaire (FHAR; Homosexual Front for Revolutionary Action) as they were in the establishment of the MLF. Their critique represented the institution of heterosexuality as doubly oppressive: internally, because it legitimized and indeed idealized unequal relations between a woman and a man, and externally, in that the hegemony of the heterosexual model oppressed all those whose desires it excluded. Though lesbian groups remained central elements of the feminist movement, the radical lesbian line on heterosexuality led to some conflicts with straight feminists, as the latter struggled to reconcile sexual and emotional ties to individual men, with recognition of male privilege and power to oppress in a patriarchal culture. Tensions surfaced periodically throughout the 1970s, and received a very public airing in 1980–1, when the feminist journal *Questions féministes* foundered on the split between its lesbian and straight contributors. 'The lesbian choice', wrote the radical lesbian group, in an Open Letter to the MLF on International Women's Day 1981, 'is awareness that male violence against women is at work everywhere, especially in "private" life, with its traps of emotional attachment or heterosexual "desire"' (Duchen 1987: 89). Straight feminists could agree with the analysis, but nonetheless found themselves grappling with emotions and desires that could not simply be dismissed by the use of ironic quotation marks.

In literary terms, romance, not surprisingly, was low on the agenda of feminist women writers of the 1960s and 1970s. Christiane Rochefort's novels had foretold the post-1968 feminist deconstruction of romantic love—*Les Petits Enfants du siècle* (1961) and *Les Stances à Sophie* (1963),

---

[2] The text in question, 'Logique masculine' (pp. 72–7), tells the story of how the author's husband or lover dismisses her first novel with the words 'Ma pauvre fille, tu ferais mieux de raccommoder des chaussettes' ('My poor girl, you'd do better to get on with darning socks'), and thereby saps her confidence to the extent that (for a time) she can no longer write. Rochefort recounts exactly the same story in her autobiographical *Ma vie revue et corrigée par l'auteur* (Rochefort 1978: 67). In a pre-1968 novel, *Les Stances à Sophie* (1963), Rochefort had subjected the whole romance script to a bitingly comic attack—see below.

in particular, caustically reveal the dangers of falling for the discourse of romance. Josyane, narrator-heroine of the first novel, condemns herself to the same joyless domestic drudgery as her mother by finally giving in to the powerful myth of True Love, while Céline (*Les Stances à Sophie*) takes the reader on a comic but instructive journey through her initial passion for the charming bully Philippe, her total loss of identity in marriage, and her triumphant self-liberation. Throughout Rochefort's work, where love is an authentic value it tends to be either homosexual (*Printemps au parking*, 1969), incestuous (*Archaos ou le jardin étincelant*, 1972), or—by mutual consent—transient, polygamous, and non-committed (*Les Stances à Sophie*, 1963). Although the 1970s saw an expansion in the publication of women's writing, with the development of new women's presses and publishers' lists (Fallaize 1993: 16), the heterosexual love story had little place either in the experimental *écriture féminine* that sought to forge a new, woman-centred form of language, or in the more realist, confessional strand evident (for example) in the early work of Annie Ernaux (*Les Armoires vides*, 1974; *Ce qu'ils disent ou rien*, 1977) or that of Marie Cardinal (*La Clé sur la porte*, 1972; *Les Mots pour le dire*, 1975).

Second-wave feminism, then, contested the hegemony of romance as the 'natural' form of women's lives or of their writing. Central as it was to the attack of the 'soixante-huitards' ('sixty-eighters') on the traditional family, feminism had a marked effect on social mores: in the years following the MLF's most active and visible phase, the marriage rate in France, after a long period of steady increase, went into steep decline: from 416,000 marriages in 1972, it dipped to 334,000 in 1980, 315,000 in 1981, and 265,000 by 1987 (Picq 1993: 80). In serious 'literary' writing by women, the love story was a rare genre in the 1970s. And yet two factors in particular suggested that romantic love would not disappear easily from female, or indeed feminist, culture. One was the evidence of the popular literary market, where the sales of Delly, Max du Veuzit, Magali, and their successors never faltered, even at the height of the feminist movement,[3] and the international romance industry swept into France with the immediate success of Harlequin-France in 1977.[4] The other was the fact that despite their insistence on the liberation of female sexuality from the straitjacket of a repressive, man-centred culture, feminists often found themselves opposed to their male comrades on the question of the

---

[3] The number of Delly titles (re)published each year is consistently high (between 5 and 48) from 1944 to 1984, but peaks in the 1970s with an average of 15.5 titles per year (Saint-Germain 1995: 198–200).

[4] The nature of the Harlequin romance, and its success on the French market from its arrival in 1977 to the present, is discussed below in Chapter 6.

relationship between sex and love. The difference between (broadly) male and female conceptions of sexual freedom surfaced in the magazine *Tout!*, nominally edited by Jean-Paul Sartre who lent his fame and stature to the publication's defence of total sexual liberation when it was prosecuted for offences against public morality in 1971. *Tout!* proclaimed 'le droit à l'homosexualité et à toutes les sexualités' ('the right to homosexuality and to all forms of sexuality'), and preached the liberation of desire from all moral strictures, but the MLF women who worked on it, both straight and gay, were soon expressing doubts about the ideal of a total separation between eroticism and emotion. Issue No. 16 (1972), largely written by women, was more concerned to try and imagine how love might take on new forms once released from the sexual inequality and heterosexist imperative that currently shaped it.

There were some attempts, in different forms of feminist publication, to theorize a relationship between love and liberation, perhaps the most notable being in Marie Cardinal and Annie Leclerc's collaborative *Autrement dit* (1977), which I discuss briefly below. As feminist ideas became more embedded in social and personal practice, and the heady days of forging and performing new concepts of the feminine muted into less visible practical and political struggles, a concern with how romantic and erotic love relations might be lived resurfaced at all levels of women's writing, from popular 'middlebrow' to highly 'literary'.[5] Marie Cardinal's 1979 *Une vie pour deux* is a formally complex love story that interrogates the possibilities of the heterosexual couple, and its relationship with love between women. In 1983, Régine Deforges's rollicking tale of romance and resistance under the Occupation, *La Bicyclette bleue*, became a massive bestseller in France, demonstrating both the durability and the flexibility of the romance form. And the 1980s also saw the development of what might be called the mainstream lesbian romance: novels of love between women that represent the gendered specificity of lesbian relationships, and the subversive perspective they provide on a heterosexist culture, but also work simply as compelling stories of love and desire. The third section of this discussion of romance in the 1980s will take as its central text Mireille Best's *Camille en octobre*.

---

[5] Duras's L'*Amant* (1984), '*the* text of the 1980s' (Davis and Fallaize 2000: 37) in the sense that it achieved a remarkable fusion of critical and popular success, also confirms the strong presence of romance in the decade's literature. L'*Amant* belongs to the genre in as far as central to its narrative is a passionate encounter between a man and a woman, the memory of which will transcend time and separation. It is also, however, just as much a novel about mother–daughter relations, colonialism, madness, and writing itself.

Marie Cardinal and *Une vie pour deux* (1979)

Marie Cardinal (1929–2001) achieved international fame with her sixth book, *Les Mots pour le dire* (1975), a fictionalized account of her own psychoanalysis. The story of a woman's self-liberation from psychosis through the appropriation of language, *Les Mots* foregrounds the mother–daughter relationship, and the profoundly repressive effect of a colonialist, bourgeois, Catholic female education. Love and the couple are a secondary theme, but the narrator's husband plays an important role by responding to her writing of her own story with a renewed assertion of his love and admiration, thus affirming her simultaneously as a woman and a writer. His supportive presence by her side, after a long period of living apart, is an important element in the story's happy ending. *Les Mots* concludes the narrator's personal story with a final, one-line chapter: 'Quelques jours plus tard c'était Mai 68' ('A few days later it was May 68', Cardinal 1975: 345), the spatial foregrounding of this epilogue emphasizing the collective significance of the individual female story. The very form of *Autrement dit*, co-written with Annie Leclerc and published in 1977, is indicative of the new feminism:[6] rather than the singular voice and the private, personal story, it is in a dialogue between women that the truth can be forged, and the loose, improvisational structure refuses to assume the authority of the traditional (normally male-authored) discursive essay. The book explores the everyday texture of women's lives, and the question of how to give this appropriate literary form, with Cardinal rejecting the 'hermetic' obscurity of experimental 'écriture féminine' in favour of a more transparent and referential style, 'celle de la masse, celle des gens' ('the kind of writing that most people understand', 62). Cardinal and Leclerc agree that 'the couple' in the traditional sense, as a domestic unit based on gender-differentiated roles, can only wither away as women refuse their prescribed identities (162), but they seek alternative models of how 'deux êtres libres peuvent former un couple … en dehors de la quotidienneté, en dehors des enfants, des tâches matérielles et de l'argent' (156).[7] The perspective here is clearly heterosexual: somehow, the desire and liking for men ('Je trouve

---

6 The collective female voice of militant texts like *Le Livre de l'oppression des femmes* (see above) found an echo in more 'literary' collaborations such as Marguerite Duras's *Les Parleuses* (*entretiens avec Xavière Gauthier*) (1974), and *Autrement dit*. Feminist sisters Flora and Benoîte Groult, ahead of their time, had already practised collaborative writing in, for example, *Journal à quatre mains* (1962), republished by Gallimard in 1974.

7 'two free beings can form a couple … without becoming immured in the everyday, children, material chores and money.'

leur tendresse aussi précieuse qu'un diamant. J'aime leur odeur, j'aime leurs grandes mains,'⁸ says Cardinal, 183) must be reconciled with the rebarbative qualities that are also part of the way that masculinity is currently constructed: 'Je n'aime pas leur prétention, leur aveuglement, leur méprise totale en ce qui concerne les femmes' (183–4).⁹

In *Une vie pour deux*, which she was writing as she worked with Leclerc on *Autrement dit*, Cardinal used fiction to address the question of the heterosexual couple, and the issue that underlies the genre of romance: how far can a woman reconcile an intense and lasting love for a man with self-fulfilment? Simone and Jean-François are a middle-aged couple with grown-up children, beginning a long holiday on the coast of Ireland. Through Simone's narration, the reader learns that their marriage has been long and troubled, with Jean-François living and working for many years in Canada, while Simone has brought up the children alone in France. Simone's dream is to use this holiday to set their relationship on a new footing, to have it finally take on that 'forme parfaite, belle, pleine, ronde, que nous cherchions depuis tant d'années' (14).¹⁰

Simone's ideal of the perfect couple has two sources. One is the powerful force of social expectation based on the institution of the family: by marrying, she takes her place in a trans-generational chain of women who ensure the reproduction and well-being of the clan. To form a unit that contributes to the time-defying solidity of the family is profoundly reassuring (the roots of the couple 'enfoncent solidement un homme et une femme—jusqu'a ce que mort s'ensuive—dans la terre de l'humanite' (14)),¹¹ even if it is also antithetical to any drive towards personal, extra-social fulfilment. Though the reality of life together has been disordered, conflictual, unstable, Simone longs to recapture some of the simplicity and ordered happiness that marriage promised. The other source of Simone's ideal is more personal and passionate. Simone recalls her first meetings with Jean-François, and the attraction of his otherness, figured in part through the contrast between her southern volatility and dark-skinned ease in the sun and the sea, and his more northern, muted, rational distance from the natural world. Through their long, if difficult, relationship, and particularly in lovemaking, she has known at once the delight of understanding 'le langage, l'esprit, l'ensemble des signes' ('the language, the mind, the whole set of signs') that make up another, uniquely different person, and that of the fleeting

---

⁸ 'To me their tenderness is as precious as a diamond. I love their smell, I love their big hands.'
⁹ 'I don't like their conceit, their blindness, their complete misunderstanding of women.'
¹⁰ 'perfect, lovely, fully rounded form that we had been trying to find for years'.
¹¹ 'plant a man and a woman firmly—until death—deep in the earth of humanity'.

'sensation de n'être qu'un' ('feeling of being one', 88). She both wants to fulfil the social ideal of the perfect marriage, and yearns for a bond that would at once maintain the magic of difference, and allow complete fusion with the other.

Distanced from their social environment by the holiday, in a setting whose subtle, temperate charm—'la pluie, la grisaille, le fermé, la flamme des dedans'[12] (12)—is, for Simone, at once alien and seductive, the narrative traces the couple's slow, fraught achievement of a relationship that the novel represents as viable and enriching for both, but that is significantly different from Simone's initial ideal. This process is given narrative shape and colour by Jean-François's discovery of the drowned corpse of a woman on the beach. Mary MacLaughlin, as the dead woman turns out to be called, becomes the focus of the couple's conflicts and the catalyst for the reinvention of their marriage. At first she is the object of Simone's jealousy, for Jean-François's fascination with her story echoes his numerous infidelities with women Simone has perceived as more desirable and interesting than herself. But as Simone herself engages with the mystery of Mary's death, and begins to write for her a story of rural childhood, desire and seduction, conflict between autonomy and motherhood, that mirrors and interprets her own life, so she abandons the role of jealous victim and instead struggles on even terms for possession of Mary's story. In writing the other woman's life, in a female voice that combines identification with the freedom of invention, Simone encounters parts of herself that she has suppressed as incompatible with the 'belle statue de la mère-épouse' ('imposing statue of the wife-and-mother', 92) she has allowed herself to become. The act of writing itself means emerging from the reproductive role she has accepted as her lot to 'appropriat(e) the power of the Logos, traditionally associated with the Father' (Cairns 1992: 176). To envisage Mary not as a rival, but as a seductively mysterious other both like and unlike herself, breaks the patriarchal pattern in which women compete to win male love. Bitter conflicts surface as Simone insists on the ruthless selfishness of the men in Mary's life. Choosing to make Mary a single mother allows her to write of the hard work, exhaustion, and loneliness of motherhood, and of all the sacrifices that have been her own lot. The storytelling reveals that beneath the veneer of the united 'couple', Simone and Jean-François have lived as two separate, opposed individuals. But the battle for narrative power, like the honest admission of anger, repositions them as equal subjects, and the elaboration of Mary MacLaughlin's story finally becomes a project

---

[12] 'the rain, the grey, enclosed, dullness, and the flame beneath'.

that can be shared. As in *Les Mots pour le dire*, a woman's assertion of her own voice through writing leads not to the loss of love, but to its renewal. Towards the novel's close, as Simone narrates their attendance at the inquest on the real Mary, the emphasis is on their mutual understanding and on her renewed desire for Jean-François:

> **Cette harmonie qui existe aujourd'hui entre nous, cette capacité de nous séduire mutuellement, cette impression que je suis lui et qu'il est moi, me semble être ce qu'il y a de plus important dans une vie d'humain, la première chose à protéger.[13] (322)**

In the narrative centrality and the high value it accords to love, *Une vie pour deux* belongs to the genre of romance. Moreover, it is that rare form of the genre, a heterosexual feminist romance that ends happily, with female self-discovery and self-assertion being rewarded by male love and desire. Like Colette's *L'Entrave*, the story ends with the couple on a beach, facing the immensity of the sea as they contemplate their future lives together—but here there is no allocation of the roles of vagabond and captive, for each will maintain both positions: 'Décidés à ce que jamais l'un ne soumette l'autre. Fuyant la résignation et sa sécurité' (343).[14] The utopian dénouement echoes the MLF's occasional dream of a future where love might be lived in equality, with both men and women having achieved 'la totalité d'être humain' ('human wholeness'), and shares with the mass-market romance the perfect reconciliation of female self-fulfilment with commitment to the couple. However, for a feminist romance to reach this conclusion demands a number of significant changes to the norms of the genre.

In formal terms, the novel both resembles and differs from the standard romance. Aimed, like most romances, primarily at a female readership, the novel has the accessible transparency and narrative coherence Cardinal found appropriate to a democratic feminism. Nonetheless, it departs considerably from the straightforward third-person narrative of popular romance, and the multi-layered, at times poetic narration is, as we have seen, essential to the theme of women's need to claim linguistic and narrative authority. Moreover, if Simone's story concludes in classic romance mode with a united couple facing a happy future, Mary's story, as written by Simone, eschews the romance form and concludes with a freely chosen, solitary death. The text offers the pleasure of closure

---

[13] 'This harmony that now exists between us, this power we have to seduce each other, this impression that I am him and he is me, seems to me to constitute what is most important in human life, and what it is most essential to protect.'

[14] 'Resolved that neither one will ever subjugate the other. Fleeing from resignation and security.'

in happy love, but also undercuts any sense of this as the only proper conclusion to women's stories.

Thematically, Simone's struggle to articulate the relationship between socially prescribed role and subjective desire re-addresses the fundamental question of romance. But whereas the mass-market romance concludes with a perfect convergence between the socially prescribed roles of wife and mother, and the heroine's personal happiness, Cardinal's novel concludes with their absolute incompatibility. Only by refusing the gender-differentiated structures of the traditional family, which privileges male freedoms and turns resentful women into censorious, stoically repressed *mère-épouses*, can love achieve that 'forme parfaite' Simone sought. Rather than the smooth, seamless form she had envisaged, which would have made private happiness perfectly compatible with social expectations, the ideal couple will have the variable, complex form needed to accommodate two freedoms, two subjectivities. Writing Mary's story out of the material of her own life has enabled Simone to 'exorciser mes démons et conquérir . . . ma . . . liberté. Parce que c'est le seul royaume de l'amour. Je comprends aujourd'hui seulement que je ne peux pas aimer en dehors d'elle' (340).[15]

What differentiates Cardinal's happy ending most clearly from that of the popular romance, though, is the determining role played by bonds between women. Simone's achievement of authentic love involves a complete transformation of her relations with other women. The mass-market romance, like the patriarchal nuclear family itself, highlights only the bond between man and woman, husband and wife: the principal narrative function of women other than the heroine is that of rival. Simone's admission of a fascination with the dead woman not only allows her to reinterpret her own story, but also enables her to face what she had always refused to acknowledge: a passionate interest in other women, including her rivals, that carries a strong current of desire. A repressed memory resurfaces, of walking in on her employer/lover making love to a beautiful woman, Angèle, and of being at once deeply shaken and transfixed by the close-up vision of Angèle's sexual body, and the revelation of its beauty. Vulva and vagina are described in lyrical terms—'Et la trouée, ce passage non dit, non vu, non osé, qui entonne les roses et les rosés, les pâleurs vives' (108).[16] This powerful, sensuous, inviting body is both empowering because it is the same as Simone's

---

[15] 'exorcise my demons and win . . . my . . . freedom. Because freedom is love's only kingdom. It's only now that I realize I can't love unless I am free.'

[16] 'And the hole, that unspoken, unnamed, unseen passage, with its chorus of rose and pinks and its pale brilliance'.

own ('je n'imaginais pas ma fente si belle' ('I hadn't imagined my own slit to be so beautiful', 109)), and enriching because it provokes new forms of desire: she longs to take Angèle in her arms, 'l'abreuver du champagne le plus doré, de la fleurir des pois de senteur les plus roses, d'apaiser sa bouche, et sa poitrine, et sa nuine, par mes baisers frais, par ma bouche de femme' (109).[17] Acceptance of herself as a desirable, sexual body comes through identification with other female bodies, and acceptance of the plurality of desire, rather than its exclusive dependence on sexual difference, contributes to Simone's release from dependence on Jean-François. The happy-ever-after ending is signified not only by the couple's closeness, but also by a playful fantasy sequence in which Simone frolics naked in the sea with Angèle and Mary, her two principal female 'others' (315).

Cardinal's is a romance of maturity, not so much the discovery of love as its redefinition on new terms. Reconciling the utopian longings of the genre with feminist scepticism, *Une vie pour deux* makes the happy romance conditional upon women's appropriation of language, refusal to be confined to a domestic and maternal role, and capacity to love themselves and each other.[18]

Régine Deforges and *La Bicyclette bleue* (1981)

Marie Cardinal became a well-known name in France; most of her books (including *Une vie pour deux*) were printed and reprinted in paperback, and widely translated for non-francophone markets. Her readership, however, was small and specialized when compared with the publishing phenomenon of Régine Deforges's *La Bicyclette bleue*, one of the best-selling French novels of the twentieth century. Deforges (b. 1935) has played a pioneering role in French publishing, particularly in relation to women's writing. She was the first woman to own a publishing company in France (founding first L'Or du Temps in 1968, then the Éditions Régine Deforges in 1976), braving prosecutions for obscenity to publish erotic texts by, among others, Apollinaire and Aragon, and specializing in writing by women, including important and long unavailable works such as the lesbian poetry of Renée Vivien. Deforges published her own first

---

[17] 'to quench her thirst with the most golden champagne, to deck her with the pinkest of sweet peas, to soothe her mouth, her breasts, and her sex with my fresh kisses, with my woman's mouth'.

[18] Cardinal's emphasis on strong bonds between women as a condition for female self-fulfilment, and for positive relations between the sexes, has much in common with the 'Psych et Po' strand of post-1968 French feminism, and notably with Luce Irigaray's concept of an 'entre-femmes' (Irigaray 1986).

novel, *Blanche et Lucie*, in 1976, and followed this with a series of erotic fictions, including the autobiographically based novel *Le Cahier volé* (The Stolen Notebook, 1978). *La Bicyclette bleue*, set under the Occupation, was the first of her novels to find a mass popular readership: it was followed by eight best-selling sequels (1983–2003) that trace its heroine's story through the major events of Occupation and post-war French history, to the Algerian war. Deforges now writes a regular column for *L'Humanité*[19] and continues to publish books that position themselves, implicitly or explicitly, as feminist.[20]

La Bicyclette bleue is very closely based on that most popular of all twentieth-century romances,[21] *Gone with the Wind*, first published in 1936, translated into French in 1939. Deforges never made a secret of the fact that her novel was an affectionate pastiche of Margaret Mitchell's blockbuster, transposed from Civil War America to Second World War France. Sued by Mitchell's notoriously litigious heirs in 1987, she was first found guilty of plagiarism (1989) then cleared on appeal (1990); her skilful reworking of Mitchell's plot and characters was finally judged to be a case of legitimate intertextuality, rather than one of intellectual theft. Like *Gone with the Wind*, *La Bicyclette bleue* is an epic romance, a pleasurably melodramatic narrative driven by a compelling current of desire and attraction between hero and heroine, played out against historical events in which they are also protagonists. Where Scarlett O'Hara's privileged life as a Southern belle is turned upside down by the American Civil War, Léa Delmas—like Scarlett, 17 as the novel opens—finds her secure and carefree existence as the daughter of rich Bordeaux winegrowers disrupted by the outbreak of the Second World War. The novel came out at a time of renewed interest in the Occupation period,[22] and the history of invasion, exodus, collaboration, and resistance provides a colourful dramatic framework for the heroine's adventures. Like Scarlett, Léa faces the terrors of exodus before invading armies, suffers the occupation of her beloved home by enemy troops, and resists the invader out of an instinctive pride and a passionate refusal to countenance personal defeat. Each heroine's narrative is driven at once by external events,

---

[19] Collected in Deforges 1998 and 1999.

[20] *L'Érotique des mots*, 2004, is co-written with Chantal Chawaf, an author generally claimed by critics as among the best practitioners of *écriture féminine*; its form recalls Cardinal's collaboration with Annie Leclerc in *Autrement dit*.

[21] *Gone with the Wind* has sold more copies world-wide than any book except the Bible, at least according to Margaret Mitchell's website (**www.gwtw.org/**).

[22] Ophuls's documentary *Le Chagrin et la pitié*, made in 1970, was finally shown on French TV in 1981; Louis Malle's story of a collaborator, *Lacombe Lucien*, had come out in 1975, and Truffaut's feature film *Le Dernier Métro*, set in the Occupation, came out in 1980; Marguerite Duras's *La Douleur* would appear in 1985.

and by her own imperative desires: for self-affirmation, for belonging, and for love. Like Scarlett, Léa at first misrecognizes her own desire, believing herself to be in love with a good, honourable man (Mitchell's Ashley Wilkes becomes Laurent d'Argilat) whose marriage to his gentle, sober cousin Camille (Melanie in *Gone with the Wind*) devastates her early in the plot. But with the double focalization typical of romance, the reader is granted a wider and more knowing vision than the heroine, and it soon becomes apparent that the true hero is rather the seductive, dissident outsider whose aggressive desire and irreverent clarity of vision mask a passion that is more than sexual. Rhett Butler becomes François Tavernier, and the narrative returns insistently to the sparring, erotically and emotionally charged encounters between François and Léa. Both novels avoid a closed dénouement: Scarlett's famous refusal to accept Rhett's final rejection of her ('After all, tomorrow is another day') offers the reader the option to imagine a future for the couple, and Deforges separates her lovers to leave the way open for sequels. Nonetheless, both end with a re-posing of the central question of romance: can these two people find happiness together?

Scarlett O'Hara's appeal for women readers (and spectators) was and is immense.[23] Women—in particular—enjoy the mix of admiring identification and scandalized disapproval that she invites: Scarlett's energetic determination to have her own needs fulfilled pleasurably flouts all the rules of acceptable femininity, while her impatient misreading of other people, like her indifference to their feelings, invites the reader to mingle intense sympathy with the exercise of critical judgement. Léa is also a heroine of powerful, and at times unscrupulous, appetites and desires; she shares Scarlett's hot temper, robust constitution, and relentless will to happiness, never losing her appetite for food even at moments of crisis or extreme emotion, and displaying—in a way that by the 1980s was tolerable, if still unexpected, in a teenage heroine—an open, explicit, and shameless appetite for sex, which she often initiates: 'Je t'aime et je te veux', she announces to a shocked and prudish Laurent, 'Je te désire autant que tu me désires' (42).[24] Léa is a less transgressive heroine than her original, in the sense that half a century after *Gone with the Wind*, a woman's incursions into the 'masculine' territory of armed combat and public affairs, like the assertion of her sexual freedom, could be more easily accommodated into mainstream values. Nonetheless, even with the map of gender partially redrawn by feminism, Léa's

---

[23] See Helen Taylor's *Scarlett's Women: Gone with the Wind and its Female Fans* (Taylor 1989) for detailed demonstration of Scarlett's popularity as a heroine.

[24] 'I love you and I want you. I desire you as much as you desire me.'

uncompromising pursuit of her own pleasures, and irreverent dismissal of the social norms of her own era, still make her a contestatory heroine. But whereas Scarlett's 'unfeminine' ambition and egoism are finally punished by the narrative, through her social isolation, the death of her daughter, and the loss of Rhett's love, Léa is positively rewarded for her refusal to conform to the rules of her gendered role, by the respect and admiration of the novel's good characters, by inclusion in the nascent community of the Resistance, and by the answering desire of the men she chooses.

Successful popular romances, like their more 'literary' counterparts, always offer some reflection on what it means to be a (good) woman. Deforges also draws on *Gone with the Wind* to reaffirm the value of certain traditionally 'feminine' virtues, which her heroine—albeit less radically than Scarlett—appears to reject. Both heroines love and lose mothers who are models of devoted, domestically competent, morally uncompromising womanhood, and if Scarlett and Léa carry their readers with them in choosing an entirely opposing way of being a woman, the maternal bond remains an important element of their characterization. This, as Helen Taylor puts it, 'allows women readers . . . a space in which to celebrate the mother's virtues and values, but also to challenge and disregard them' (Taylor 1989: 9). The maternal model has a more sustained role in Deforges's narrative through the character of Camille, based on *Gone with the Wind*'s Melanie. Camille could have stepped out of a Delly novel: she is pure, fragile, utterly selfless, and monogamously devoted to her man, Laurent. But as with Melanie, and as with Delly's heroines, beneath the delicate exterior lies an unshakeable sense of integrity: in the defence of honour and justice, and of those she loves, Camille can reveal nerves of steel and unsuspected strength. As oblivious to gossip as she is to Léa's jealous coldness towards her, Camille maintains an unswerving tenderness for and loyalty to Léa: sick and pregnant during the 1940 exodus before the invading army, she still manages to shoot a looter who threatens Léa; later she will be an intrepid supporter of her Resistance activities. If Léa's model of the heroine suggests a valorization of 'masculine' qualities (autonomy, physical courage, self-affirmation) at the expense of those positive qualities traditionally aligned with the feminine (concern for others, sensitivity, selflessness), the latter are reinstated in the character of Camille. Deforges proposes alternative models of strong femininity, and (like Cardinal) has her heroine's happiness depend not solely on union with the hero, but also on a learned appreciation of bonds with other women.

The massive popular success of *La Bicyclette bleue* in some ways suggests the capacity of romance to adapt to a more feminist era. Here a strong, resourceful, passionate heroine achieves both historical agency and the love and desire of the man she wants, the latter without sacrificing her independence, and in a way that clearly captured the imagination of millions of women. It is interesting, then, that in its characterization of the hero—presumably also a major factor in its success—the novel should have remained very close both to its original, and to the traditional mass-market romance. François Tavernier, tall, mocking, indifferent to social convention, and devastatingly seductive ('Pourquoi cette faiblesse soudaine dans tout le corps, ce poids délicieux au creux des cuisses?'[25] wonders Léa (46)), is a familiar kind of hero, evoking not only Margaret Mitchell's Rhett Butler, but also the heroes of Delly and the Barbara Cartland school of traditional romance. He is knowledgeable and powerful: François disappears from the narrative for chapters at a time, but when he reappears, it is always to bring much-needed solutions to problems (food at times of shortage, transport for the exodus before the German army, information), or to provide—for Léa and the reader—a satisfyingly erotic interlude, a brief escape from the tensions of war. Like all true heroes, he is ethically and politically aligned with the novel's positive values: though his confident indifference to public opinion allows him to be taken for a collaborator, he is in reality a Resistance hero. And whereas Léa is often uncertain of his feelings, motivations, and even whereabouts, he is sufficiently perceptive and well informed to always, unfailingly, know precisely what she is thinking, feeling, and doing. The sexual and emotional appeal of the romance hero seems to be disturbingly consistent in its identification with mastery, strength, and control, as if even a narrative of female agency and freedom needed, to be profoundly satisfying, a fantasy of self-abandonment to the benevolent power of a greater force.

However, the pleasures of a hero like François Tavernier are not necessarily politically regressive. We can explain why he constitutes such an enjoyable fantasy, but also recognize that readers of romance, on the whole, make their own distinctions between fantasy and what they seek in their own lives, and that Deforges's text encourages such a reading. François is surely the impossibly perfect combination of what Jessica Benjamin calls 'the holding mother and the exciting father' (Benjamin 1988: 131). He is the exciting father, he who represents the adventure and the challenge of the world beyond childhood and family, and who encourages and rewards the daughter's wish to emulate him. François introduces a whiff of the forbidden and the illicit into Léa's safe world,

---

[25] 'Why this sudden weakness throughout her body and this delicious heaviness between her thighs?'

for he is associated with gun-running and the Spanish Republican cause; it is he who introduces her to Parisian nightlife, initiates her sexually, and sends her off to confront the dangers of the exodus, always assuming that she has the competence, energy, and passion to match his own, and rewarding her with his love when she lives up to this. At the same time, he provides the unconditional, unqualified love of the idealized mother. François's immediate and total understanding of Léa—like Rhett with Scarlett, he is never taken in by her pretences—is not only a sign of his power, it also means that what he loves her for is her 'real' self, the core beneath the performances presented to others. Unlike Laurent, who is not strong enough to match Léa's passions, or her childhood friend Mathieu, whose love turns to anger when she offers only sex without commitment, François always survives her rejection, her unemotional use of him for sexual pleasure, her bad behaviour—and returns, still loving. Deforges situates the first time the two make love during a brief stopover on the flight south. After the violence, heat, and terror of the journey, in which Léa has been wholly responsible for driving the pregnant Camille to safety as German planes strafe the fleeing hordes of refugees, the relief of François's sudden appearance is intensified when he finds an old well and obtains sufficient water for them to wash each other, cleaning away the dust and blood of the day. The act of washing Léa's naked body is both erotic and maternal: François is at once thrillingly desirable, his body focalized from Léa's perspective (185), and warmly comforting. The perfect fantasy requires both: Mathieu (who chooses the path of collaboration, not resistance) can satisfy Léa sexually, but lacks the ethical solidity to love deeply, but when Léa finally achieves her aim of making love with the brave but too virtuous Laurent, she finds herself 'le cœur comblé' ('her heart satisfied', 368) but her body decidedly not so. François brings together 'the constituent elements of desire' (Benjamin 1988: 131): the exuberance of the sensual, adventurous figure, traditionally the father, and the warmth, containment, and acceptance identified with the mother.

The effectiveness of Deforges's re-creation of Mitchell's iconic hero partly explains the success of *La Bicyclette bleue*. However, it is important to bear in mind that, irresistible as he is for most heterosexual women readers, Rhett Butler is not essential to Scarlett's survival, or even, possibly, her happiness. Scarlett survives and on the whole thrives with or without Rhett, and the novel closes with her making alternative plans, since he is about to leave her. Deforges maintains this additional dimension of readerly pleasure in the text: this is a dense and complex story with many characters and sub-plots, and neither narrative interest nor the continuation of Léa's adventures, erotic and otherwise, depends entirely on François Tavernier. Alternative sources of maternal warmth can be found, in Camille as well as a host of minor motherly figures, just as other characters offer love, desire, and adventure. François, uniquely and perfectly, marries the two, but life—in the novel as in readers' lives—can also be survived, even happily, without perfection.

Lesbian romance: Mireille Best and *Camille en octobre* (1988)

Many post-1968 romances, then, show the impact of feminism in their inclusion of relationships between women as essential to the heroine's well-being. Though the central narrative focus remains on the hetero-sexual couple, its successful formation no longer represents absolute, self-contained happiness: even in the fantasy world of the romantic blockbuster, other kinds of bonding are granted narrative importance. The late 1970s and the 1980s also saw the publication of many lesbian romances—by no means a new sub-genre, but one that after the post-1968 emergence of a visible and articulate lesbian movement could achieve greater prominence. By 'the lesbian romance', I mean a love story between two women that conforms broadly to the parameters of the genre: a narrative centred on a single love relationship, in which the ideal of a perfect union with the beloved Other encounters obstacles which may be overcome, or may prove insuperable so that the plot ends in loss or renunciation.

One important difference of the same-sex romance lies in the rela-tionship between desire and social acceptance, for if (at least in later twentieth-century western cultures) a woman's freely assumed desire and love for a man can take the socially sanctioned form of marriage, no such institution exists to reconcile same-sex love with social structures. Thus post-feminist hetero-romances may locate the obstacles to desire precisely in the institutions that sanction but can also distort and neut-ralize the initial impulse (as in *Une vie pour deux*), and a satisfying fantasy of perfect love may demand the avoidance of closure in definitive com-mitment (*La Bicyclette bleue*). But for lesbian love, the conflict between personal fulfilment and social belonging is more straightforward: in romances of this period, love between women encounters incompre-hension, disapproval, and a paralysing absence of available linguistic or social expression. The conflict between romantic desire and social acceptance is starker, and the emphasis tends to fall on the struggle to achieve a durable, mutual commitment, rather than on the intrinsic problems of relationship.

Régine Deforges's *Le Cahier volé* (1978) is a story of lesbian love set in 1950s provincial France, though it is more a brief 'sentimental education' than a romance. The 15-year-old narrator-heroine, Léone, is an earlier model of Léa: headstrong, beautiful, and shamelessly sexual. Attracted to individuals of both sexes, Léone's most intense and durable love is for her school friend Mélie. When Léone's personal diary is stolen and made public by a jealous young man, she discovers the severity with which her society is prepared to defend its principles of universal heterosexuality and male authority: Church, school, and family combine to ostracize and bully her into giving up Mélie. The power of what Lucille Cairns terms 'heteronormativity' (Cairns 2002) is also a central theme in Deforges's 1986 *Pour l'amour de Marie Salat*, a love story narrated through the letters of two married, working-class young women in 1903-4. Marguerite and Marie meet when the former moves with her husband to Marie's village, and their immediate affinity rapidly turns to passionate love. The experience of absolute fascination with another person, like that of sexual ecstasy, is completely new to both, for marriage for each has meant no more than a tolerable cohabitation. But here it takes no external intervention to separate the lovers: recognizing the impossibility of finding any social form for their love ('Ensemble, nous n'aurions connu rapidement que honte et déchéance',[26] 150), Marie moves away, so that their 'belle histoire' ('beautiful story', 150) may at least end with dignity, and remain intact as a memory. These novels address one of the central questions of romance, that of the possibility of reconciling personal fulfilment through love with social belonging—and declare it impossible, at least within their diegetic contexts.

Jocelyne François's 1980 novel *Joue-nous 'España'* (1980), like *Le Cahier volé*, is a first-person narrative with a strong element of autobiography. Here too, the orthodox family is negatively portrayed: there is little love between the narrator's parents, or from parents to children, and their repeated, purportedly joking question 'Où sommes-nous allés la pêcher?' ('Where did we get her from?', 12) expresses that sense of not belonging that defines the narrator's childhood. The women-only community of the convent boarding school to which she is sent, as part of the family's effort to achieve bourgeois respectability, turns out to be both a refuge and the scene of the romantic encounter. For Marie-Claire, whom she later renames Sarah, the narrator experiences a sudden, absolute *coup de foudre* : 'A partir de ce moment rien n'est pareil' (164).[27] The sensations of love—the fascination with the other's difference, the

---

[26] 'Together, we would soon only have known shame and loss.'
[27] 'From that moment on, nothing is the same.'

desire for 'l'union, la fusion complète avec quelqu'un' ('union, complete fusion with someone else', 180)—are described more vividly than the beloved herself, who remains an idealized but shadowy presence. Torn apart by a cruel collaboration between Church and family, the lovers spend seven years living 'normally', during which time the narrator marries and has three children. But the couple re-find each other, and despite the bitter opposition of their families establish a life together:[28] 'Tu as ouvert le désir, le plaisir, l'écriture, états qui étaient en gésine dans mon corps . . . Bien que tu sois venue très tôt, longue a été l'attente de toi, puis ta lumière a fait pâlir la préfiguration de toi en moi' (195).[29] When love is socially forbidden, the emphasis of the romance falls to a greater extent on the conflict between desire and social orthodoxy, and it is often the utopian bliss of mutual love, rather than its internal conflicts, that dominate the narrative.

Of the numerous lesbian love stories published in the 1970s and 1980s,[30] Mireille Best's *Camille en octobre* (1988) was one of the more highly acclaimed both by the literary mainstream and by lesbian readers and critics (Cairns 2002: 280). It shares with the novels outlined above a diegetic location in the past (1960s France), a highly critical depiction of the 'normal' family, and a vivid sense of the difficulty of 'crystallizing and socially constituting' (Cairns 2002: 291) lesbian love, in a culture that refuses its existence. It is also stylistically inventive, darkly humorous, and moving in its depiction of both sibling love and frustrated sexual love. Camille, the narrator-heroine, grows up in a working-class milieu in a northern French seaport, with her two younger siblings Ariane and Abel. If she suffers from a sense of uncertain identity, and of not belonging ('Je n'ai jamais très bien su QUI j'étais', 13),[31] this is not only because she is more bookish and academic than the rest of the family, nor simply because of a dawning recognition of her own sexuality, but also because all children in this inhospitable world of oppressed, distracted mothers and angry, overworked fathers seem lost or bent on escape. The novel's perspective on the sheer misery of women and men trapped in poverty and loveless marriages mixes caustic humour with sympathy. The survival strategy of

---

[28] *Joue-nous 'España'* is one of a quartet of autobiographically based, if chronologically non-sequential, novels by François. The utopian quality of the relationship between the narrator and her lover is also present in the other volumes, though issues of jealousy and conflicting desires for others of both sexes arise in *Les Amantes* (1978) and *Histoire de Volubilis* (1986).

[29] 'You opened in me the springs of desire, pleasure, writing, states which were lying latent in my body . . . Though you came to me so early in my life, the wait for you was long, then when you came your light was so much brighter than that first prefiguring of you in me.'

[30] See Cairns 2002.

[31] 'I've never really known WHO I was.'

'Les Mères' (The Mothers) is to meet together daily to drink overstewed coffee and gossip, dream, and share their resignation, before returning to the routine of endless domestic work, childcare, and husbands who 'leur montaient dessus, cognaient parfois, pesaient sur leur conscience autant que sur le rythme de leurs jours' (32).[32] The men's strategies are drink, silence, and varying degrees of violence. While Ariane, precociously lucid and pragmatic, defends herself from this 'monde morne et flou' ('bleak and shapeless world', 12) with a single-minded goal of escape (which she achieves, though only into a more affluent version of family life), the mentally damaged Abel seems to concentrate the whole family's pain in his complete alienation from the social world, his copious tears, and his dramatic and medically inexplicable fainting fits. Camille responds to her father's gruff brutality and her mother's passivity with a series of apparently accidental attempts at patricide—attempts rendered semi-comic by their very explicit Oedipal overtones (the father returned from the Second World War to usurp the infant Camille's exclusive bond with her mother), and their repetitiveness ('J'ai tué papa. Encore, a bougonné ma sœur Ariane', 65).[33] Camille fails (but only just) to knock him out with a metal 'boule', break his skull with an iron, and drown him in the canal. But she also seeks an alternative vision of who she is, and how life could be, by falling in love.

Even before Camille, and the reader, meet Clara, with her 'yeux très noirs et très beaux, sous le regard desquels on se sent quelqu'un de très bien' (56),[34] the novel has undermined heteronormative assumptions: through the juxtaposition of the Mothers' absolute acceptance of the need for a man in their lives with the unpleasant reality of their marriages, through the minor but important—and relatively happy—character of the street cleaner Marie-qui-a-les-deux-sexes (Mary-who-is-both-sexes), and through Ariane's staunch refusal to let normative views on gender get in the way of loyalty to her sister. Mylène, daughter of one of the 'Mères', plays the Princess and promises to choose the suitor who brings the prettiest flower. Seeing that Camille wants to compete with the boys, Ariane helps her to obtain the best flower, and refuses to accept the boys' complaints that a princess 'can't choose another girl'.

> - Et d'abord, dit Ariane, est-ce que Mylène choisit entre les garçons, les filles, ou les fleurs? Quelle fleur tu préfères, Mylène?
> - Celle de Camille, dit Mylène, avec une certaine hésitation, mais . . .

---

[32] 'mounted them, sometimes hit them, weighed on their minds as they did on the rhythms of their days'.

[33] ' "I've killed Dad." "Oh not again", groaned Ariane.'

[34] 'very black, very beautiful eyes, under whose gaze you felt like someone really worthwhile'.

- C'est celle de Camille qui est la plus belle, oui ou non?
- Oui, oui sûrement . . . Mais . . .
- Bbbbon. C'est bien cette fleur-là que tu préfères?
- Oui . . . Mais.
- Alors il y a pas le moindre 'mais', dit Ariane. Attrape![35] (60)

Ariane's sisterly irreverence for orthodox gender roles leads straight to Camille's discovery of love, for the flower Ariane has in mind has to be stolen from the dentist's waiting room, and Clara is the dentist's wife. The flower—deceptive in its beauty, because artificial, and leading only to an empty victory (Mylène does not really accept Camille's offering)—functions as an image of Clara's relationship with Camille.

Immediately attracted to her eyes, her smile, her gentleness, Camille never forgets Clara and returns to the dentist's four or five years later, when she is almost 16. The relationship that ensues is passionate on Camille's side, and Clara's encouragement of Camille's visits, invitations to her holiday house by the sea, and cautiously restrained gestures of tenderness ('En détournant à la toute dernière seconde un geste de sa main qui s'en allait vers mon genou', 148)[36] imply an answering desire. Their most sensual physical contact is during the motorcycle journeys to the seaside house, when Camille rides pillion and is transported in more sense than one: 'Je suis soudée au cuir de sa veste Au corps que je devine dessous A sa chaleur de bête solaire A son odeur d'herbe exotique poussée a l'autre bout du monde' (119).[37] At last, on a trip to the house to celebrate Camille's birthday and her success in the baccalauréat, they make love. Unpunctuated, but with spaces indicating both simultaneity and (possibly) pauses for retrospective wonder, this passage mingles active and passive verbs to make clear the mutual nature of their passion.

J'ai bu et j'ai mangé en pleurant le corps de Clara   L'eau du corps de Clara   L'odeur tellement violente oh mon Dieu de Clara   J'ai eu ses dents contre mes dents et sur la nuque et sur les flancs   J'ai été sucée dévorée dissoute   J'ai été rouleée empoignée lissée projetée en cercles concentriques dans une merveilleuse succession de gouffres.[38] (165)

---

[35] ' "Look", said Ariane, "is Mylène choosing between boys, girls, or flowers? Which flower do you like best, Mylène?" "Camille's", said Mylène, with some hesitation, "but . . ." "Is Camille's the prettiest, yes or no?" "Yes, yes it is, but . . ." "Oookay then. That is the flower you like best?" "Yes . . . but . . ." "Then there's no but about it", said Ariane. "Here, catch!" '

[36] 'Stopping right at the very last moment the movement of her hand towards my knee'.

[37] 'I am welded to her leather jacket. To the body I sense beneath. To her warmth, like some creature from the sun. To her smell, like some exotic herb from the other end of the earth.'

[38] 'I drank and ate Clara's body weeping   The water of Clara's body   The smell so violent a smell oh my God of Clara's body   I had her teeth against my teeth on the back of my neck on my sides   I was sucked devoured dissolved. I was rolled over grabbed stroked hurled in concentric circles into a wonderful series of chasms.'

But Clara is firmly established in a heterosexual life that has a structure, a future, a recognized place in the social order, and in the cold light of day she can neither articulate nor acknowledge her feelings for Camille. It is shortly after this episode that she announces that she is pregnant, and leaving the town with her husband. The novel ends a year later, with Camille now a university student, feeling herself radically estranged from both her new milieu and the one she has left behind—'jamais une "vraie". Nulle part. Ni chez les miens, ni chez les autres' (208).[39] Clara returns to see her, bringing her little daughter, also named Camille, and in the adult Camille's feelings of tenderness for her small namesake, and in Clara's response to Camille's account of the flower that began their story, there is at least the hint of a shared acknowledgement of the value of what passed between them.

> ...Tu te rends compte, c'était la plus belle fleur que j'aie vue de ma vie, et elle n'existait pas.
> ...
> - Tu vois partout des choses très belles, dit Clara, qui n'existent pas ...
> ...
> - ...Mais ce sont elles qui ont tort, dit Clara. Elles devraient, AURAIENT DÛ être comme tu les vois ...
> ...
> ...Tu sais, Camille ... D'une manière ou d'une autre, elles ont tout de même plus ou moins existé ... Tu ne crois pas?[40] (219)

Nonetheless, the dénouement is bleak, and made more so by the death of Abel, for which Camille feels responsible, and the awkward, constantly interrupted, long-distance call with Ariane, now living on the other side of the world, which punctuates the narrative and underlines Camille's solitude. Clara's formulation of their relationship almost qualifies it out of existence: it is a set of 'things', that 'all the same', 'more or less' existed. For Clara, and for the society Camille inhabits, love between women cannot lead to a happy ending because it has no language to bring it into social existence.

Conclusion

Second-wave feminism rejected the classic romance scenario as a dangerous myth that seduced women into acceptance of their own

---

[39] 'never the "real thing". Not anywhere. Not with my own lot, nor with the others.'

[40] ' "... Do you realize, it was the loveliest flower I had seen in my life, and it didn't exist.". ..."You see lovely things that don't exist everywhere", said Clara. ... "But it is the things that are wrong", said Clara. "They should exist, they SHOULD HAVE existed as you saw them ...". ..."You know, Camille ... in one way or another, they did more or less exist ... don't you think?" '.

subordination. Yet the deconstruction of romance could not be the whole story, for to jettison the ideal of intense, durable, and mutual passion was to relinquish one of the most recurrent and compelling images of human happiness, and to dismiss a major (and unwaveringly popular) strand of female culture. By the 1980s, feminist writers were reclaiming the romance form as a means both to re-imagine heterosexual desire, outside the androcentric terms in which it had traditionally been framed, and to dispute the exclusively heterosexual nature of romantic love. If a woman's love for a man encountered the problem of ready-made social institutions—the Couple, marriage, family—that at once endorsed a relationship and distorted it, pulling it away from the initial equality of mutual desire, a woman's love for another woman met the opposite problem—that of an absence of social or even linguistic form to reconcile personal emotion with social living. Writing and reading stories of love played an important part, both in negotiating the con-flicts between romantic love and its consecrated social outcomes, and in rendering visible, and speakable, love and desire between women.

6 Love in a Postmodern Age: Contemporary Romance in France

Where second-wave feminism came to terms with romance, it was to assert female desire and the right to love freely against the traditional narrative of love which meant compulsory heterosexuality, acceptance of male authority, and a domestic and maternal role. In its contestation of what had been the structuring principles of social life, feminism was part of a broader wave of rebellious thinking—thinking that was authentically liberating, but that achieved some of its goals because it also converged with major material and economic developments in the late twentieth century. The emphasis on individual freedom rather than obedience to family, and on the right to one's desires, both follow the liberatory logic of May 1968 and befit a sophisticated consumer society requiring a mobile, adaptable workforce and a public convinced of its right to consume ('because you're worth it', as L'Oréal's advertising slogan assured us).[1] The postmodern culture of the 1990s and early 2000s can be characterized as a culture shaped both by the wave of utopian iconoclasm that shook western societies in the late 1960s, and by the logic of globalized consumerism: it is a culture suspicious of absolutes, whose positive values are change and variety rather than stability and consistency, the provisional and the fluid rather than the definitive and the solid.

The romance narrative of the encounter with unique and transcendent love might seem ill adapted to such a climate. However, a widespread investment in love—'love', that is, meaning a mutual commitment based on passionate desire and affinity—is also a significant feature of contemporary culture, despite the shift from a dominant model of marriage-for-life to less permanent, more sequential and complex family structures. As, across the centuries, the choice of partner has come to be determined less and less by the material and dynastic interests of the extended family, and more and more by individual inclination, so the love story has become the essential basis, the *raison d'être*, and the *sine qua non* of the family unit.[2] Romantic love is not only assumed to be a

---

[1] In French, 'Vous le valez bien.'

[2] In his 1993 postscript to *L'Ère du vide*, a series of essays that define postmodern culture, Gilles Lipovetsky sees the 1990s as an age of 'individualisme *à la carte*, hédoniste et psychologique, faisant

source of extreme personal fulfilment, it is also accepted as the crucial determinant of successful living arrangements: partnerships and families may well have to dissolve and re-form if one or other of the couple live out a new love story with a different partner. Social institutions reflect and enable this valorization of love, and the acceptance of its impermanence. Divorce on the grounds of the breakdown of a relationship—or the ending of love—is now relatively easy and socially acceptable, in France as elsewhere in the West. In France the PaCS (Pacte Civil de Solidarité, 1999) provides state ratification of cohabiting partnerships between same-sex as well as different-sex couples, thus endorsing desire and affinity between two people as sufficient basis for formal recognition as a social unit. The concern with finding, keeping, or replacing a partner in love runs throughout the culture of the everyday, in popular songs, in films and television, in magazines.

As in the past, though, the genre of romance—the telling and consuming of stories of love—remains a predominantly female domain. Popular romantic fiction, almost entirely written and read by women, remains the most widely read, if also the most critically despised, genre in France. And though rigorously excluded, in its popular form, from serious bookshops, female-authored romance also maintains a very visible presence on the shelves of contemporary literature. Titles such as *Passion simple* (Annie Ernaux, 1991), *Dans ces bras-là* (In Those Arms, Camille Laurens, 2000) and *L'Amour, roman* (Love, a Novel, Laurens, 2003), *La Conversation amoureuse* (The Amorous Conversation, Alice Ferney, 2000), *Je l'aimais* (I Loved Him, Anna Gavalda, 2002), *D'amour* (Of Love, Danièle Sallenave, 2002), *Envie d'amour* (Desire for Love, Cécile Beauvoir, 2002), and *Politique de l'amour* (A Politics of Love, Alina Reyes, 2002), attest visibly to the widespread presence of romance themes in recent work by authors who are acknowledged—through publication by respected publishing houses, reviews in the serious press, appearances on TV arts programmes, the award of book prizes—to be fully 'literary'. Though the titles are less explicit, the romance script also structures novels such as Emmanuèle Bernheim's *Vendredi soir* (1998), Christine Angot's *Pourquoi le Brésil?* (2002), Marie Nimier's *La Nouvelle Pornographie* (2002), Christine Jordis's *La Chambre blanche* (2003).

All of the authors mentioned so far are white: the category of contemporary French women's writing least to deploy romantic forms and themes is that of ethnic minority authors. While some francophone

de l'accomplissement intime la fin principale des existences' ('individualism *à la carte*, hedonistic and psychological, that makes a private, intimate form of self-fulfilment the major goal of life', Lipovetsky 1993: 316).

writers—notably the Algerian Assia Djébar (b. 1936)[3]—have made the love story an important element of their exploration of colonialism and of female identity, French writers from Maghrebi or African-French communities have tended, so far at least, to focus more on the tensions of biculturalism, on the search for identity and belonging by young female subjects constructed by both cultures as 'other', and on the formation of a viable identity as a woman, caught between conflicting versions of what this means. In the 1980s, Leila Sebbar's heroine Shérazade[4] had encountered love and desire as one element of her journey of self-discovery through France, but romantic love is certainly not what drives the plot, any more than it is for Leïla Houari's *Zeida de nulle part* (1985). Zeida's quest for a sense of belonging seems to find its answer in the handsome Watani, encountered on a visit to her family in Morocco—but Watani's realism about the incompatibility of their worlds defeats her romantic dreams, and the quest continues elsewhere. In the 1990s and 2000s too, the *roman d'apprentissage* (novel about growing up and forming an identity) has dominated postcolonial women's writing.[5] The critically admired work of Nina Bouraoui (b. 1967) has explored, above all, themes of split identity, both in terms of the conflict between French and Algerian cultures, and in terms of gender. If the 2002 novel *La Vie heureuse* traces its teenage heroine's passion and—for a time—requited love for a classmate, Diane, the narrative is equally concerned with broader issues of forging identity, and with a first close encounter with death. Sexual love has its place in current black and Maghrebi-French women's literature,[6] but it is one strand in a closely woven thread of urgent themes rather than—as in the genre of romance—the narrative's central concern. However, whilst we do know what black and Maghrebi-French women are writing, it is much harder to know what they are reading, and it is more than likely that patterns of readership apply, to some extent, across France's different ethnic groups, and that the readership for the various forms of romance is not limited to white women.

[3] For example, Djébar's 1967 *Les Alouettes naïves* is a passionate love story as well as a novel about the war for Algerian independence. The women's stories in *Femmes d'Alger dans leur appartement* (1980) are interwoven with themes of love and desire, as is *Oran, langue morte* (1997).

[4] In *Les Carnets de Shérazade*, 1985.

[5] For example Ferrudja Kessas's *Beur's Story* (1990); Soraya Nini's *Ils disent que je suis une beurette* (1993); Nina Bouraoui's *Garçon manqué* (2000).

[6] Odile Cazenave identifies in the work of the Cameroonian-French writer Calixthe Beyala a 'search for a new sexual ethics' (Cazenave 2003: 130) that suggests some overlap with the themes of romance (see also Cazenave 1996). Contemporary representations of romantic love in the context of postcolonial writing would be a rewarding topic to pursue, but it is too large to address here.

Situated between the mass-market formula romance, now dominated by the multinational Harlequin, and 'literary' love stories, lie the best-selling novels of Madeleine Chapsal. 'Méprisée par la critique et ignorée des hommes' ('despised by the critics and ignored by men', Frey 1997), Chapsal finds a huge and loyal female readership for her numerous novels, the plots of which revolve around the pursuit of love, and the possibility—for contemporary women—of reconciling heterosexual love and personal freedom. Her autobiographical writing also echoes romance themes: the 2004 *L'Homme de ma vie* (The Man of my Life) recounts her teenage *coup de foudre* for Jean-Jacques Servan-Schreiber, their thirteen-year marriage (during which they founded one of France's major weekly news magazines, *L'Express*), its ending in divorce—and their enduring love that (according to Chapsal) survived Servan-Schreiber's remarriage to confirm the durability of romantic love. 'Jean-Jacques et moi nous aimons toujours. Je peux dire comme au jour de notre mariage. L'amour véritable est intemporel' (Chapsal 2004).[7]

This chapter will explore the persistent popularity of romance for women, in an age where marriage is no longer assumed to be a woman's only proper destiny, and where love—while idealized and endlessly evoked—is rarely assumed to be 'till death do us part'. Discussion of popular romance will focus on the main romance 'brand' of the late twentieth and early twenty-first century, Harlequin, and on a lesbian response to the overwhelming heterosexuality of Harlequin. Out of the wealth of possible 'literary' romance texts, discussion of how women writers use, reshape, and reflect upon the most traditional of feminine genres will be centred on Emmanuèle Bernheim's *Vendredi soir* (1998), a romance narrative condensed into a single night, which has also been adapted by the author into a very successful film directed by Claire Denis, and on Camille Laurens's critically acclaimed *L'Amour, roman* (2003).

Harlequin comes to France

In France, as we have seen, the popular romance novel has a long and very successful indigenous history. If the genre can be traced all the way back through the eighteenth century *roman sentimental* to the medieval

---

[7] 'Jean-Jacques and I still love each other. I might even say, as we did on the day we were married. True love lies outside time' (From the back cover and web publicity for *L'Homme de ma vie*). Chapsal has been publishing at least one novel each year since the 1970s, with titles such as *Adieu l'amour* (Farewell to Love, 1987), *Une femme heureuse* (A Happy Woman, 1995), *Les Amoureux* (1999). Even before they appear in paperback (they are all published in the Livre de Poche series), they normally sell some 70,000 or 80,000 copies.

roman courtois, it is in the twentieth century that publishers began to employ the term as a marketing category, and that the popular romance, marketed in low-cost, high-turnover series, came to dominate the reading practices of the female population. For most of the century, Delly—and to a lesser extent writers like Max du Veuzit and Magali, who offered less pious variations on the Delly model—dominated the French market. But globalization or, more specifically, Americanization of popular culture reached romantic fiction in 1978, when the Canadian/American publishers Harlequin opened a French subsidiary. Harlequin—founded in 1949, but achieving worldwide dominance of the romance market after the 1971 takeover of the leading British romance brand, Mills and Boon—was already established in the Netherlands, West Germany, Austria, and Switzerland, and has gone on to set up companies all over the developed and developing world including Japan, Australia, and Eastern Europe. Harlequin novels are all written by English-language, mainly North American, authors, and mainly set in the USA: the job of the local company—in this case, Harlequin-France—is to study the local market, select the most marketable novels, employ and oversee a team of translators, and deploy a sales strategy in line with Harlequin's global policy, but adapted to the local culture. Marketing methods resemble those for domestic or beauty products, rather than books: with consumer response closely observed through surveys and focus groups, the novels are sold in supermarkets, by mail order, or over the web, and readers are encouraged to think of themselves as an important part of a shared Harlequin world.[8] These techniques have been rewarded, in France as elsewhere, by stunning sales figures. Some sixteen different series (the precise number varies as categories are added and discontinued) provide for all tastes within the genre, from *Horizon: la magie du rêve et de l'amour* (Horizon: The Magic of Dreams and Love), to *Passion: Rencontres Audacieuses et Jeux de Séduction* (Passion: Exciting Encounters and Games of Seduction) or (from 2003) *Red Dress Ink*, the 'chick-lit' series for 'citadines branchées' (modern city women). If Harlequin-France themselves are to be believed, they sell about twelve million volumes a year (Harlequin website, August 2005) and are read by approximately 20 per cent of the French female population (Lucet, n.d.: 2).

Harlequin can of course be seen as the McDonald's or the Coca-Cola of western capitalist patriarchy: offering immediate, easy gratification,

---

[8] The website Harlequin-France, for example, offers readers a monthly 'horoscope amoureux' and a free on-line novel as well as detailed product information including a list of 'les incontournables' (the indispensable current Harlequins). Information about Harlequin-France is based on or confirmed by an interview with the marketing director and the deputy dditor, 12 Jan. 2004, and subsequent e-mail correspondence.

Harlequin makes huge profits and disseminates a powerful ideology by seducing consumers to enjoy what is bad for them. Apart from the political criticisms that could be made of Harlequin's consistent celebration of consumer culture, through stories in which 'romance itself is inseparable from an abundance of wealth and possessions' (Darbyshire 2000: 1), good feminist arguments exist to explain why this kind of romance is bad for women's health. Harlequins feature those same rich, socially privileged, virile heroes and beautiful, needy heroines familiar from Delly romances, and play out the heroine's story to a happy dénouement of marriage and, sometimes, pregnancy. They can be plausibly argued to eroticize male power and female submission, and to impose the heterosexual couple as the sole path to female self-fulfilment—in short, to be a highly effective mode of patriarchal propaganda.

The argument here will take account of the genre's peculiar fidelity to a narrative logic from which women, at least in the West, could be thought to have escaped. But I also want to contend that, despite their unpromising conditions of production, Harlequin romances maintain the traditional function of romance as a fictional space where women can address fears and anxieties raised by the conditions of their lives, and define positive values by imagining pleasurable solutions. Like most romances, Harlequin books create an almost entirely female circuit of communication: with few exceptions, it is female authors (all anglophone) who write the books; the mainly female team at Harlequin-France select appropriate novels for their market on the basis of rigorous consumer consultation; a team of largely female translators reproduce the texts in French; women readers buy, read, and often provide feedback; authors' guidelines reflect reader response. The aims of the company are straightforwardly commercial, but Harlequin's very effective marketing strategy demands sensitivity to readers' values and close attention to what they find sufficiently pleasurable to motivate repeated purchases. In its formulaic way, popular romance deals with questions that matter; moreover, these questions are equally central to many contemporary women-authored novels published and reviewed within the field of serious or elite literature.

What do the Harlequin novels provide then that can explain the scale and consistency of their success? There is no doubt about the efficiency of their narratives, which play apparently infinite variations on the same basic plot: meeting establishes the possibility of mutual desire, obstacles keep the reader in (often highly erotic) suspense until the inevitable, blissful closure in the couple's union. The attention Harlequin pay to their readers has certainly kept them alert to social change, and despite the fundamental similarities to the earlier twentieth-century *roman d'amour*, Harlequin romances clearly recognize that women's lives and identities have altered. Although gender difference remains central to the dynamics of the plot, the implied definition of what constitutes successful, desirable femininity and masculinity has changed in line with shifting performances of gender in the real world. The blonde fragility that characterized the heroines in Coquillat's corpus (Coquillat 1988: 25) has largely given way to more robust beauty, like that of the tall, auburn-haired Stéphanie in *Le Secret de la mariée* (*The Groom said Maybe!*), whose effect on the love-struck hero connotes power rather than the need for protection: 'Elle irradiait, brûlait comme un soleil' ('She radiated, she burnt like a sun', Marton 1999*b*: 26). Romance heroines have always had a certain feistiness about them, but the contemporary Harlequin heroine may well manifest this through professional success; she is no longer innocent and sexually passive but knowingly desiring, with sexual desire for the hero in many cases preceding love; in some series she tends to be older than her predecessors (in her thirties or forties), so that love arrives not as life's one great adventure, but initially (even if the reader knows better) as a complication in an already well-furnished existence. Female friendship plays a minor role, but secondary female characters are much more likely to be supportive friends in the background than (as in Delly) malicious rivals whose function is to confirm that emotional salvation lies only in the hero's arms. Heroes remain large, muscular, imposingly handsome, but to win the heroine's love they must respect her right to a degree of independence, often in the form of work.

Frequently, the clash between the romance's premiss of a one, true, transcendent love, and the social context of a world characterized by what Zygmunt Bauman describes as 'pair relationships... notorious for their institutional underdetermination, flexibility, mutability and fragility' (Bauman 1993: 1), is self-consciously acknowledged in the text. Unlike the popular romances of earlier periods, Harlequin plots unfold in a rootless, globalized society where transient commitments are the norm and there are no shared moral absolutes. Typically, the hero of *Épouse malgré elle* (*The Bride Said Never!*, Marton 1999*a*) begins the novel at his nephew's traditional church wedding, reflecting on the absurdity of the whole proceeding and of marriage itself, and planning a compensatory night of uncommitted sex with his mistress—though he will of course end it happily married to the heroine who erupts into his life immediately after these cynical musings. The credibility gap that the modern reader might encounter is recognized, respected, and enjoyably demolished as the protagonists themselves move from scepticism to belief, helpless before the evidence of overpowering emotion.

But the continuing appeal of the love story seems to depend as much on certain generic constants as on its capacity to reflect a changing social climate. As Janice Radway and other feminist critics have argued, the romance offers the female reader identification with a heroine who is the active agent of the narrative: it is her quest that structures the story, and this quest involves the negotiation of her needs and if necessary the transformation of the hero to meet these. 'Le véritable chasseur, celle qui mène la quête, c'est la femme' ('The real hunter and seeker here is the woman', Reuter 1990: 219). Thus Gina, the convent-educated and apparently ingénue heroine of *Le Fruit défendu* (*Educating Gina*, Rawlins, 2003), determinedly overcomes the scruples of the young man her uncle has asked to chaperone her around New York, becomes his lover, and ends the book married to him and engaged in the exciting career that her parents refused her. And the quest narrative can equally well be seen as the retelling of a story even more fundamental than that of romantic love: the romance, as argued above and as several critics have contended, restages a woman's Oedipal drama, and gives it a happy ending. The heroine always starts her story in some form of solitude, displaced from family, or from a familiar way of life, and at once vulnerable and determined to prove her autonomy. In what may be read as the stage of individuation and separation from the mother, she asserts herself as independent against her growing attraction to the hero. By at once resisting him—the hero is generally impressed by her spirit and competence—and by appealing to that deeper self concealed beneath his masculine arrogance, she wins his love and achieves a feeling of perfect, utopian wholeness ('enlacés dans les bras l'un de l'autre, ivres de bonheur' ('wrapped in each other's arms, drunk with happiness', Marton 1999a: 151). Thus she both wins the father's love (the hero is always larger, physically and metaphorically more powerful), and (less obviously but more interestingly) regains her lost union with the mother, that 'paradis perdu des origines, paradis d'autant plus interdit qu'il est homosexué' (Houel 1990: 278).[9] The big, authoritative but nurturing, sensual hero represents (in a culturally acceptable way) the maternal body lost to the girl child when the heterosexual imperative demands that she turn her desire toward the father, so that (as *La Bicyclette bleue* also showed) the romance satisfies in fantasy those needs that the female Oedipal drama leaves unmet.

This psychoanalytic interpretation is persuasive because it accounts for the mesmerizing, apparently limitless pull of the romance for many readers, the desire to relive again and again a happy version of a fundamental

---

[9] 'lost paradise of her origins, a paradise that is all the more forbidden because it is homosexual'.

drama of identity. It also helps to account for the strange survival of quite extreme forms of sexual difference in the romance, at a period when gender roles in western societies have seen a marked degree of convergence. The Harlequin hero, just like the Delly hero, is distinguished by his size, his bulk, and his hard, muscular body ('dur comme de l'acier', ('as hard as steel'), Marton 1999*a*: 65). These, like his air of male authority, are irresistible to the heroine (even if she finds him at first thoroughly objectionable[10]); conversely, in passages focalized by the hero, the heroine's curves, softness, and grace produce at once sexual arousal (described more or less explicitly depending on the series) and a fascinated tenderness that makes desire the sign of love. At one level, the accentuated difference between the two confirms the hero's function as a figure who blends the paternal and maternal; at another, it is a means of acknowledging the difficulty of reconciling utopian dreams of togetherness with a culture in which male and female aspirations and energies are still likely to diverge. This is registered through the heroine's initial pain at the hero's harshness or at his apparent separation of sex from love; the romance can then provide a fairytale resolution by revealing tenderness beneath the indifference, love as the true meaning of desire. There is clearly still some pleasure to be gained from identifying with the heroine's fear of male violence and will-to-domination, then discovering with her (or more often, before her) that behind the mask of aggression lies love. However, the fantastical (rather than realist) nature of such a resolution is implicitly recognized and indeed marked in most Harlequin romances. The stories are already located in an affluent, glamorous, and simplified world far removed from that of most readers, a 'dépaysement' (sense of pleasurable unfamiliarity) that is heightened for French (and other non-anglophone) readers by the characters' English names and the North American or occasionally English setting. At the point of romantic resolution, the narrative often shifts to a location more explicitly coded as fantasy: the couple find themselves alone in a luxurious house on an otherwise uninhabited island (*Noces de cristal*), on a small private Greek island (*Épouse malgré elle*), or simply in a pastoral rather than urban space. Here, in a world clearly marked out as imaginary, the utopian pleasure of perfect complementarity, and of desire uncomplicated by social or practical constraints, can be fantasized: it is in an empty hotel on a deserted island that Annie discovers that she

---

[10] Laura in *Épouse malgré elle*, faced with Damian's aggressive desire and assumption of knowledge about her feelings, experiences a desire to 'lui arracher les yeux' ('scratch his eyes out')—or alternatively 'de se jeter dans ses bras faire l'amour' ('to throw herself into his arms and make love to him', 49).

still loves and desires her divorced husband, and that the dominance she resists elsewhere in the plot becomes a source of erotic pleasure: 'D'un seul coup puissant, il prit possession d'elle. Anne sentit la vague l'emporter et se fracasser sur les rivages du plaisir' (Marton 1999c: 128).[11] The Harlequin-France editors were eager to point out, in interview, that the 'relation fantasmatique' ('fantasized relations') of extreme sexual difference diminished, in Harlequin novels, in proportion to the realism of plot and setting.

Perhaps it could also be argued, if more tentatively, that the accentuation of *difference* works to address an important ethical issue that both encompasses and transcends that of gender: the relationship between self and other, the tension between respect for the other's difference—their otherness or alterity—and sufficient acknowledgement of sameness to encompass caring, concern, and equality. Clearly, the Harlequin romance is unlikely to be informed by theoretical work on ethics,[12] or to offer any analytical discussion of such issues. Nonetheless, one of the most fundamental forms of encounter between self and other is the erotic encounter, about which popular romance in its highly repetitive yet endlessly varied way continues to speak, mainly to women. Beyond the marked bodily differences between them, hero and heroine experience each other as incomprehensible, enigmatic, seductive precisely because each is irreducible to the other's ways of thinking and feeling. For the novel to conclude, they must both discover the common human ground beneath the sexual difference (she recognizing his softness and he her capacity for 'hard' independence) and maintain the seductive sense of each other's otherness: the constraints of the genre ensure that the story stops short of a domestic familiarity that would attenuate alterity. Although desire, paradoxically, wills the destruction of that space between self and other that impedes total fusion, impelling the subject in Zygmunt Bauman's terms to 'close the gap to alterity' (Bauman 2003: 9), the Harlequin romance ends with two still radically different people locked in each other's arms. Difference here is figured solely as the most clichéd form of sexual difference—but it could also be read as evoking that irreducibly unknown quality of all other human beings, and as registering the ambivalence of desire that both depends on separation, and longs to obliterate it in total fusion with the other.

---

[11] 'With one powerful thrust, he took her. Annie felt the wave carry her away and break on the shores of pleasure.'

[12] The work of theorists such as Lévinas and Bauman has made the self/other relation one of the key ethical issues of the age. See Lévinas 1989; Bauman 1993.

In *Liquid Love*, Bauman writes of the 'radical overhaul of kinship structures' in the late twentieth century: with a far weaker material and social imperative to tie sex and falling in love to lifelong heterosexual unions, individual freedom is increased, but sex and relationships are also in danger of becoming consumer activities, only sustained until a better product appears, satisfying the confident, active, curious aspect of the self, but also producing anxiety and fear. 'Sex stripped of its former social standing and socially endorsed meanings encapsulated the harrowing and alarming uncertainty that was to become the major bane of liquid modern living' (Bauman 2003: 51). The inclination to connect sex with emotional commitment may well be stronger in women, because of their early emotional development,[13] because the sexual double standard has by no means disappeared from contemporary western culture, and because women still form the large majority of primary carers for children, with or without a partner. One of the reasons for the success of contemporary Harlequin novels is undoubtedly their capacity to provide imaginary good sex, in a way that satisfies their readers by reconnecting eroticism with affective needs, and indeed with ethics. The plots promise but delay satisfaction, heightening sexual tension by narrative devices that keep the couple in physical proximity, but prevent them from making love, until at last the reader is offered the vicarious enjoyment of a top of the range, star-quality male body ('très grand, athlétique, ténébreux' ('very big, athletic, and dark'), Marton 1999*b*: 17), revealing when naked 'une virilité aussi impressionante qu'elle se l'était imaginée' ('a virility as impressive as she had imagined', ibid.: 69), plus skilful and sensitive lovemaking, and always, essentially, the revelation that the true meaning of desire is love. When the hero—making love to her for the first time—says, 'je veux tout connaitre de vous' ('I want to know all of you', ibid.: 67), the reader knows that this goes far beyond the desire to explore her body. In interview, the Harlequin-France editors were adamant that 'il y a une éthique dans le roman Harlequin' ('there is an ethic in the Harlequin novel') and that any failure to respect this would alienate readers: the ethic is that while sex is no longer tied to marriage, good sex unites body and emotions, passion and tenderness, and forms the basis for a long-term relationship. In its often banal prose, and despite its clichéd representations of gendered bodies and roles, Harlequin romance still contains a utopian defence of sexual intercourse as necessarily also emotional intercourse, based on a 'two-way recognition of the difference of the other, separate from the subject' (Abel-Hirsch 2001: 3).

[13] See Ch. 1.

Le bonheur est à tous: lesbian popular romance

Harlequin romances can be argued to stage the thrill and the difficulty of self/other relations, but their representation of difference is extremely limited. All the characters in French Harlequin novels are white,[14] and all romances are heterosexual. Lesbian romances can be found in France, many of them translated from English-language texts, but there is no series of 'formula' romances available for the lesbian reader. It was to fill this gap that Marine Rambach and Anne Rousseau, founders of the publishing company Éditions Gaies et Lesbiennes, invented *Le Bonheur est à Tout le Monde* (Happiness is for Everyone), a collection of gay and lesbian romances. The popular romance, they argue in their editors' foreword, 'avec ses conventions, son style enflammé, ses intrigues passionnées', is a 'merveilleuse machine à fantasmes'[15]—but is positively hostile to homosexuality. Their series will extend the 'bonheur' of romance reading to gay and lesbian readers.

Les Lois de l'amour (The Laws of Love), Rambach and Rousseau's 1998 novel, duly follows the narrative structure of the Harlequin romance: an encounter marked by a *coup de foudre* or sudden, intense, mutual attraction, the struggle against a series of obstacles, closure with the final, ecstatically happy union of the couple. As with Harlequin, the plot takes the reader to enjoyably glamorous and exotic settings: if the action is centred on Paris, the two women's more idyllic encounters transport us to the snowy coastal cliffs of Brittany in winter, the banks of the Bosporus, and (albeit more semi-pastoral than glamorous) the zoo at Vincennes. The difference lies in the nature of the obstacles that divide the lovers and, inevitably, since gender can no longer figure the lover's alterity, in the way that otherness is presented and resolved.

Chiara is a helicopter pilot who works for a medical rescue team. At a car crash on a snowy motorway, she rescues an extraordinarily beautiful, dark-skinned young woman, who turns out to be a Turkish student, Zeyneb. Chiara's efforts to trace the girl she cannot stop thinking about fail, but the two meet by chance in a lesbian nightclub in Paris, and despite Zeyneb's initial reluctance, they maintain contact and soon become passionate lovers. Two linked factors divide them. One is Zeyneb's emotional turmoil, torn as she is between family and love, for though

---

[14] This was confirmed by the editors at Harlequin-France. A small number of original English-language Harlequins do have non-white heroes or heroines, but despite the marketing of Harlequin-France in non-metropolitan francophone countries, to date Harlequin-France have published none of these.

[15] 'with its conventions, its colourful style, its passionate plots' is a 'wonderful fantasy machine'.

she is desperately homesick, she has fled to France because her own culture imposes heterosexuality, if necessary by force. The other is French immigration policy, for Zeyneb, like many of her friends, is a 'sans-papiers' or illegal immigrant, whose stay permit has run out with little hope of renewal. Zeyneb's clandestine status at first merely limits their affair, but halfway through the narrative she is caught and forcibly expelled from France. In a dramatic dénouement, Chiara borrows a yacht and, with the help of two American lesbian friends, rescues Zeyneb from Istanbul and carries her back to France. Peace is made from a distance with Zeyneb's (relatively liberal) Muslim family, and the two hope, if uncertainly, for a future legalization of Zeyneb's status. The novel closes with the same inseparability of desire, love, and mutual commitment as a Harlequin romance:

> Leur avenir était incertain mais cette incertitude n'était pas de leur fait. Sous leurs paupières suspendues, dans leurs pupilles brillantes, dans leur respiration commune, leur amour se lisait, indiscutable et confiant. Les lèvres se joignirent dans un baiser profond. Déjà renaissait en elles ce qui les avait à peine quitté: le désir.[16] (137)

The conservatism of the mainstream popular romance is thus reversed to show that the formula can accommodate a very different politics, on both sexual orientation and ethnicity, without ceasing to be an effective 'machine à fantasmes'.

The authors' aim here is to reproduce the absorbing but undemanding narrative style, and the erotic charge, that characterize contemporary formula romance. This demands rapid, colourful characterization, and sufficient difference between characters to produce the shock of desire and some degree of potential conflict, which the narrative can then resolve. In the Harlequin romance, this is largely achieved through an exaggerated form of gender difference: the source of attraction and conflict between hero and heroine is their opposed, but finally complementary, sexual identity. Here difference must be established in some other way. Chiara and Zeyneb are immediately differentiated by nationality and background, and by appearance, the former tall, lean, short-haired and the latter smaller, dark, curly-haired, and strikingly pretty. The distribution of qualities between them maps to some extent onto traditional gender roles. Chiara is exceptionally tall and slender,

---

[16] 'Their future was uncertain, but this uncertainty was not of their doing. Under their half-open eyelids, in their shining eyes, the shared rhythm of their breath, their love was visible, undeniable, and confident. Their lips met in a deep kiss. Already that force that had scarcely left them was returning to life: desire.'

confident, tough, and professionally skilled; Zeyneb is shorter, softer in appearance, and her illegal situation also makes her more vulnerable. Because of her legal status and practical competence, Chiara is the more active agent in the plot: she rescues Zeyneb twice, the second time with all the dash and adventure of the fairytale hero. However, the authors are careful to avoid a simple reproduction of gender stereotypes: both women are strong and independent (Zeyneb makes a living on the black market as a plumber), and the erotic scenes allocate active and passive roles very evenly. Moreover, when the distribution of activity/passivity, or hardness/softness between two characters is no longer tied to gender, it can be deployed to create a sense of complementarity in love without at the same time confirming deeply rooted social inequalities.

As we might expect, secondary female characters play a more important role here than in the Harlequin novels. Whereas in Harlequin (or Delly), all the key scenes in the progression of romance are played out between the couple alone, Chiara and Zeyneb spend one of their happiest days in the women-only space of a hamman (steam baths) in Paris, in the company of several other gay, immigrant women, most of them with insecure legal status in France. The sensual pleasures of this 'royaume perdu' ('lost kingdom', 76), with its warm, fragrantly steamy rooms and icy blue pools, extend those of the specifically—and graphically—erotic scenes, and provide a plausible setting for the women to tell their stories which echo and elaborate on Zeyneb's own.

The market for the lesbian formula romance is undoubtedly a lot smaller than that for heterosexual *romans d'amour*, and the apparently limited success of this collection may reflect this—as well, of course, as reflecting the commercial might of a multinational company like Harlequin.[17] Both hetero- and homosexual romance for women now provide their readers with a form of mild pornography, that is, with texts part of whose pleasure lies in the creation of sexual tension and its vicarious, always perfect satisfaction, and whilst there can be pleasure in reading about forms of sexuality not one's own, most readers, given the choice, will choose a story that reflects their own desires. Indeed, this is the premiss of the Rambach and Rousseau collection. Romance of either sexual persuasion can address the tensions between the desire for active autonomy and the desire to be loved and possessed, between the attraction of alterity and the fear it can provoke—but only in the

---

[17] So far, only three titles seem to have appeared in the series. The two lesbian novels *Cœur contre cœur* (1997) and *Les Lois de l'amour* (1998) have been republished in a single volume (2005). *Embarquement pour l'amour* (1997) is a love story between two men.

heterosexual romance are these mapped onto gender in a way that reflects the experience of the majority of women. What this experiment with a 'lesbian Harlequin' demonstrates is that the formula romance does not have to be politically conservative in order to produce the readers' pleasure: that it is not tied exclusively to a heterosexual script, nor to its current very limited view of ethnicity, nor to an exoticism that depends solely on the celebration of affluence.

Romance in literary fiction and film: Emmanuèle Bernheim

The narrative structures and themes that typify mass-market romance form part of a broader cultural climate and reappear, albeit somewhat differently, in love stories that seek to present a more original and personal vision. Amongst the plethora of women-authored fictions that have recently appeared in France, many are centrally concerned with love and address the thematic concerns of romance, some of them through the deployment of the romance narrative. Where the popular and the literary differ is in the degree of resolution they provide: the function of the Harlequin romance is to provide an imaginary experience of needs happily fulfilled, whereas 'literary' novels may explore needs and desires in their tension with reality, and without offering solutions.

Emmanuèle Bernheim (b. 1955) is the author of five short novels (published 1985-2002) and several film screenplays. In 1993 she won the Prix Médicis for her novel *Sa femme* (translated as *The Other Woman*), the brief, spare narrative of a woman doctor's passionate affair with a married man, and the unexpected contraction of desire that tinges her delight when she discovers that the wife and children who have stood in the way of their relationship do not in fact exist. In *Vendredi soir* (Friday Night), Bernheim's elliptical, pared-down narrative style condenses a love story into a single night. Laure is on the eve of moving out of her own flat to begin a shared life with her boyfriend François. Driving across Paris to see friends on that last evening, she finds herself caught in the traffic jam caused by a public transport strike, gives a lift to a stranded pedestrian, and ends up spending a passionate night with him in a hotel. The *coup de foudre* is unspoken but mutual and unmistakable. Into their one night together are compressed the main components of a shared life: they make love, share a room and a bed, go out to eat and drink together and return to the now familiar bedroom: 'Ça y est. Ils étaient chez eux' ('There—they were back home', Bernheim 1998: 61). In the very early morning, Laure leaves to return to her life, and to move in with François.

Vendredi soir has all the elements of romance, whilst being very much a novel of the 1990s. This is the heroine's story: Bernheim's characteristically laconic, third-person narration makes Laure the principal focalizer throughout, her voice at times inflecting the tone of the narration with the use of *style indirect libre*, as in the example above where the present tense 'ça y est', like the sense of the room being 'chez eux', belong to Laure rather than the narrator.[18] Though the heroine has a profession (she is a radiographer), a sketched-in past, and friends, and though the city is an important context for the story, the narrative focus remains unswervingly on the relationship between the central couple. Laure, like so many heroines of the popular romance, starts her journey at a transitional point in her life, alone and in an unfamiliar, unnerving setting (here the gridlocked city). The chance encounter carries an odd sense of fatality: Laure notices the man, and assumes from his expression that he is seeking someone, 'une femme sans doute' ('a woman, no doubt', 16), among the drivers, but when his face registers recognition and he heads for a car, it is her own. He has the mystery (Laure and the reader learn nothing beyond his name, Frédéric), the competence (at one point he takes over and drives the car, well), and the irresistibly seductive aura of the hero, the latter signified here by his smell of mingled 'tabac, cuir et eau de toilette' ('tobacco, leather, and cologne', 19)[19] of which Laure is immediately and intensely aware. If the mutual nature of this attraction is implied by his unexplained choice of her car, as by his willingness to entrust himself to her ('Déposez-moi où vous voulez, n'importe où' ('Drop me wherever you like, anywhere will do'), 17), their coming together is delayed by a series of classic romance obstacles. Laure loses him when she suddenly misreads his prolonged presence in her car as a threat, imagining possible rape or kidnap; he walks off into the night, and she pursues him, finding him, to her relief, in a café. There are imagined rivals, like the young girl playing pinball in the café, and later the woman in the pizzeria where they go to eat, with whom Laure imagines him making love. But fear and jealousy—both components of and impediments to

---

[18] So central is Laure's point of view that the novel has sometimes been mis-described as a first-person narrative (e.g., Dawson 1993).

[19] Colette uses precisely the same combination of smells to connote seductive masculinity: Farou's hands in *La Seconde* (The Other One) carry a sensual 'odeur de peau brune, de tabac, de lotion parfumée' ('smell of dark skin, tobacco and scented lotion', Colette 1991b: iii. 414) that Fanny finds irresistible; in *Le Toutounier* what most poignantly evokes the memory of her dead husband for Alice is 'la faible odeur de cuir, d'eau de toilette parfumée, de tabac et de papier imprimée' ('the faint smell of leather, toilet water, tobacco and printer's ink', Colette 1991c: iii. 1237) that lingers in his study.

desire—are resolved in his arms: the sense of uniqueness, transcendence, and transformation of the self that characterize romantic love are present here.

> Elle lui sourit.
> Et, sans se voir, elle sut que jamais encore elle n'avait souri ainsi.[20] (61)

Vendredi soir, then, follows the narrative structure of the romance. It is also firmly on romance territory in the tension between *amour-passion* and socialized love that determines the novel's ending. Laure's planned cohabitation with François is not presented as an unwanted social obligation: neither family nor convention has obliged her to make this decision, rather, she has made a free choice to move to a more secure, economical, and agreeable organization of her life, based on the couple's mutual affinity. Nonetheless, the loss of her own living space, car (François insists they can manage with one), and right to irresponsibility is depicted, in Bernheim's understated way, as painful:

> Elle leva les yeux vers les deux fenêtres, tout là-haut. Chez elle.
> Depuis huit ans et pour une nuit encore, c'était chez elle.[21] (11)

Though we never meet François, he is aligned with reason, order, and the limitation of possibilities: despite being Laure's freely chosen partner, he represents a socialized form of heterosexual union that shapes and limits her. Once she moves in with him, she is to give up her car, which in the story means not only her mobility but also the space of her desire; François is the dispenser of rational knowledge (wondering why '16 valve' written on the car in front has no plural 's', Laure reflects that 'Elle poserait la question à François. Il saurait' ('She would ask François. He would know', 15)), and the red skirt she puts on as part of her seduction of the stranger is a garment François has always hated. François constitutes the reality of a future life, but he does not belong within the charmed circle of desire.

The episode that forms the plot, on the other hand, is situated outside 'normal' time and space, in a city immobilized out of its familiar routine, on an evening when no one knows Laure's whereabouts, and she can enjoy a last reassertion of the free self she is about to sacrifice for the sake of a reasonable happiness.

---

[20] 'She smiled at him.
And though she could not see herself, she knew that she had never before smiled in that way.'
[21] 'She looked up at the two windows, way up there. Her home.
For the last eight years, and for one more night, this was her home.'

Personne ne l'attendait. Personne ne savait où elle se trouvait.
Ce soir, elle aussi, elle était seule.
Et elle était libre.[22] (44)

The current of desire that connects Laure and Frédéric is outside any social framework: they know nothing of each other's lives, they scarcely use language, each steps outside the determining logic of the everyday to give themselves over to chance and to the other: 'Elle eut la certitude qu' . . . elle aurait pu l'emmener où elle voulait' ('She was suddenly certain that she could have driven him wherever she liked', 29); 'Il pouvait l'emmener où il voulait' ('He could take her wherever he liked', 35). The syntactical simplicity of Bernheim's style, with its single-clause sentences and near absence of grammatical connectives, renders the way that sensual and affective experience take over from the logic of reason. The world is apprehended through sight, smell, touch, but far from being a hedonistic interlude that asserts an asocial desire for uncommitted pleasure, this fleeting relationship is both passionate and full of tenderness for the other: a tenderness signified by small gestures like his insertion of his hand into her glove, to join hers, her gentle caressing of his blistered foot, their identical choices from the menu in the restaurant. The intensity of feeling for this unknown man is such that Laure briefly envisages changing her plans, and merging this unexpected episode into her 'real' life:

Soudain son sourire se figea
Elle ne pourrait plus quitter cet homme.[23] (97)

If she re-emerges from the hotel to resume the life she had briefly left, it is because the novel suggests perhaps not an absolute incompatibility, but at least a radical tension between *amour-passion* and socialized love. Laure has glimpsed a sensual and emotional intensity that leaves her both saddened and enriched—she ends the novel in a taxi on her way back to the flat, smoothing down the red skirt over her thighs—but that ecstatic intensity, by its very nature, could only be glimpsed in the suspended time of the defamiliarized city. There is no magical Harlequin-style convergence of passion and social existence, nor any sense of a conflict between them caused by oppressive social institutions, and hence—in the longer term—perhaps resolvable. The romance here has little impact

---

[22] 'No one was waiting for her. No one knew where she was.
This evening, she was alone too.
And she was free.'
[23] 'Suddenly her smile froze. She would be unable to leave this man.'

on the overall narrative of its heroine's life. Martine Beugnet's comment on the ending of Claire Denis's film of *Vendredi soir* can equally well be applied to the novel itself: it 'belong(s) to the postmodern in so far as [its] denial of the comfort of the progressive unfolding and of the "logical" ending seems to echo the contemporary fading of the belief in safe, "grand narratives" ' (Beugnet 2004: 43).

Claire Denis's 2002 film of *Vendredi soir*, co-scripted by Bernheim herself, is at once closely faithful to the novel and intensely cinematic. It thus highlights some of the particular qualities of Bernheim's novel, and raises a question that is largely outside the scope of this study but may be briefly addressed here: how does the romance narrative translate into cinema? Like women novelists, women film directors in France have demonstrated some predilection for and fascination with the love story: late twentieth-century examples include Coline Serreau (*Romuald et Juliette*, 1989), Diane Kurys (*Un homme amoureux*, 1987; *Après l'amour*, 1992; *Les Enfants du siècle*, 2002), Tonie Marshall (*Vénus beauté*, 1999), although the romance has only been one of a wide variety of genres French women directors have chosen to develop.[24] And in the case of cinema, male directors have been equally willing to explore the genre—the majority of French directors have made romance films, and many of the most celebrated love stories in French cinema have been directed by men, from Marcel Carné's *Quai des brumes* (1938), to François Truffaut's *Jules et Jim* (1961), and on to (most recently) Jean-Pierre Jeunet's *Le Fabuleux Destin d'Amélie Poulain* (*Amélie*, 2001) and *Un long dimanche de fiançailles* (*A Very Long Engagement*, 2004).This is certainly due, at least in part, to the fact that female directors came late to the medium, with only a handful of women behind the camera until the 1980s, whereas women were known to make up a substantial part of the cinema audience. In film as in literature, romance has been assumed to be a genre that appeals particularly to women ('the women's film'), but—in France perhaps more than in the USA and Britain—it has also been a genre well received by both sexes, and one that (given the small numbers of women in the profession) has attracted more male than female directors.

Denis reproduces the novel's central narrative focus on the meeting, magical night together, and return to normality, though certain filmic techniques enable her to add a new dimension by situating the single love story within all the other potential stories that a city contains: a long opening pan across lighted windows precedes the singling out of

---

[24] See Tarr (2001).

Laure's window, and Laure's story; similarly, the traffic jam produces a number of unrealized encounters, signified by close-ups on the faces of drivers and passers-by, before the main encounter occurs (Beugnet 2004: 186). The novel's use of its heroine as the principal focalizer translates into the film's rendering of her impressions through point-of-view shots, and through a soundtrack that includes both ambient noise and a musical score whose long, insistent chords are sometimes urgent, and sometimes poignantly gentle. Laure's car feels like a warm refuge from the cold, chaotic world outside its windows, and the desirable aura of the stranger is conveyed by close-ups of his hands and profile, from Laure's perspective, and by the way she feels and smells the lingering warmth of his hands on the driving wheel. The sense of inexplicable rightness that each has in the other's presence is vividly evoked by their physical ease—his relaxed body as he settles into the passenger seat, her drowsiness once he is beside her—and by the minimal dialogue. The sense of a banal reality magically transformed is created through the slow ballet of the semi-motionless cars, light reflecting off their metal surfaces, filmed through a mixture of smooth travelling shots and gentle dissolves, whilst Laure's sudden fear of Jean (his name is changed in the film) as a potentially dangerous stranger is registered through the sudden speed of both camera movement and montage, as he finds a less crowded route and drives them through dark unknown streets. Denis finds a filmic equivalent for Bernheim's spare narrative style, with its lack of syntactical connections, in her use of dissolves, simple cuts, fades to black and even (once) an iris to link narrative events, Laure's perceptions and imaginings, and a wider 'third-person' vision of the city, in a montage that is more impressionistic than tightly chronological.

Denis's film also maintains the novel's discreet and unglamourized sensuality. Rather than the perfect choreography of passion that marks the union of Harlequin lovers,[25] desire in both the novel and the film of *Vendredi soir* is realized in a world that includes cold hotel bedrooms, awkward layers of clothing, and the need to purchase condoms. In the film, the couple's first kisses, filmed in extreme close-up and without a musical soundtrack, are warm and slightly clumsy, as are their movements when making love. Neither actor has a flawless star body, and the camera frames not the standard signifiers of the erotic (breasts, chests, buttocks) but rather two bodies entwined, and from an angle so close that it precludes any harmonious aesthetic patterning of the scene. The perspective is essentially Laure's: sex here is the urgently passionate

---

[25] Harlequin sex works smoothly and perfectly, bringing to mind Erica Jong's eloquent phrase the 'zipless fuck' (Jong 1973).

fulfilment of the desire so vividly evoked in the film by the scenes of close proximity in the car, and it is suffused with tenderness for the liberating otherness of this casual stranger, and for the details of his physical presence. Yet when Laure leaves him to return to her own life, the dawn light on the empty streets, the rapturous slow motion with which Denis films her run towards her abandoned car, convey too the exhilaration of choosing 'the familiar logic of a known reality' (Beugnet 2004: 191). There is no happy-ever-after convergence of passionate desire with a socially viable future, but nor does the ending of the romantic encounter mean the grim acceptance of an impoverished reality. Laure chooses to leave her romance behind, but also carries the experience with her into her chosen future. *Vendredi soir* provides a concise illustration of how the romance narrative, with its representation of female subjectivity and desire, can lend itself equally well to cinematic form.

In defence of romance: Camille Laurens

Camille Laurens (b. 1957) was already the author of four well-received novels, a brief memoir (*Philippe,* 1995), and an essay on language (*Quelques-uns*, 1999), when she published two auto-fictional texts that are mainly about love. *Dans ces bras-là* (2000) deploys, semi-parodically, the narrative structure of romance. A framing narrative opens with the narrator-heroine's *coup de foudre* for a stranger; since he turns out to be a psychotherapist, she becomes his patient, and the therapeutic relationship between them both mirrors the growing intimacy of the conventional romance plot, and finally merges with it when her attempts to seduce him conclude in partial success. Meanwhile, the novel explores the central themes of romance through the narrator's memories and reflections on sexual difference, on male otherness, and on desire.[26] Like *Dans ces bras-là*, but more explicitly, *L'Amour, roman* draws attention to its own connections to the popular love story. The novel follows an auto-fictional thread of plot to underpin a complex reflection on love, which also becomes a defence of the centrality of romance in women's culture.

The narrative of *L'Amour, roman* follows its auto-fictional narrator, Camille, as she writes a book on the seventeenth-century author of maxims and memoirs La Rochefoucauld, goes through a painful break-up from her husband Yves, and lives a passionate affair with the film director Jacques Blin. Onto this framework of plot are woven her reflections, which

---

[26] The reworking of romance conventions in *Dans ces bras-là* is discussed in more detail in Holmes (2005*a*).

follow three main paths: the interrogation of her own life experience, both contemporaneous with the composition of the text, and through memory; the re-creation of the lives, and especially the love stories, of three preceding generations of her female family (mother, grandmother, great-grandmother); the citation of and commentary on other texts, from La Rochefoucauld's celebrated maxims, to Paul Géraldy's once popular, now forgotten love poetry, and the lyrics of popular love songs. The experience of love and its cultural representations are seen to interact, language determining as much as representing the way that love is lived: 'L'amour, c'est des mots, et le mot invente la chose; aimer, c'est donner au sentiment qu'on éprouve le nom d'amour' (Laurens 2003: 36).[27]

The love story is represented as an important form of female legacy and exchange between generations. Up to the narrator's own generation, born after the Second World War, the choice of husband is the single most determining factor in a woman's adult life: the lives of mother, grandmother, and great-grandmother are remembered and imagined mainly in terms of their romantic relationships with men, and hence of the love stories that they have handed down. It is not simply a matter of one-way transmission: each story is retrospectively re-created as each generation embroiders the past in the colours of their own experience, and according to shifting cultural paradigms of love: 'on brode, on invente, on entremêle les leurs et les nôtres, on n'est pas fidèle, mais qu'importe?' (16).[28] Despite their different generational experiences, love is a shared terrain of encounter and exchange: Sophie (b. 1889) and her great-granddaughter Camille (b. 1957) both read and are moved by the poetry of Géraldy,[29] a poetry situated, like romantic fiction, on a fine line between banal sentimentality and compelling emotion. The novel begins with the narrator's grandmother walking in on a 20-year-old Camille making love with her boyfriend in the grandmother's house, and asking later, anxious and genuinely uncertain, the question that will form the book's refrain: 'est-ce que c'est ça, l'amour?' ('is that what love is?'). The process of shared reflection on the experience and language of love is both narrated and performed by the novel, as Laurens extends the chain of transmitted stories to the reader.

[27] 'Love is words, and the word invents the thing itself; to love is to give to one's emotion the name of love.'

[28] 'We embroider, invent, mingle their stories with our own, our versions are not faithful to theirs, but what does it matter?'

[29] Paul Géraldy (1885–1983) was a poet and playwright whose work, sentimental and popular, was mainly concerned with love and couple relationships. His readership was (at least assumed to be) mainly female. In the novel, Camille rediscovers her copy of Géraldy's 1913 poetry collection, *Toi et moi*, and recalls how the poems moved her when, aged 12, she read them in an original edition that had belonged to her great-grandmother.

In the narrator's reconstruction of each generation's love story, and in the primary narrative of her own, the ideal of *amour passion* constantly comes up against a more complex and compromised reality of unfaithful or disappearing husbands, unintended pregnancies, new loves replacing the old, the fading of desire repeatedly symbolized by the replacement of the marital double bed by twin beds. Laurens's text is situated not in the mythical world of romance, but on the awkward, conflicted territory of late twentieth-century couple relationships. Yet, despite this sustained demonstration of the gap between myth and experience, the novel defends the romantic ideal as a valuable female legacy, handed down from each generation to the next, like the never-used crystal glasses that Camille inherits in her turn, glasses 'qui ne sont là que pour être transmis, . . . un secret qu'on raconterait de mère en fille . . . comme une Idée de l'amour, un idéal: une belle forme à la beauté transparente, dont on ne saurait jouir sans la voir voler en éclats' (203).[30] In practice, the ideal is unlivable, but Laurens refuses to see women's dreams of perfect love as dangerous delusions that simply sugar the pill of oppression. Though Camille acknowledges the value of positive role models for girls, and the achievement of feminists in banishing from children's literature the passive 'femmes à la fenêtre, symbole de l'emprisonnement et de l'attente du prince charmant' (218),[31] she also defends the right to dream at the window, for to imagine the ideal lover is a creative act, a means of transcending through imagination the contradictions of the human condition: 'Est-ce qu'on fait autrement pour les poèmes et les romans? Est-ce qu'on fait autre chose que d'espérer ce qui ne vient jamais—la forme pure, le souffle divin, le mot juste?' (221).[32] 'Le Prince Charmant' represents not a naively idealized version of a limited destiny, but a utopian imagining of a relation with the other that combines freedom and belonging, that maintains the other's difference while closing the painful gap of separation, and that satisfies desire without destroying it: 'quelque chose qu'on pourrait saisir sans détruire le désir qu'on a de lui?' (221).[33] *L'Amour, roman*, like the *romans d'amour* it constantly evokes, expresses a doubly utopian aspiration: to the experience of desire as a passionate curiosity about and tenderness for the other, which affirms the identity of each ('dans son lit', she writes of the affair with Jacques,

---

[30] 'which are only there in order to be passed on, . . . a secret told by mothers to daughters . . . like an Idea of love, an ideal: a lovely form of transparent beauty, impossible to enjoy without seeing it fly apart into tiny pieces'.

[31] 'women at the window, the symbol of imprisonment and of the wait for Prince Charming'.

[32] 'Is what we do with poems and novels any different? Are we not simply hoping for that which never comes—the pure and perfect form, the divine breath, the exact word?'

[33] 'something that one can grasp without destroying the desire for it?'.

'je me retrouve'[34]) and extends it (in a characteristic play on words, 'connaître l'autre' becomes 'co-naître, naître au monde avec lui' (22));[35] and to a form of desire for the other that is confirmed rather than abolished by its own realization. Camille's own experiences of love deny its permanence—she is in the process of leaving Yves, of whom she had thought 'C'est Lui' ('he's the One', 49), and the affair with Jacques is uncertain and painful—but the book's words and narrative are spun from the imagination of a perfect love, and from its glimpses in experience.

The difference between Laurens's text and a Harlequin novel, apart from their very different degrees of narrative and linguistic complexity, is that the latter provides an imaginary experience of this perfection, always stopping short before the divergence between dream and reality makes the 'Idéal de l'amour' (in Laurens's words) 'voler en éclats' ('the Ideal of love fly apart into tiny pieces', 203). Laurens's novel, on the other hand, deals with the painful but often creative tension between the ideal and the real: like *Vendredi soir*, it refuses both of the traditional forms of closure to the romance narrative, ending neither happily, with the perfect union of the lovers, nor tragically, with their separation. Rather, it defends the practice of seeking and imagining ideal love, both reflecting and reflecting on the centrality of the romance script to women's lives and culture across the generations.

> Voilà pourquoi il ne faut pas éloigner les petites filles des fenêtres dans les manuels scolaires, mais y mettre les petits garçons—parce que le visage à la fenêtre, c'est le rêve, c'est l'art et c'est l'amour: ni la prison, ni l'oisivité, non, au contraire, une activité riche d'avenir—une libre pratique de l'impossible.[36] (222)

Conclusion

If the mass-market romance continues to provide the traditional satisfactions of clearly patterned narrative and neatly happy closure (though even there, we have seen some self-conscious highlighting of the gap between reality and fiction), the literary romance of the late 1990s and early 2000s shares the edgy self-awareness and the suspicion of too much

---

[34] 'in his bed, I re-find myself.'

[35] 'connaître l'autre' means 'to know the other'. Broken down into 'co-naître', the verb means 'to be born with', hence 'to be born with him, to come into the world with him'.

[36] 'So that is why we should not take little girls away from their windows in the textbooks, but rather put little boys there too—because to gaze out of the window is to dream, it is art, and love: it's not a prison, or idleness, no, on the contrary, it is an activity full of future—a free practice of the impossible.'

coherence that characterize the postmodern sensibility. The underlying presence of a whole tradition of romance is not merely implicit in contemporary love stories: with a typically postmodern emphasis on intertextuality, they point to their own reworkings of classic romance plots and formulations,[37] and thus reflect on the ways in which romantic narrative at once gives expression to shared emotions, and plays its own part in the cultural construction of love. Contemporary literary romances also refuse, on the whole, to deploy the genre's 'grand narratives'. Marriage is no longer to the same extent the central, defining event or absence in a woman's life, and this social change is in harmony with a broader cultural scepticism about absolute values and definitive life choices. Modern love stories end neither in perfect closure in the lover's arms, nor in tragic separation, nor in a painful but finally positive renunciation of love in the name of freedom. Rather, the stories tend to end with the heroine's life continuing in its complicated, multi-stranded, familiar reality, touched, altered, enriched by love, but not fundamentally reordered. Generic continuity is strong: like earlier romances, both popular and literary, these novels make love the driving force of their narrative, and represent love as a uniquely privileged form of self/other encounter, an emotion composed of both tenderness and passion, sameness and difference, an extraordinary experience of plenitude that opens up the world. Passionate love is highly valued, but rather than the unique transformative experience of a woman's life, it is cast as an ideal to be endlessly re-imagined, provisionally experienced, handed on through art, treasured as a glimpse of how relations with the other may be.

---

[37] In Christine Jordis's *La Chambre blanche*, the coolly erudite narrator is contemptuous of her culture's vulgarization of emotion, but the experience of falling in love convinces her of 'la vérité profonde des contes de fées' ('the deep truth of fairy tales', 46), and her subsequent narration of the experience of love and desire reproduces many of the commonplaces of romantic discourse. For example, she describes the sense that in the lover's arms is the only place that she belongs: 'pressée contre lui, serrée à étouffer, comme pour annuler toute distance entre nos deux corps, enfermée dans ses bras, le seul lieu au monde auquel je me sentais appartenir' ('pressed against him, held so tightly that I couldn't breathe, as if to cancel any distance between our bodies, held in his arms, the only place in the world I felt that I belonged' (Jordis 2003: 107).

Conclusion

The romance has been one of the twentieth century's most popular and enduring forms of fiction. Consistency of narrative structure, themes, and values justify its definition as a genre, or as a distinct sub-genre of (primarily) the novel, but this consistency has gone hand in hand with extreme flexibility: the romance, as we have seen, has accommodated a broad spectrum of political views, addressed readers of all social classes, appeared at all levels of the hierarchy of literary distinction, from mass-market 'formula' fiction to the avant-garde novel. Its appeal for readers has survived world wars, women's political emancipation, changes of regime, feminist attacks, critical ridicule, and massive upheavals in the publishing trade, to leave it, at the start of the twenty-first century, still perhaps the most widely read story form, from the popular to the most literary end of the market. Romance has also remained a genre primarily produced and consumed by women.

One reason for this is straightforwardly historical: because, for most of the century, the achievement of economic and social independence has been made much harder for a woman than a man, the whole process of finding a life-partner and negotiating the terms of relationship has been more central to women's lives, in a very practical as well as an emotional sense. The romance plot has addressed a set of issues that have been of unavoidable importance to most women. What kind of man is worthy of love and can make his partner happy? How might he be won, and at what cost? Can personal freedom and integrity be compatible with a permanent relationship, when marriage is an institution firmly imprinted with patriarchal values? How can one adapt to the demands of a new, shared life? Can passion be reconciled with the permanence of commitment? What happens if the object of passion is not a member of the opposite sex, but of one's own? Is romantic love a heartfelt emotion, or the imaginary signified of a powerful and omni-present cultural discourse? The romance, in many instances, has explored such questions, proposing and evaluating alternative responses, revealing and contesting the ideologies of love and sexuality that have privileged men's needs and desires. For the reader, this provides reassurance of the collective nature of conflicts and dilemmas often experienced as personal and isolated, as well as the pleasure of finding the complexity of lived emotion expressed in language, and given the shape and coherence of narrative form. If romance can be—and has been—accused of reconciling its readers to the restricted destiny of being a wife, that is because it has also offered the less worthy but equally appealing pleasure of fantasy, imagining—in the case of the formula romance repeatedly and exclusively—a perfect, utopian solution to the conflicts raised. Even in Delly or Harlequin, though, where female stories have only one form of truly happy ending, the genre demands some degree of affirmation of female subjectivity and agency. Without this, the narrative lacks that friction that drives it to a conclusion, and readers miss both the narrative momentum and the invitation to positive self-recognition that characterize the most popular of popular romances. The twentieth-century romance is overwhelmingly, if not uniquely, a woman's story: it is about the heroine's quest for self-discovery and self-affirmation, even where a utopian ending represents these goals as utterly compatible with the most traditional and patriarchal form of marriage.

The love stories discussed here have all subscribed, though with varying degrees of explicitness, to what the Harlequin editors like to call the 'ethic' of the genre. That is, they propose an ideal of relationship that would mean both intense intimacy, founded on reciprocal desire and tenderness, and a maintained respect for the beloved other's difference, their uniqueness, their freedom. The heroine's separate integrity as a self is as important to the reader as is the imagined pleasure of that self's unconditional endorsement through love. The 'otherness' of the beloved, their opacity and irreducible difference, are also central to romance, for the representation of desire demands that its object be compellingly evoked from the perspective of the lover, in all his—or her—uniqueness, and the ideal ending to a love story maintains that 'otherness' intact despite the fusional impetus of mutual passion. Romance proposes an ideal of relationship that is inseparably physical and emotional, sexual and moral, and that accepts the Other in their difference as well as in their close affinity with the self. In more everyday terms, romance is a genre that aspires to the reconciliation of individual freedom with a capacity for emotional attention to the other person, and with commitment.

In many of the love stories discussed here, and perhaps most notably in the bleak mid-century romances of Françoise Sagan, an unresolved struggle takes place between, on the one hand, an ideal of the self as autonomous and self-determining and, on the other, a model of the self as necessarily and desirably a 'self-in-relation'. The dominant ideal of selfhood through most of the century, in western or at least in French culture, has surely been the first of these, reaching its most extreme form in existentialism's insistence on the subject's responsibility to transcend all constraints and freely invent the self, but evident too in the wider culture's consistent admiration for the self-made man, the lone adventurer, the independent spirit. It is predominantly a model of male identity, but in struggling for emancipation, women too have resisted definition in terms of family or emotional relationships (someone's daughter or mother or lover or wife) and sought to impose a sense of self as individual, independent, and self-sufficient. But, as feminist theorists such as Nancy Chodorow and Jessica Benjamin have convincingly argued, while parenting has remained (for most children) primarily a maternal function, the Oedipal imperative to separate from the mother has been less powerful for the female subject, and women have tended to maintain a stronger sense of their own identity as closely entwined with that of others. Social factors (women's more central caring role in the family often from an early age, the social meanings of motherhood as opposed to fatherhood) have reinforced this tendency to female identity as relational, male as (ideally) autonomous. The pull of the romance for twentieth-century women readers surely points to a widely shared need to assert the self-determining agency of the female self, without thereby sacrificing the emotionally precious ideal of relationship as an essential element of identity, and of love as an ideal form of relationship. Mutating, as it has in twentieth-century France, through a variety of forms, from pleasurable fantasy to cautionary feminist tale, from pious parable to erotic blockbuster, from call to Resistance to postmodern soliloquy, romance has remained a genre in which the human subject's adventure of self-realization is generally played out in the female gender, and in which the goal of the adventure—whether realized or not—becomes the achievement of a passionately loving relationship with another.

References

Abel-Hirsch, Nicola (2001), *Eros* (Cambridge: Icon Books).

Angot, Christine (2002), *Pourquoi le Brésil?* (Paris: Stock).

Anon. (1971), 'les femmes', *L'Idiot-Liberté-Le Torchon brûle* (no. 0). Article unsigned.

Anon. (1972), *Le Livre de l'oppression des femmes* (Paris: Éditions Pierre Belfond).

Atack, Margaret (1990), 'Narratives of disruption 1940–44', *French Cultural Studies*, 1: 233–46.

Bard, Christine (1999), *Un siècle d'antiféminisme* (Paris: Fayard).

Barthes, Roland (1977), *Fragments d'un discours amoureux* (Paris: Éditions du Seuil).

Bauman, Zygmunt (1993), *Postmodern Ethics* (Oxford: Blackwell).

—— (2003), *Liquid Love: On the Frailty of Human Bonds* (Cambridge: Polity).

Beauvoir, Cécile (2002), *Envie d'amour* (Paris: Éditions de Minuit).

Beauvoir, Simone de (1954), *Les Mandarins* (Paris: Gallimard).

—— (1963), *La Force des choses* (Paris: Gallimard).

—— (1972), *The Second Sex*, trans. H. M. Parshley, 1st pub. 1953 (Harmondsworth: Penguin).

—— (1976), *Le Deuxième Sexe*, vols. i and ii, 1st pub.1949 (Paris: Gallimard, Folio).

—— (1979), *The Mandarins*, trans. Leonard M. Friedman, 1st pub. 1957 (London: Fontana).

Beer, Gillian (1970), *The Romance* (London: Methuen).

Belsey, Catherine (1994), *Desire: Love Stories in Western Culture* (Oxford: Blackwell).

Benjamin, Jessica (1988), *The Bonds of Love: Psychoanalysis, Feminism and the Problem of Domination* (London: Virago).

—— (1995), *Like Subjects, Love Objects: Essays on Recognition and Sexual Difference* (New Haven: Yale University Press).

Bergoffen, Debra (2003), 'Beauvoir: (re)counting the sexual difference', in Claudia Card (ed.), *The Cambridge Companion to Simone de Beauvoir* (Cambridge: Cambridge University Press), 248–65.

Bernheim, Emmanuèle (1993), *Sa femme* (Paris: Gallimard).

—— (1998), *Vendredi soir* (Paris: Gallimard, Folio).

Bertaut, Paul (1909), *La Littérature féminine d'aujourd'hui* (Paris: Librairie des Annales).

Best, Mireille (1988), *Camille en octobre* (Paris: Gallimard).

Bettinotti, Julia (1995), 'Crime et châtiment dans l'œuvre de Delly; une lecture "Gothique" ', in Bettinotti and Noizet 1995: 137–56.

—— and Noizet, Pascale (1995), *Guimauve et fleurs d'oranger* (Quebec: Nuit Blanche).

Beugnet, Martine (2004), *Claire Denis* (Manchester: Manchester University Press).

Bonvoisin, Samra-Martine, and Maignien, Michèle (1986), *La Presse féminine.* Que sais-je, 2305 (Paris: Presses Universitaires de France).

Bouraoui, Nina (2000), *Garçon manqué* (Paris: Stock).

—— (2002), *La Vie heureuse* (Paris: Stock).

Bourdieu, Pierre (1993), *The Field of Cultural Production: Essays on Art and Literature*, ed. Randal Johnson (Cambridge: Polity Press).

Cairns, Lucille (1992), *Marie Cardinal: Motherhood and Creativity* (Glasgow: University of Glasgow French and German Publications).

—— (2002), *Lesbian Desire in Post–1968 French Literature* (Lewiston: Edwin Mellen).

Cardinal, Marie (1972), *La Clé sur la porte* (Paris: Grasset).

—— (1975), *Les Mots pour le dire* (Paris: Grasset).

—— with Leclerc, Annie (1977), *Autrement dit* (Paris: Grasset).

—— (1979), *Une vie pour deux* (Paris: Grasset).

Cazenave, Odile (2000), *Rebellious Women: A New Generation of Female African Novelists* (London: Lynne Rienner).

—— (2003), 'Francophone women writers in France in the nineties', in Roger Célestin, Éliane Dalmolin, and Isabelle de Courtivron (eds.), *Beyond French Feminisms: Debates on Women, Politics, and Culture in France, 1981–2001* (New York: Palgrave Macmillan), 129–42.

Chapsal, Madeleine (1987), *Adieu l'amour* (Paris: Fayard).

—— (1997), *Une femme heureuse* (Paris: Fayard).

—— (1999), *Les Amoureux* (Paris: Fayard).

—— (2004), *L'Homme de ma vie* (Paris: Fayard).

Chodorow, Nancy (1994), *Femininities Masculinities Sexualities: Freud and Beyond* (London: Free Association Books).

—— (1999), *The Reproduction of Mothering*, 1st pub. 1978 (Berkeley and Los Angeles: University of California Press).

Colette (1960), *The Vagabond*, trans. Enid McLeod (Harmondsworth: Penguin).

—— (1961), *Lettres de la Vagabonde* (Paris: Flammarion).

—— (1964), *The Captive*, trans. Antonia White (Harmondsworth: Penguin).

—— (1979), *Break of Day*, trans. Enid McLeod (London: Women's Press).

—— (1984), *La Vagabonde*, 1st pub. 1910, in *Œuvres*, i (Paris: Gallimard, Bibliothèque de la Pléiade), 1067–236.

—— (1986*a*), *L'Entrave*, 1st pub. 1913, in *Œuvres*, ii (Paris: Gallimard, Bibliothèque de la Pléiade), 325–474.

—— (1986*b*), *Mitsou, ou comment l'esprit vient aux filles*, serialized 1917, 1st pub. 1919, in *Œuvres*, ii (Paris: Gallimard, Bibliothèque de la Pléiade), 649–716.

—— (1991*a*), *La Naissance du jour*, 1st pub. 1928, in *Œuvres*, iii (Paris: Gallimard, Bibliothèque de la Pléiade), 275–371.

—— (1991*b*), *La Seconde*, 1st pub. 1929, in *Œuvres* iii (Paris: Gallimard, Bibliothèque de la Pléiade), 373–491.

—— (1991*c*), *Le Toutounier*, 1st pub. 1939, in *Œuvres*, iii (Paris: Gallimard, Bibliothèque de la Pléiade), 1215–71.

—— (2001*a*), *L'Étoile Vesper*, 1st pub. 1946, in *Œuvres*, iv (Paris: Gallimard, Bibliothèque de la Pléiade), 763–881.

—— (2001*b*), *Le Fanal bleu*, 1st pub. 1949, in *Œuvres*, iv (Paris; Gallimard, Bibliothèque de la Pléiade), 963–1060.

Combe, Dominique (1992), *Les Genres littéraires* (Paris: Hachette).

Constans, Ellen (ed.) (1990), *Le Roman sentimental: actes du colloque des 14–16 mars 1989*, vols. i and ii. (Limoges: Trames).

—— (1997), 'Du roman sentimental au roman d'amour: qu'en est-il du déclassement?', in Migozzi 1997: 349–78.

—— (1999), *Parlez-moi d'amour: le roman sentimental. Des romans grecs aux collections de l'an 2000* (Limoges: PULIM).

Coquillat, Michèle (1988), *Romans d'amour* (Paris: Odile Jacob).

Cosnier, Claire (1999), 'Maréchal, nous voilà! ou *Brigitte* de Berthe Bernage', in Bard 1999: 241–54.

Darbyshire, P. (2000), 'Romancing the world: Harlequin romances, the capitalist dream, and the conquest of Europe and Asia', Studies in Popular Culture 23/1 (http://pcasacas.org/SPC/spcissues/23.1/darbyshire.htm accessed 10 Aug. 2005).

Davis, Colin (2000), *Ethical Issues in Twentieth-Century French Fiction: Killing the Other* (London: Palgrave Macmillan).

—— and Fallaize, Elizabeth (2000), *French Fiction in the Mitterrand Years: Memory, Narrative, Desire* (Oxford: Oxford University Press).

Dawson, Tom (1993), *Vendredi soir* (Friday Night) (www.bbc.co.uk/films/2003/07/11/vendredi_soir_2003_review.shtml).

Deforges, Régine (1978), *Le Cahier volé: petite chronique des années 50* (Paris: Fayard).

—— (1983), *La Bicyclette bleue* (Paris: Fayard).

—— (1986), *Pour l'amour de Marie Salat* (Paris: Albin Michel).

—— (1998), *Péle-méle: chroniques de l'humanité* i (Pairs: Fayard).

—— (1999), *Péle-méle: 'chroniques de l'humanité* ii (Pairs: Fayard).

—— with Chawaf, Chantal (2004), *L'Érotique des mots* (Paris: Éditions Du Rocher).

Delly (1910), *Esclave ... ou reine?* (Paris: Éditions Plon-Nourrit & Cie).

—— (1920), *La Vengeance de Ralph* (Paris: Éditions Gautier-Languereau).

—— (1920), *Les Hiboux des roches rouges* (Paris: Éditions Gautier-Languereau).

—— (1929), *Une misère dorée* (Paris: Flammarion).

—— (1934), *La Douloureuse Victoire* (Paris: Flammarion).

—— (1935), *Comme un conte de fées* (Paris: Flammarion).

—— (1950), *Rue des Trois Grâces* (Paris: Éditions Du Dauphin).

—— (1953), *Le Repaire des fauves* (Paris: Éditions Tallandier).

—— (1956), *La Biche au bois* (Paris: Éditions Tallandier).

—— (1960), *Les Deux Fraternités* (Paris: Éditions Tallandier).

Delphy, Christine [published under the name C. Dupont] (1970), 'L'Ennemi principal', *Partisans*, 'Libération des femmes: année zéro', Oct.–Dec.

Didier, Béatrice (1981), *L'Écriture-femme* (Paris: Presses Universitaires de France).

Dinnerstein, Dorothy (1977), *The Mermaid and the Minotaur: Sexual Arrangements and Human Malaise* (New York: Harper Colophon).

Djébar, Assia (1962), *Les Alouettes naïves* (Paris: Julliard).

—— (1980), *Femmes d'Alger dans leur appartement* (Paris: des femmes).

—— (1997), *Oran, langue morte* (Paris: Actes Sud).

Duchen, Claire (ed.) (1987), *French Connections: Voices from the Women's Movement in France* (London: Hutchinson).

—— (1994), *Women's Rights and Women's Lives in France 1944–1968* (London: Routledge).

Dudovitz, R. (1990), *The Myth of Superwoman: Women's Bestsellers in France and the United States* (London: Routledge).

Duras, Marguerite (1958), *Moderato cantabile* (Paris: Éditions de Minuit).

—— with Gauthier, Xavière (1974), *Les Parleuses* (Paris: Éditions de Minuit).

Ernaux, Annie (1974), *Les Armoires vides* (Paris: Gallimard).

—— (1977), *Ce qu'ils disent ou rien* (Paris: Gallimard).

—— (1991), *Passion simple* (Paris: Gallimard).

Evans, Mary (1985), *Simone de Beauvoir: A Feminist Mandarin* (London: Tavistock).

Fallaize, Elizabeth (1988), *The Novels of Simone de Beauvoir* (London: Routledge).

—— (1993), *French Women's Writing: Recent Fiction* (Houndmills: Macmillan).

Felski, R. (1989), *Beyond Feminist Aesthetics: Feminist Literature and Social Change* (London: Hutchinson Radius).

Ferney, Alice (2000), *La Conversation amoureuse* (Paris: Actes Sud).

Finch, Alison (2000), *Women's Writing in Nineteenth-Century France* (Cambridge: Cambridge University Press).

Firestone, Shulamith (1972), *The Dialectic of Sex: The Case for Feminist Revolution*, 1st pub. 1970 (London: Paladin).

Fishman, Sarah (1987), 'Waiting for the captive sons of France: prisoner of war wives, 1940–45', in Margaret R. Higonnet, Jane Jenson, Sonya Michel, and Margaret C. Weitz (eds.), *Behind the Lines: Gender and the Two World Wars* (New Haven: Yale University Press), 182–93.

Fishwick, Sarah (2002), *The Body in the Work of Simone de Beauvoir* (Oxford: Peter Lang).

Flaubert, Gustave (1983), *Madame Bovary*, 1st pub. 1857 (Paris: Livre de Poche).

—— (1992), *Madame Bovary*, trans. Geoffrey Wall (Harmondsworth: Penguin).

Fletcher, John (1989), 'Freud and his uses: psychoanalysis and gay theory', in Simon Shepherd and Mick Wallis (eds.), *Coming on Strong* (London, Unwin and Hyman), 90–118.

Fowler, Brigid (1991), *The Alienated Reader: Women and Romantic Literature in the Twentieth Century* (Hemel Hempstead: Harvester Wheatsheaf).

François, Jocelyne (1980), *Joue-nous 'España'* (Paris: Mercure de France).

Fray, Pascale (1997), 'Chapsal rassure', *Lire*, Apr. 1997 (www.lire.fr/critique. aop/idC, accessed 10 Aug. 2005).

Gamman, Lorraine, and Marshment, Margaret (eds.) (1988), *The Female Gaze: Women as Viewers of Popular Culture* (London: Women's Press).

Gavalda, Anna (2002), *Je l'aimais* (Paris: Le Dilettante).

Gengembre, Gérard (1997), *Réalisme et naturalisme* (Paris: Seuil).

Geraldy, Paul (1913), *Toi et moi* (Paris: Stock).

Giet, S. (1997), 'La Presse du cœur, avatar du récit illégitime', in Migozzi 1997: 83–96.

—— (1997) *Nous deux 1947–1997: Apprendre la langue du cœur* (Leuven: Peeters Vrin).

Goldberg, Nancy Sloan (1999), *'Woman, Your Hour is Sounding': Continuity and Change in French Women's Great War Fiction, 1914–1919* (Houndmills: Macmillan).

Greer, Germaine (1970), *The Female Eunuch* (London: MacGibbon & Kee).

Groult, Benoîte, and Groult, Flora (1974), *Journal à quatre mains*, Ist pub. 1960. (Paris: Gallimard).

Guérin, Marie, and Paulvé, Dominique (1994), *Le roman du Roman rose* (Paris: Éditions Jean-Claude Lattès).

Hall, Martin (2000), 'Eighteenth century women novelists: gender and genre', in Stephens 2000: 102–19.

Hamer, Diane (1990), 'Significant others: lesbianism and psychoanalytic theory', *Feminist Review*, 34 (Spring): 134–51.

Hawthorne, Melanie (2000), *Contingent Loves: Simone de Beauvoir and Sexuality* (Charlottesville: University Press of Virginia).

Holmes, Diana (1995), 'Angry young women: sex and conflict in bestselling first novels of the 1950s', in Renate Gunther and Janice Windebank (eds.), *Violence and Conflict in French Culture* (Sheffield: Sheffield University Press), 199–214.

—— (1996), *French Women's Writing 1848–1994* (London: Athlone).

—— (1998), ' "Quel fleuve noir nous emportait…": sex and the woman reader at the *fin-de-siècle*', in Jean Mainil (ed.), *French Erotic Fiction: Ideologies of Desire: Nottingham French Studies*, 37/1: 51–69.

—— (2005*a*), 'Romancing the text: love stories in recent French women's writing', in Gill Rye (ed.), 'A new generation: sex, gender, and creativity in contemporary women's writing in French', *L'Esprit créateur*, 45 (Spring): 97–109.

—— (2005*b*), 'Novels of adultery: Paul Bourget, Daniel Lesueur and what women read in the 1890s', in Sarah Capitanio, Lisa Downing, Paul Rowe, and Nicholas White (eds.), *Currencies: Fiscal Fortunes and Cultural Capital in Nineteenth-Century France* (Oxford: Peter Lang),13–28.

—— (2005*c*), 'Daniel Lesueur and the feminist romance', in Holmes and Tarr 2005: 197–210.

—— and Tarr, Carrie (eds.) (2005), *A 'Belle Époque'? Women in French Society and Culture 1890–1914* (Oxford: Berghahn).

Houari, Leïla (1985), *Zeida de nulle part* (Paris: L'Harmattan).

Houel, Annik (1990), 'L'Amant Harlequin', in Constans 1990: 277–84.

Irigaray, Luce (1986), 'Créer un entre-femmes', *Paris-Féministe*, 31–2 (Sept.): 37–41.

Jackson, Stevi (2001), 'Love and romance as objects of feminist knowledge', 1st pub. 1993, in Weisser 2001: 254–64.

Jones, Ann R. (1986), 'Mills and Boon meets feminism', in Radford 1986: 194–218.

Jong, Erica (1973), *Fear of Flying* (Orlando, Fla.: Holt, Rinehart and Winston).

Jordis, Christine (2003), *La Chambre blanche* (Paris: Le Seuil).

Jumelais, Yann (1990), 'De Delly à Dailey: les obstacles dans le roman sentimental', in Constans 1990: 225–38.

Kern, Stephen (1992), *The Culture of Love: Victorians to Moderns* (Cambridge, Mass.: Harvard University Press).

Kessas, Ferrudja (1990), *Beur's Story* (Paris: L'Harmattan).

Klaw, Barbara (1995), 'Sexuality in Beauvoir's *Les Mandarins*' in Margaret A. Simons (ed.), *Feminist Interpretations of Simone de Beauvoir* (Philadelphia: Pennsylvania University Press), 193–222.

—— (2000), 'Simone de Beauvoir and Nelson Algren: self-creation, self-contradiction, and the exotic, erotic feminist other', in Hawthorne 2000: 117–52.

Kristeva, Julia (2002), *Le Génie féminin iii: Colette* (Paris: Fayard).

Lafayette, Madame de (1972), *La Princesse de Clèves et autres romans*, 1st pub. 1678 (Paris: Gallimard, Folio).

Larnac, Jean (1929), *Histoire de la littérature féminine en France* (Paris: Éditions Kra).

Larsson, Flora (1990), 'Approche du roman sentimental durassien', in Constans 1990: 77–94.

Laurens, Camille (2000), *Dans ces bras-là* (Paris: POL).

—— (2003), *L'Amour, roman* (Paris: POL).

Leroy, Gérardi, and Bertrand-Sabiani, Julie (1998), *La Vie littéraire à la Belle Époque* (Paris: Presses Universitaires de France).

Lesueur, Daniel (1897), *Calvaire de femme*, i: *Fils de l'amant*; ii: *Madame l'Ambassadrice* (Paris: Alphonse Lemerre).

—— (1904), *Le Masque d'amour*, i: *Le Marquis de Valcor*; ii: *Madame de Ferneuse* (Paris: Alphonse Lemerre).

Lévinas, Emmanuel (1989), *The Lévinas Reader/Emmanuel Lévinas*, ed. Seán Hand (Oxford: Blackwell).

Lewallen, A. (1988), '*Lace*: pornography for women?', in Gamman and Marshment 1988: 86–101.

Lipovetsky, Gilles (1993), *L'Ère du vide: essais sur l'individualisme contemporain*, 1st pub. 1983 (Paris: Gallimard).

Lucet, Catherine (n.d.), 'Le Roman sentimental en France: Harlequin', in X-Passion no. 6. *Le Roman sentimental* (www.polytechnique.fr/eleves/binets/xpassion).

McMillan, James (2000), *France and Women 1789–1914* (London: Routledge).

Magali (1931), *Le Jardin de l'enchantement* (Paris: Tallandier).

—— (1942), *Un baiser sur la route* (Paris: Tallandier).

Makinen, M. (2001), *Feminist Popular Fiction* (Houndmills: Palgrave).

Margueritte, Victor (1922), *La Garçonne* (Paris: Flammarion).

—— (1923), *Le Compagnon* (Paris: Flammarion).

—— (1924), *Le Couple* (Paris: Flammarion).

Marion, Henri (1900), *Psychologie de la femme* (Paris: Armand Colin).

Marks, Elaine (1960), *Colette* (New Brunswick, NJ: Rutgers University Press).

Martin-Mamy (1909), *Marcelle Tinayre*, Les Célébrités d'Aujourd'hui (Paris: E. Sansot).

Marton, Sandra (1999*a*), *Épouse malgré elle* [*The Bride Said Never!*], trans. J. B. André (Paris: Harlequin).

—— (1999*b*), *Le Secret de la mariée* [*The Groom Said Maybe!*], trans. J. B. André (Paris: Harlequin).

—— (1999*c*), *Noces de cristal* [*The Divorcee Said Yes!*], trans. J. B. André (Paris: Harlequin).

Maryan (1882), *Les Chemins de la vie* (Paris: Bloud et Barral).

—— (1885), *Une dette d'honneur* (Paris: H. Gaulier).

—— (1890), *Anne de Valmoët* (Paris: Librairie Blériot).

—— (1903), *Mariage moderne* (Paris: Firmin-Didot, Bibliothèque des Mères de Famille).

Mercier, Michel (1976), *Le Roman féminin* (Paris: Presses Universitaires de France).

Migozzi, Jacques (ed.) (1997), *Le Roman populaire en question(s): actes du colloque international de mai 1995 à Limoges* (Limoges: PULIM).

Miller, Judith Graves (1988), *Françoise Sagan* (Boston: Twayne).

—— (1991), 'Françoise Sagan', in Eva M. Sartori and Dorothy W. Zimmerman (eds.), *French Women Writers: A Bio-bibliographical Source Book* (Westport, Conn.: Greenwood Press), 392.

Milligan, Jennifer E. (1996), *The Forgotten Generation: French Women Writers of the Inter-war Period* (Oxford: Berg).

Mitchell, Margaret (1936), *Gone with the Wind* (New York: Macmillan).

Modleski, Tania (1984), *Loving with a Vengeance: Mass-Produced Fantasies for Women* (London: Methuen).

Morello, Nathalie (1998), *Sagan: Bonjour tristesse*, Critical Guides to French Texts 122 (London: Grant and Cutler).

—— and Rodgers, Catherine (eds.) (2002), *Nouvelles Écrivaines: nouvelles voix?* (Amsterdam: Rodopi).

Némirovsky, Irène (2004), *Suite française* (Paris: Denoël).

Nimier, Marie (2002), *La Nouvelle Pornographie* (Paris: Gallimard).

Nini, Soraya (1993), *Ils disent que je suis une beurette* (Paris: Fixot).

O'Brien, Catherine (1996). *Women's Fictional Responses to the First World War: A Comparative Study of Selected Texts by French and German Writers* (New York: Peter Lang).

Ohnet, Georges (1884), *Le Maître de Forges*, 1st pub. 1882 (Paris: Ollendorf).

Olivier-Martin, Yves (1980), *Histoire du roman populaire en France* (Paris: Albin Michel).

Paizis, George (1998), *Love and the Novel: The Poetics and Politics of Romantic Fiction* (Basingstoke: Macmillan).

Péquignot, Bruno (1997), 'Le Sentimental et le populaire', in Migozzi 1997: 65–81.

Pert, Camille (1899), *Leur égale* (Paris: H. Simonis Empis).

Picq, Françoise (1993), *Libération des femmes: les années-mouvement* (Paris: Seuil).

Quefferec, L. (1989), *Le Roman-feuilleton français au XIXe siècle* (Paris: Presses Universitaires de France, Qu sais-je).

Raabe, J. (1985), 'Ce roman que l'on dit rose', *Le Magazine littéraire*, 331 (Apr.) 60–4.

Radford, J. (ed.) (1986), *The Progress of Romance: The Politics of Popular Fiction* (London: Routledge and Kegan Paul).

Radway, Janice A. (1987), *Reading the Romance: Women, Patriarchy and Popular Literature*, Ist pub. 1984 (London: Verso).

Rambach, and Marine, Rousseau, Anne (1998), *Les Lois de l'amour* (Paris: Éditions Gaies et Lesbiennes).

—— (2005), *Cœur contre cœur* and *Les Lois de l'amour* (Paris: Éditions Gaies et Lesbiennes).

Rawlins, Debbi (2003), *Le Fruit défendu [Educating Gina]*, trans. Cécile Besson (Paris: Harlequin).

Reuter, Yves (1990), 'Le Roman sentimental: système des personnages et circulation sociale de la thématique amoureuse', in Constans 1990: 209–24.

Reyes, Alina (2002), *Politique de l'amour* (Paris: Zulma).

Richebourg, Émile (1899a), *Une haine de femme* (Paris: E. Flammarion).

—— (1899b), *Les Hontes de l'amour* (Paris: E. Flammarion).

Richet, Charles (1931), 'La Vraie Place de la femme' (Woman's true place), in *Le Matin*, 5 Nov. 1931.

Roberts, Mary-Louise (2002), *Disruptive Acts: The New Woman in Fin-de-Siècle France* (Chicago: University of Chicago Press).

Rochefort, Christiane (1961), *Les Petits Enfants du siècle* (Paris: Grasset).

—— (1963), *Les Stances à Sophie* (Paris: Grasset).

—— (1969), *Printemps au parking* (Paris: Grasset).

—— (1972), *Archaos ou le jardin étincelant* (Paris: Grasset).

—— (1978), *Ma vie revue et corrigée par l'auteur* (Paris: Stock).

Ross, Kristin (1995), *Fast Cars, Clean Bodies: Decolonization and the Reordering of French Culture* (Cambridge, Mass.: MIT Press).

Rougemont, Denis de (1972), *L'Amour et l'Occident*, 1st pub. 1939 (Paris: Plon).

Rousset, J. (1981), *Leurs yeux se rencontrèrent* (Paris: Librairie José Corti).

Sagan, Françoise (1954), *Bonjour tristesse* (Paris: Julliard).

—— (1956), *Un certain sourire*, Pocket (Paris: Julliard).

—— (1957), *Dans un mois, dans un an* (Paris: Julliard).

St-Onge, Marian (1984). 'Narrative strategies and the quest for identity in the French female novel of adolescence: studies in Duras, Mallet-Joris, Sagan and Rochefort', unpublished Ph.D. dissertation, Boston College.

Saint-German, Richard (1995), *Bibliographie*, in Bettinotti and Noizet 1995: 157–200.

Sallenave, Danièle (2002), *D'amour* (Paris: Gallimard).

Sand, George (1863), *Mademoiselle la Quintinie* (Paris: Michel Lévy Frères).

—— (1868), *Mademoiselle Merquem* (Paris: Michel Lévy Frères).

—— (1977), *Laura ou, voyage dans le cristal*, 1st pub. 1864 (Paris: Nizet).

Sartre, Jean-Paul (1947), *L'Âge de raison* (Paris: Gallimard).

Schaeffer, Jean-Marie (1989), *Qu'est-ce qu'un genre littéraire* (Paris: Seuil).

Schor, Naomi (1988), 'Idealism in the novel: recanonizing Sand', *Yale French Studies*, 75: *The Politics of Tradition: Placing Women in French Literature*, 56–73.

Sebbar, Leïla (1985), *Les Carnets de Shérazade* (Paris: Stock).

Shiffrin, Anya (1987), 'Studying the romantics', *New Society*, 27 Nov.: 17–19.

Stephens, Sonya (ed.) (2000), *A History of Women's Writing in France* (Cambridge: Cambridge University Press).

Strassburg, Gottfried von (1960), *Tristan* (Harmondsworth: Penguin).

Sullerot, Evelyne (1965), 'Condition de la femme', in A. Sauvy (ed.), *Histoire économique de la France entre les deux guerres* (Paris: Fayard).

Tarr, Carrie, with Rollet, Brigitte (2001), *Cinema and the Second Sex: Women's Filmmaking in France in the 1980s and 1990s* (London: Continuum).

Taylor, Helen (1989), *Scarlett's Women: Gone with the Wind and its Female Fans* (London: Virago).

Thiesse, Anne-Marie (1984), *Le Roman du quotidien: Lecteurs et lectures à la belle époque* (Paris: Le Chemin Vert).

Thomas, Édith (1944), *Contes d'Auxois* (Paris: Éditions de Minuit).

Tinayre, Marcelle (1905), *La Rebelle* (Paris: Calmann-Lévy).

—— (1915), *La Veillée des armes: le départ: août 1914* (Paris: Calmann-Lévy).

Todd, Christopher (1994), *A Century of Bestsellers in France (1890–1990)* (London: Edwin Mellen).

Todorov, Tzvetan (1970), *Introduction à la littérature fantastique* (Paris: Seuil).

Treacher, Amal (1983), 'What is life without my love? Desire and romantic fiction', in Susannah Radstone (ed.), *Sweet Dreams: Sexuality, Gender and Popular Fiction* (London: Lawrence and Wishart), 73–90.

Triolet, Elsa (1945), *Les Amants d'Avignon*, 1st pub. 1943, in *Le Premier Accroc coûte deux cents francs* (Paris: Denoël).

—— (1959), *Roses à crédit* (Paris: Gallimard).

d'Urfé, Honoré (1966), *L'Astrée*, 1st pub. 1607–27 (Geneva: Slatkine).

Vareille, Jean-Claude (1994), *Le Roman populaire français (1789–1914): idéologies et pratiques* (Limoges: PULIM).

Vercors (1944), *Le Silence de la mer* (Paris: Éditions de Minuit).

Veuzit, Max du (1980), *Nuit nuptiale*, first date of publication unobtainable (Paris: Tallandier).

Waelti-Walters, Jennifer, and Hause, Steven C. (1994), *Feminisms of the Belle Epoque: A Historical and Literary Anthology* (Lincoln: University of Nebraska Press).

Weiner, Susan (1993), 'Le Repos de la critique: women writers of the fifties', *French Literature Series*, 20: 93–102.

Weisser, Susan Ostrov (2001), *The Romance Reader* (New York: New York University Press).

Williams, Linda (1991), 'Film bodies: gender, genre and excess', *Film Quarterly*, 44/4 (Summer): 2–13.

Zola, Émile (1990*a*), *Au Bonheur des Dames*, Les Rougon-Macquart III, 1st pub. 1883 (Paris: Gallimard, Bibliothèque de la Pléiade).

—— (1990*b*), *Germinal*, Les Rougon-Macquart III, 1st pub. 1885 (Paris: Gallimard, Bibliothèque de la Pléiade).

Index